SCOTLAND:
THE MAKING AND UNMAKING OF THE NATION
c.1100-1707

SCOTLAND
THE MAKING AND
UNMAKING OF
THE NATION
c.1100 – 1707

VOLUME I : THE SCOTTISH NATION:
ORIGINS TO C.1500

Edited by
Bob Harris and Alan R MacDonald

DUNDEE UNIVERSITY PRESS

and

THE OPEN UNIVERSITY IN SCOTLAND

First published in Great Britain in 2006 by
Dundee University Press

University of Dundee
Dundee DD1 4HN

www.dundee.ac.uk/dup

ISBN 10: 1-84586-004-7
ISBN 13: 978-1-84586-004-2

British Library Cataloguing-in-Publication Data
A catalogue record for this book is available on request from the British Library

Typeset by Hewer Text UK Ltd, Edinburgh
Printed and bound by Bell & Bain Ltd, Glasgow

Contents

Preface

This volume and the series of which it is a part represent the completion of a project that began in the mid-1990s to facilitate the study of Scottish history in Scotland and beyond. A milestone was reached in 1998 with the launch of a module in Modern Scottish History – *Modern Scottish History: 1707 to the Present*. This module, and the five volumes which accompany it, have won consistently high praise from the students who have taken it, as well as strong commendation from many professional academics. Appropriately perhaps, with the project's completion in 2007 – the 300th anniversary of the parliamentary union with England – anyone who wishes to will be able to study Scottish history from c.1100 to present day by distance learning.

In 1998, the editors said that it was a particularly appropriate moment to bring Scottish history to a new and wider readership and audience. In the first place, this reflected the outcome of the 1997 Referendum, but also the evident depth of contemporary interest (expressed in a large variety of ways) in the Scottish past. It is no less true today. Indeed, if anything, the need and desirability of reflecting this interest is only greater with the first flush of post-devolution excitement over, and the place of Scottish history in universities and schools not necessarily any stronger than it was a few years ago. And while popular history books are being written and published – and from 2003 *History Scotland* has been available on newsagents' shelves – long–established myths and preconceptions about the Scottish past still exert a very firm grip on general opinion, and even on those who really should know better. Scottish history and Scotland deserve better than this.

These volumes aim to present recent academic research to a wide readership. As such, they should be of interest to anyone with an interest in knowing about the Scottish past as well as the essential historical background to many present-day concerns and issues. They also provide a way for readers to develop their own skills as students of history, focusing on issues relating to the use (and abuse) of primary sources and the conceptual questions and challenges raised by specific topics. While we have left out some of the overtly pedagogical material that was included in the Modern Scottish History volumes, there is still plenty of discussion on sources and methods for interested readers to follow up.

The potential scope of these volumes is enormous, and this despite the fact that the sources and scholarship for the medieval and early modern periods are considerably less abundant than for the modern one. Any decision we might have taken about how to present the history of periods as long as c.1100–c.1500 and c.1500–1707 would have involved some awkward compromises. Volumes 1 and 3, comprising new essays by expert authors, start with a number of broadly chronological chapters, furnishing readers with a basic narrative. These chapters are followed by a range of more thematic ones. All the chapters are designed to offer a reasonably comprehensive introduction to recent work and, as importantly, a context or contexts for further reading and investigation. There is some overlap between the chronological and thematic chapters, which offers scope for comparison between authors and for looking again at topics and themes from alternative perspectives. Some themes span the two volumes – for example, the Highland-Lowland divide, urbanisation, Scottish identity, Anglo-Scottish relations – so they can be traced over the 'long durée' and across conventional period divisions. There are no separate chapters on gender. Rather this theme has been deliberately blended in with other themes and topics. Some will find this not to their taste, but the aim is to present an inclusive, broad vision of the Scottish past, not one which segregates particular experiences. We have also chosen to include greater coverage of areas of cultural history than in the modern volumes. In part, this reflects recent trends in the writing of history – the so-called 'cultural turn' in historical studies – but also the wealth of scholarship which exists on such topics. It may also reflect something of an emancipation of scholars from the primacy of documentary sources, but then this is no new thing for medievalists. Throughout both volumes a key theme that emerges (in terms of how we study the Scottish past, and also the patterns and meanings present in this past) is the importance of Scottish relationships and involvement in a broader European past. Let's hope the anniversary of the Union does not mask or detract from this theme, or from the great strides that have been made in recent decades to recover this dimension of the Scottish past. The second and fourth volumes contain selected readings to accompany the topic/theme volumes, and should prove a great resource for those wishing to explore a particular subject further. The fifth volume is a collection of primary sources for the history of Scotland from c.1100–1707, designed to accompany the other volumes. It makes documents of both local and national importance accessible. Quite a few of these have been specially transcribed for this volume. All students of history should want to read primary sources for the uniquely rich insight they furnish into the past. We also hope that they may encourage some readers to make their own forays into local archives.

This book is another product of the University of Dundee-Open University collaboration that offers modules in Scottish history to distance learning students. The modules are offered at honours level for undergraduates. However, all the volumes are designed to be used – singly or as a series – by anyone with an interest in Scottish history. Our hope is that they will inspire and deepen enthusiasm for the investigation of the Scottish past, perhaps even encouraging some to examine aspects of their own community history based on themes covered in the volumes.

From the outset, this project has depended on the efforts and enthusiasm of many people, and there are several major debts to acknowledge. Financial support for the development of these volumes was provided initially from the strategic fund of the Faculty of Arts and Social Sciences at the University of Dundee under the guidance of the then dean, Professor Huw Jones. His successor, Professor Christopher A.

Whatley, has been a constant supporter, and has contributed his expertise to these volumes, as well as being an editor and contributor to the Modern Scottish History volumes. The Strathmartine Trust generously provided further vital financial support to facilitate the production of these volumes. Within the Open University, invaluable supporting roles have been played by Peter Syme, Director of the Open University in Scotland, and Ian Donnachie, Reader in History at the Open University in Scotland. It is the shared commitment of individuals in both institutions, stimulated by the success and quality of the Modern Scottish History course, which has driven forward the continued development of the project. John Tuckwell, who published the Modern Scottish History volumes, and who commissioned the present volumes, has been a sage and encouraging adviser to the editorial team. The authors produced their contributions to agreed formats and, for the most part, to agreed deadlines. While they are responsible for what they have written, they have also been supported by other members of the writing team and our editors. Particular thanks are also due to Sharon Adams for sterling support to the editors at a crucial stage, to Mrs Johanne Phillips, the former secretary and administrator of the Modern Scottish History course, and to Mrs Helen Carmichael and Mrs Sara Reid, secretaries in the Department of History, University of Dundee for their administrative support. Thanks are also due to Jen Petrie who typed many of the texts for inclusion in the articles and documents volumes.

Finally, a word about the title of these, volumes – *Scotland the Making and Unmaking of the Nation* – is perhaps required. Some may be tempted to see this as betraying a nationalist bias in the editors, with 1707 being deliberately framed as a moment of natiional erasure and shame. It is certainly designed to provoke, but bear in mind this preface was written by an English-born British historian who knows very well that Scotland's history, like all histories, is wonderfully resistant to simple gernalizations if it were otherwise, its study would not be so rewarding.

USING THIS BOOK

The chapters in volumes 1 and 3 include lists of books and articles for further reading. These lists are intended simply as guides to those who wish to follow up issues and topics covered in the volumes. They are not intended as obligatory further reading.

Bob Harris, Professor of British History, University of Dundee

Illustrations

Maps

Picture Acknowledgements

The following are thanked for permission to reproduce illustrations in their collections:

The Parker Library, courtesy of the Master and Fellows of Corpus Christi College, Cambridge: *illus 8*, CCC MS 171 f. 165r.; Historic Scotland: *illus 1, 2, 4, 5, 7, 9*; the Royal Commission on the Ancient and Historical Monuments of Scotland: *illus 3, 6, 10*; Edinburgh University Library: *illus 11, Registrum Cartum Ecclesie Sanctii Egidii de Edinburgh*.

Maps 1 and 3 are reproduced by permission of the Trustees of the Conference of Scottish Medievalists; map 2 is reproduced by permission of the Trustees of Scottish Medievalists, 1996.

List of Contributors

Michael Asselmeyer, medieval historian and architect. Has held academic appointments at the universities of Münster and Berlin, as well as scholarships at the universities of Cambridge and Bologna. Lecturer in Architecture at the University of Dundee from 2002–04. His current research, funded by the British Academy, is on 'The Invention of the Middle Ages – A Critical Review of the Periodisation' and is being conducted at the Warburg Institute in London.

Geoffrey W S Barrow, Professor Emeritus, University of Edinburgh. Has published very widely on the history of Scotland from the eleventh to the fourteenth centuries. His main publications include *Robert the Bruce and the Community of the Realm of Scotland* (1965; 3rd edn, 1988) and *Kingship and Unity: Scotland, 1000–1306* (1981).

Dauvit Broun, Lecturer, Department of History (Scottish), University of Glasgow. Main research interests focus on Scottish identity and historiography in the middle ages. His book *The Irish Identity of the Kingdom of the Scots was published in* 1999.

Michael Brown, Lecturer, School of History, University of St Andrews. Principal interests lie in political society of Scotland between c.1250 and c.1500. His publications include *James I* (1994), *The Black Douglases* (1998) and, most recently, *The Wars of Scotland 1214–1371* (2004).

David Ditchburn, Senior Lecturer in History, School of Divinity, History and Philosophy, University of Aberdeen. Writes on medieval Scotland's relations with Europe. The first part of a two-volume study on this theme, *Scotland and Europe: The Medieval Kingdom and its Contacts with Christendom c.1215-1545: Volume 1, Religion, Culture and Commerce* was published in 2001.

Elizabeth Ewan, Professor of History and Scottish Studies, University of Guelph. Has written widely on urban history and history of women and gender in medieval Scotland. Her book *Town Life in Fourteenth-Century Scotland* was first published in 1990. She co-edited *Women in Scotland, c.1100–c.1750* (1999).

Janet Foggie was recently appointed mental health care chaplain for NHS Tayside. Her book *Renaissance Religion in Urban Scotland: the Dominican Order, 1450-1560* (2002) was awarded the Hume Brown Prize for the best 'first' book in the field of Scottish history published in 2002–03.

Derek W Hall and **Catherine Smith** are archaeologists based at the Scottish Urban Archaeology Trust.

R Andrew McDonald, Associate Professor, Brock University. Main research interests focus on eleventh to thirteenth century Scottish history, and in particular the highlands and western islands. His main publications include *Outlaws of Medieval Scotland: Challenges to the Canmore Kings, 1058–1266* (2003) and *The Kingdom of the Isles: Scotland's Western Seaboard, c.1100–c.1336* (1997; new edns, 1998 and 2002).

Nicola Royan, Lecturer in English Literature, University of Nottingham. Her research focuses on Scottish identity and self-representation, especially as manifested in late medieval and early modern historiography. Has written a series of articles and chapters on these themes including, jointly with Dauvit Broun, a contribution to the forthcoming *The Edinburgh History of Scottish Literature*.

Fiona Watson, Senior Lecturer and Director of the Centre for Environmental History and Policy, University of Stirling. Author of *Under the Hammer: Edward I and Scotland, 1296–1305* (1998).

Ian Whyte, Professor of Historical Geography, University of Lancaster. Main research interests focus on evolution of landscape, economy and society in early modern Scotland, on which he has written widely in numerous books and articles. Recent publications include *Migration and Society in Britain, 1550–1830* (2000)

CHAPTER ONE

Scotland Before 1100: Writing Scotland's Origins

Dauvit Broun

Information from written sources is the meat and drink of the historian, but for the period before 1100 the rations are alarmingly meagre. The archaeologist and art historian, by contrast, can feast on hundreds of carved stone monuments and the riches of major excavations. If this volume was devoted to the early middle ages, then pride of place would have to be given to essays on hill forts, churches, trading centres, and sculptured stones (to name but a few). As it is, the brief is a narrow one: to approach the period as historians and explore how the lean pickings available to us might best be utilised. There are, it is true, some substantial items that should be on any historian's menu: Adomnán's *Life of Columba* (which had probably taken shape by 697); Bede's *Ecclesiastical History of the English People* (published in 731); derivatives of an Iona Chronicle (written up to 740, at least), including the so-called Chronicle of Ireland (by or soon after 912); and a northern English chronicle (beginning as continuations of Bede in the eighth century and continued to the 1120s). There are also others, which may be less bulky but are nonetheless hugely significant. Each and every text, however, only yields a harvestable crop of historical information if it is subjected to close analysis.

This chapter will concentrate on the 'beginning of Scotland' in the ninth to eleventh centuries. Even with this restricted focus some key aspects cannot be tackled – the most glaring omission is Scandinavian Scotland. On a more positive note, the topic will force us to peer into the heart of history as a discipline, recognise some of the limitations of writing national history, and look at how texts can be analysed – all issues of general relevance. A word should be said about the spelling of names. Scots forms of Gaelic personal names were once used habitually by scholars writing in English, but this is now less common. One reason for this change is that not all names have intelligible Scots or English forms. Another is that scholars internationally use medieval Gaelic spelling for Gaelic names. This mainly involves Ireland rather than Scotland, because that is where most Gaels and almost all Gaelic sources are found in this period. Scholars now tend to prefer medieval Gaelic forms in a Scottish context, too. Here are a few examples: Causantín (Constantine), Cinaed (Kenneth), Domnall (Donald), Donnchad (Duncan), Mac Bethad (Macbeth), Mael Coluim (Malcolm). Welsh names are usually rendered in modern Welsh forms, and a serious attempt is made to render Pictish names in a way that is sensitive to the little we know about Pictish (for example, Bredei for 'Brude', and Unust son of Uurgust instead of 'Oengus mac Fergusa' or 'Angus mac Fergus' for the powerful Pictish king who reigned 729-61).

THE DISAPPEARANCE OF THE PICTS
AND THE BEGINNING OF 'SCOTLAND'

It is generally recognised that Gaelic was spoken in nearly all of Scotland at some time before 1100, and that a key stage in Gaelic's advance was when it took over from Pictish as the native language in the east and north. Unfortunately there is very little information about exactly when or how this happened. The most accessible surviving sources are predominantly about kings and their families. It is tempting to link language death with a political takeover, but the lesson to be learnt from better documented times suggests that the process is better understood as primarily a consequence of social upheaval, and that even a political event as dramatic as conquest is of itself unlikely to be a sufficient explanation.

The best place to begin looking for some guidance on this issue are sources that preserve material written more or less as events occurred. There is not much of this surviving for Scotland in this period. When it is examined closely, a striking change can be seen. 'Picts' and 'kings of the Picts' are found up until the 870s, but no reference is made to them thereafter. It is as if the Picts had disappeared. Instead, a new terminology is used for the kingdom and its people, based on the Gaelic word *Alba*. In 900 the first appearance is made of a 'king of *Alba*', followed in 918 by the first mention of the 'people of Alba' (*fir Alban*). *Alba* is, of course, the Gaelic word today for Scotland, and *Albannach* (inhabitant of *Alba*) is a 'Scot'. In a very direct way, then, the year 900 marks the beginning of 'Scotland', at least insofar as this can now be perceived in surviving sources.

It seems natural to regard the coining of a new Gaelic name for the kingdom, and the disappearance of Picts from contemporary sources, as marking a crucial stage in the Gaelicisation of Scotland. This impression is strengthened by an important change in terminology in the Anglo-Saxon Chronicle (written in English and surviving in a manuscript of this period). In English the word *Scotland* originally meant Ireland. This may seem odd today, but it made perfect sense before 900 because a *Scot* was someone who spoke Gaelic, and Ireland was par excellence the land of Gaelic-speakers. But this changed. From 920 onwards the people of Alba were *Scots*, and from 933 Alba itself was referred to as *Scotland*. The simplest way to explain this is that Gaelic had become the predominant language. Given that English kings had direct dealings with kings of Alba, but not with Irish kings, it is understandable that, from an English point of view, the 'land of Gaelic-speakers' which they were most conscious of was now Alba, not Ireland. In this way the English started to use the term *Scotland* to mean something approaching what it does today; at the same time they ceased referring to Ireland as *Scotland*, and began using the term *Ireland* instead.

So far so good: all the evidence comes together to suggest that *Alba*, 'Scotland', was born as a Gaelic-speaking country in a region where there had once been Picts speaking their own language. The trouble starts once you try to discern how this came about. One curious aspect of this change which has proved particularly difficult to account for is that *Alba* before 900 had been the regular Gaelic word for 'Britain'. Unfortunately the most recent attempts to explain this have not yet been published

(Woolf unpublished; Broun forthcoming). In a nutshell, it has been argued by Alex Woolf that *Alba* was originally a term for 'Gaelic-speaking Britain', and was first used in relation to Argyll, which was the earliest part of Scotland where Gaelic was the native language. A quite different interpretation has been advanced by Dauvit Broun, based on the use by the Welsh before the twelfth century of a word for 'Britain' to refer to Wales. If a word for 'Britain' could be used for their own country by the Welsh (who inhabited only part of the island), then it is possible that the Picts did something similar, and called their country 'Britain'. It may be hypothesised therefore that *Alba* was a direct translation into Gaelic of a Pictish term that was applicable to both 'Britain' and 'Pictland'. This would account for how the Gaelic word for 'Britain' ended up being used for what had been Pictland. The best published explanation of the coining of *Alba* is Máire Herbert's. She argued that it was adopted as an ethnically neutral territorial term which both Gaels and Picts could identify with, in a similar way to how the most powerful Irish king began to refer to himself as 'king of Ireland' in the 850s because it unified his diverse following in a single identity (Herbert 2000).

The choice in explaining how *Alba* was coined as the kingdom's name can, therefore, be boiled down to one that sees it as essentially Gaelic, another which sees it as essentially Pictish, and a third in which the secret of the term's success is because it was neither Gaelic nor Pictish. Now, it might be thought that, because we are dealing here with kings and their followers, it should be possible to study this aspect of the Gaelicisation of Pictland by referring to the predominantly king-centred sources which survive from this period. If the ethnicity of the kings and their people could be established, then that would surely help to determine whether *Alba* was coined as the name of a kingdom that was self-consciously Gaelic, or recognisably Pictish, or was meant to be something else.

A good place to start, you might think, is to determine what happened in the century or so before 900. If we were to take the clock back to 775, for example, we would find a king of the Picts called Ciniod and a king of Dál Riata (the Gaelic kingdom consisting chiefly of Argyll) called Aed. If we were to fast forward to 975, we would find there was no king of the Picts or king of Dál Riata: instead we would find a king of Alba called Cinaed (a Gaelic form of the Pictish name Ciniod) who was advertised in his genealogy as a descendant of Aed who was king of Dál Riata in 775. It would appear from this that a merging of kingships had occurred, and that this may be regarded as a key to understanding the change from Pictland to Gaelic *Alba* by about 900.

But there are problems. Anyone wishing to learn some detail about what happened to the kings of Picts and Dál Riata and their kingdoms in the ninth century might naturally turn for enlightenment to academic books and articles published in the last decade. The more they read, however, they more they will be struck by the complete failure of scholars to agree on anything of fundamental importance. Was Cinaed mac Alpín a Gaelic king of Dál Riata (i.e. Argyll) who conquered the Picts in the 840s (Wormald 1996)? Or was he preceded by a dynasty of Gaelic kings who ruled the Picts between 789 and 839, and were sometimes also kings of Dál Riata (Hudson 1994)? Was the Gaelic takeover of Pictland a gradual, planned process begun in the early 800s and culminating in Cinaed's removal of

Columba's relics to Dunkeld in 849 (Bannerman 1999)? Or should the establishment of a Gaelic dynasty in Pictland and the Gaelicisation of the Picts be ascribed to Cinaed's grandsons, Domnall (d.900) and Causantín (d.952) (Woolf 2001)? Alternatively, Cinaed's precursors between 789 and 839 may not have been Gaels at all, and may instead have been a dynasty of Pictish kings who dominated Dál Riata (Broun 1998a). Even more radical is the suggestion that Cinaed mac Alpín himself may actually have been a Pict (Dumville 1997). If this plethora of possibilities is not confusing enough, a diligent reader will also be presented with the spectacle of one historian who has constructed an account of this period in which Cinaed is seen as a Gael and the kingdom of his grandsons as a radical break with the past (Broun 1994), only to disavow this and articulate a new interpretation in which Cinaed is recognised as a Pict and the kingdom of his grandsons is seen as merely a continuation of Pictland in a Gaelic guise (Broun forthcoming).

The only aspect that is uncontentious is the fact that the Picts suffered some major Viking attacks in this period: the dynasty that had held the kingship since 789 was cut down in battle in 839; Pictland was raided in 866, and Picts taken into slavery to Dublin in 871; another serious defeat was suffered in 875, and Columba's relics had to be removed to Ireland (probably from Dunkeld) in 878 because of fear of the Vikings. In 903 the Vikings raided again and stayed a whole year; in 904, however, they were decisively defeated by Cinaed's grandson, Causantín, and nothing more is heard of Viking attacks for at least fifty years. It will come as no surprise, however, that there is no agreement about the role to be ascribed to Viking pressure in the transition from Pictland to Alba.

WRITING ABOUT A NATION'S ORIGINS

The best way to make sense of this cacophony of scholarly argument is to retreat and take stock. In fact, the situation is so confusing that it is advisable initially to withdraw from the field altogether and begin again by considering some of the fundamental principles of writing history. This, plus an understanding of the sources, should make it easier to rejoin the fray without feeling completely lost. The ultimate objective is to give you a fighting chance of picking your own way through the topic.

History as a discipline can be summed up by two words: 'narrative' and 'evidence'. Narrative can be as simple as an attempt to describe 'what happened'. In a broader sense it can also be recognised as a fundamental feature of all historical writing, such as the construction of an argument, or even the way complex data is marshalled so that it can be read and understood. For the purposes of this chapter, however, I will confine myself to 'narrative' in its most obvious manifestation: 'telling the story', as it were. 'Evidence', for its part, is the building material for any piece of historical writing. In whatever form it takes, it must be identifiable as deriving from the period in question: a mute witness from the past which is given voice in a historian's narrative. The goal of all historians is, of course, to convince those who read their work. This depends not only on evidence, but also on the way it is deployed and on the rhetorical powers of the writer. Another important consideration is the audience's expectations, which are influenced crucially by genre: for example, readers may be prepared to regard direct speech by Cinaed mac Alpín as 'convincing' in a historical novel, but would regard it as out of place in a standard academic history book.

The problem that confronts anyone writing on Scotland before 1100 is that there is insufficient evidence to construct a narrative that might hope to gain general acceptance. This problem is tackled with brutal honesty by AO Anderson, who deplored the tendency to draw together all medieval writing on a topic as if it is all 'evidence' (Anderson 1940). Only a small amount can claim to pass the basic test of acceptability as a witness to what may or may not have happened. For a source to pass this test there needs to be good cause to regard it as written by someone in Scotland or with links to Scotland at or near the time the recorded events occurred; also, there needs to be some reason to assume that it was not written in a conscious attempt to fictionalise the past. As far as the period 840–920 is concerned, only the common source of extant Irish chronicles can be said to meet these requirements at all readily. Anyone seeking to write a readable narrative should therefore take heed of Anderson's warning: 'He who is determined to write history in literary form should avoid the early history of Scotland'.

If you try and write about this period, therefore, you are caught on the horns of a dilemma. If you choose to stick rigorously with the almost random scatter of credible information bequeathed to us from the past, then it is more or less impossible to produce anything readable. If, however, you try to construct a narrative, you will inevitably need to supply additional material from somewhere. The best way to achieve this is not by adding information gleaned from later texts in an uncritical way, but by overtly embracing the challenge posed by the voids in our knowledge so as to create different scenarios that take account of all the evidence. You might end up with a number of contradictory narratives: there is, however, as yet no established genre of writing history that could readily sustain such an outcome. In practice, this means that you will try to develop a single narrative that you think is the most compelling (always recognising that someone else could use the same evidence to construct a markedly different account).

Seeking to explain a nation's origins puts a special strain on this process. The most satisfactory way of writing about this period is to allow yourself to be led by the evidence. There is no point in asking questions if there is little or no information from which an answer might be constructed. In the case of a nation's beginnings, however, not only is the question posed from the outset (how did Scotland begin?), but there is a strong expectation about what will be included in the narrative, regardless of whether there is enough evidence or not: for example, it should start either with the migration of a people, or a conquest by a founding king (or both), and should describe how various regions were inexorably united to form a single country (typically by a series of conquests or dynastic unions). In Scotland's case, the standard account offered in reputable textbooks is that the Scots first arrived in Argyll around 500, that in 843 their king, Cinaed mac Alpín (Kenneth mac Alpin), effected a takeover of the Picts (by conquest or dynastic union); later, Lothian became part of Scotland after Mael Coluim (Malcolm) II's victory at the battle of Carham (1018) on the current border; and

Strathclyde (the kingdom covering most of the south west) was incorporated after the death of its last king, Owain the Bald, fighting alongside Mael Coluim II at Carham, at which point Mael Coluim intruded his grandson and successor, Donnchad (Duncan) I. This may make for a readable story, but it has some obvious weaknesses. For example, it is written with the eye fixed firmly on hindsight, rather than on trying to understand the past on its own terms; also, it headlines events, and downplays or ignores the wider context of social, political and cultural change. Its greatest weakness is that it can survive even where there is no proper evidence at all (that is, evidence as defined by Anderson, as noted above). We will investigate the claims made for 843 and 1018 shortly; the deficiencies of the idea of a migration of Scots about 500 have been exposed by Ewan Campbell and David Dumville (Campbell 1999; Dumville 2002). The 'traditional' narrative of Scotland's beginnings can survive without evidence because it is nourished chiefly by the demands of people today for an explanation of Scottish origins, not by an intimate knowledge of sources. This is also what makes it so enduring: ideas about a nation's beginnings are extraordinarily long-lived, especially where there is a lack of evidence with which to mount a powerful challenge.

THE INTEGRATION OF STRATHCLYDE

The fullest contemporary account of the battle of Carham is found in *Historia Regum* ('History of Kings') attributed to Symeon of Durham, which took shape in the 1120s. It is based on near-contemporary annals written in northern England. This is what it says during its account of the year 1018 (the translation is adapted from Anderson 1908, 82):

> A great battle was fought at Carham between the Scots and the Angles, between Uhtred, Waltheof's son, the earl of Northumbria, and Mael Coluim, king of Scots, the son of Cinaed; and with him in the battle was Owain the Bald, king of the men of Strathclyde.

Owain, king of Strathclyde, is mentioned. But does it say that he was killed, or died shortly afterwards? The answer is obvious: no! How, you might ask, have scholars been so sure that Owain died as a result of the battle? The answer partly lies in Welsh chronicles (known as *Annales Cambriae*), which are also likely to be based on contemporary annals. Here we are told that Owain son of Dyfnwal was killed in 1015. It is assumed that he was king of Strathclyde (which is plausible: a king of Strathclyde called Dyfnwal died in 975), and that he was the same as Owain the Bald who fought with Mael Coluim II at Carham. This, of course, would require that Welsh chronicles are in error in saying he was killed in 1015, and that *Historia Regum* attributed to Simeon of Durham omitted to say that Owain the Bald was killed at Carham. Should we rewrite our sources at all, though? There is nothing otherwise wrong with the chronology of Welsh chronicles at this point. A simpler solution would be to suppose that Owain son of Dyfnwal (d.1015) and Owain the Bald (alive in 1018) were *not* the same person (Duncan 2002, 29; Broun 2004).

This would mean that we don't know when Owain the Bald died. Far from dying at the battle of Carham, he may well have shared the spoils with Mael Coluim II. Carham may have resulted in Strathclyde's expansion east into Teviotdale (which could explain how Teviotdale was later within the diocese of Glasgow), rather than the point when the Borders became part of Scotland. What about the idea that Owain the Bald was succeeded by Mael Coluim II's grandson and heir, Donnchad I? The evidence for this has been re-examined by Professor Duncan (Duncan 2002, 37-41), who pointed out that the ultimate source is another early twelfth-century English text, John of Worcester's chronicle (based partly on a version of the *Anglo-Saxon Chronicle*). This has an account of a defeat of Mac Bethad, king of Scots, by Siward, earl of Northumbria in 1054, in which it is said that Siward 'constituted Mael Coluim, son of the king of the Cumbrians, as king' (Duncan 2002, 38 n.48). This has been taken as a reference to Mael Coluim III, son of Donnchad I, who killed Mac Bethad in 1057 and became king in 1058. But, as Archie Duncan has pointed out, it would be very strange if Mael Coluim III, whose father Donnchad I was certainly king of Scotland, was referred to in 1054 as 'son of the king of the Cumbrians', rather than 'son of the king of Scotland', in the context of an invasion of Scotland against Mac Bethad. Professor Duncan has therefore suggested that the Mael Coluim in 1054 was someone else, an otherwise unknown son of a king of Strathclyde (bearing in mind that 'Cumbria' and 'Strathclyde' were interchangeable in this period). This is perfectly plausible: there was, in fact, a Mael Coluim king of Strathclyde (d.997), so the name is not unprecedented. For all we know, the Mael Coluim of 1054 may have been a son of Owain the Bald (Broun 2004). The reference to Mael Coluim 'son of the king of the Cumbrians' in 1054 is the only 'evidence' for the idea that Donnchad I, king of Scots 1034–40, was made king of Strathclyde by his grandfather, Mael Coluim II (1005–34).

We may conclude, therefore, that there is no evidence for the traditional account of Strathclyde's incorporation into Scotland. A more complex case is the idea (first proposed by Kirby (1962), and often repeated by subsequent scholars) that Strathclyde had, since the early tenth century, fallen under the political control of kings of Scots, even though it had not yet been fully incorporated. This is an example of a much later source being used to supply information that is lacking in contemporary evidence. You will recall that, according to Anderson, such later material should not be regarded as evidence at all. He put the matter bluntly: 'It is the first duty of the historian to examine carefully what is offered to him as evidence, and to reject what should not be accepted as evidence. He must reject it entirely; refusing to be influenced by it, and refusing to interpret the evidence in accordance with it . . .' (Anderson 1940, 13).

Kirby gives an attractive narrative of how there were two kingdoms, Strathclyde and Cumbria, and that one was held by the heir to the Scottish throne. The idea that Strathclyde and Cumbria were separate in this period has been shown to be mistaken (Wilson 1966; see also Smyth 1984, 229). The two terms are interchangeable (as Kirby himself admits): for example, in the early twelfth century the bishop of Glasgow was the 'bishop of Cumbria' – clearly Glasgow is in Strathclyde. Kirby refers regularly to John of Fordun's *Chronicle* as a source, even though this was written sometime shortly after 1371. (Fordun may have used an earlier work, but, if so, it existed in 1285, which is still centuries adrift from the 900s.) Another problem is that Fordun's *Chronicle* is fundamentally different from annalistic texts (such as *The History of Kings* or John of Worcester's *Chronicle*): unlike them, it is a continuous narrative in which sources have been shaped and gaps filled almost imperceptibly in order to produce a smooth, coherent account. If the information derived from Fordun is placed alongside information derived from contemporary sources (or from sources based on contemporary witnesses), it is immediately apparent that they rarely, if ever, coincide. Anderson would not have regarded Fordun as 'evidence'. Unfortunately Kirby's (and Smyth's) narrative treats Fordun as of equal value to the other sources. If you discount Fordun as 'evidence' their narrative is destroyed.

If Fordun's information is rejected, then you end up with a scenario very different from what prevails in most recent writing on tenth-century Scotland. You discover that kings of Strathclyde were *not* a branch of the Scottish royal dynasty, and that they ruled a kingdom separate from Scotland (although sometimes allied with or occasionally subordinate to the king of Scots). This is one way of constructing their genealogy:

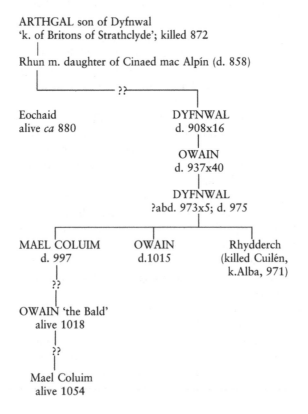

ARTHGAL son of Dyfnwal
'k. of Britons of Strathclyde'; killed 872

Rhun m. daughter of Cinaed mac Alpín (d. 858)

— ??

Eochaid
alive *ca* 880

DYFNWAL
d. 908x16

OWAIN
d. 937x40

DYFNWAL
?abd. 973x5; d. 975

MAEL COLUIM
d. 997

??

OWAIN 'the Bald'
alive 1018

??

Mael Coluim
alive 1054

OWAIN
d.1015

Rhydderch
(killed Cuilén,
k.Alba, 971)

THE UNION OF PICTS AND SCOTS

The main evidence to support the idea that Cinaed mac Alpín led the 'Scots' in a takeover of the Picts is a passage in the *Chronicle of the Kings of Alba*, but this is of uncertain value. This is a key text for this period. What other sources are available? The only material which readily passes the basic test as a credible witness to 'what happened' in the period 840-920 is the common source of extant Irish chronicles. You will look there in vain for anything about Cinaed's takeover of the Picts. In fact, as far as the Picts are concerned, it looks as if nothing fundamental had changed: the kingdom's inhabitants are still 'Picts', and Cinaed, his brother, and his sons are 'kings of the Picts'. There is nothing here to suggest that a major shift in political identity had occurred, or a new 'Scoto-Pictish' realm, never mind a conquest of the Picts. It has even been suggested that, even though Cinaed is represented in Scottish royal genealogies as a Gael – a member of Cenél nGabráin (the descendants of Gabrán, a sixth-century king of Dál Riata) – he may have been a Pict in the male line. The genealogy cannot be traced as a text earlier than the late tenth century, and could have been partially invented, perhaps to signify a fundamental association with powerful Gaelic kindreds and churchmen: genealogies were frequently concocted or altered because it was more important that they be consistent with a family's current status and political relationships than with a true account of their biological origins. In one early text of the genealogy the ruling dynasty is simply called 'the royal line', while another kindred is called *Gabranaig* (meaning 'people of Gabrán'): surely, if Cinaed was a member of Cenél nGabráin, then *Gabranaig* would have been used of the kings descended from him, rather than of another kindred altogether?

On its own this silence need not be fatal to the traditional view of Cinaed's significance for Scottish history (Wormald 1996). There is some indication, however, that the idea of Pictish kingship was boosted, not diminished, *after* Cinaed's reign. The evidence is to be found in the least 'historic' part of the longer Pictish king-list. Most of the names in the list are in a Pictish form, but there are sections at the beginning, and after Cinaed mac Alpín at the end, in which Gaelic forms are used. These Gaelic sections are clearly additions to the Pictish 'core'. The 'Gaelic' material added at the beginning represents a dramatic lengthening of the list by more than forty kings. It begins:

Cruithne mac Cinge, father of the Picts living in this island, reigned for 100 years.
He had seven sons. These are their names: Fíb, Fidach, Foltlaid [read 'Fotlaig'], Fortrenn [meaning 'of Fortriu'], Caitt, Ce, Circinn.
Circinn reigned for 60 years.
Fidach reigned for 40 years.
Fortrend reigned for 60 years.
Foltlaid reigned for 30 years.
Gatt [read 'Caitt'] reigned for 12 years.
Ce reigned for 15 years.

'Cruithne' is simply a Gaelic collective noun for 'Picts', and his seven sons, who each rule the kingdom in turn, are all names of Pictish regions: for example, *Fíb* is Fife, *Caitt* is the Gaelic name for the people of northern Scotland (as in 'Caithness', meaning 'ness of Caitt'), while *Fotlaig* is the people of Atholl (and maybe beyond: Atholl is *Ath Fotla*, 'new Fotla'). This all seems blatantly contrived: it is like beginning a list of Scottish kings with a king called 'Scots' whose sons were 'Galloway', 'Lothian', 'Moray', and so on. But it was, presumably, written this way to hammer home an obvious message: the intention was to claim that Pictland, from Caithness to Fife, was from the very beginning a united territory under a single king. This is made clear by the fact that each of Cruithne's sons is made to succeed to the kingship. We may guess that the reason this material was made up, and the reason its message was made so bluntly was because it was promoting a new idea: an idea of the king of the Picts as successor to all of Cruithne's sons, and so inheriting a right to rule all Pictland. Hitherto the Pictish king may have been essentially king of the most prominent region (Fortriu) and, at best, overking of other Pictish regions or kingdoms.

When was this vision of a stronger kingship and united Pictish kingdom concocted? The answer is likely to lie in the last section of the list, beginning with Cinaed mac Alpín. It is probable, on the face of it, that when the list was extended deep into the past by adding Cruithne's sons, it would also have been updated to include the king who was reigning at that time – that is, the king who was expected to benefit from this portrayal of a stronger, united Pictland. The updating of lists can be difficult to detect. We are dealing here, however, with something more deliberate than the mere addition of a couple of kings at the end, and might expect a definite conclusion to the list by whoever enlarged it so radically. The key here is the appearance of 'and' before two kings: the first is Bredei, last king before Cinaed mac Alpín, and the second is Cinaed's son, Causantín (d.876). This may seem insignificant, but it is very rare. It presumably served to bring the list to a deliberate close: it is like saying 'A, B, C, D, E, F, and G', in which 'G' represents Bredei. Now, Bredei was certainly once the last king in the list, because he is at the end of the section with Pictish name-forms. Cinaed mac Ailpín, his brother Domnall, and son Causantín must therefore have been added subsequently, as if the list was later continued 'H, I, and J', with Causantín son of Cinaed as 'J'. If we think now of Cruithne and his seven sons and the other kings with Gaelic name-forms added at the beginning, then this must have happened *after* Bredei's reign in the early 840s –presumably at the same time as the list was updated (using Gaelic name-forms) to Cinaed's son Causantín. The promotion of a united Pictland under a single Pictish king in this king-list would therefore belong to Causantín's reign. This, of course, runs counter to what you would expect according to the 'traditional' view of Cinaed taking the Picts over and founding a new Scottish monarchy. But it is in keeping with the Irish chronicles (the only readily acceptable source of contemporary information), where Causantín is recorded at his death as 'king of Picts'.

Now let us consider the *Chronicle of the Kings of Alba*. It begins with a striking statement of how Cinaed established a new order:

So Cinaed son of Alpín, first of the Scots, ruled this Pictland prosperously for 16 years. Pictland was named after the Picts, whom, as we have said, Kenneth destroyed; for God deigned to make them alien from, and void of, their heritage, by reason of their wickedness; because they not only spurned the Lord's mass and precept, but also did not wish to be equal to others in the law of equity. Two years before he came to Pictland, he had received the kingdom of Dál Riata.

There are problems with the central passage. The destruction of the Picts 'as we have said' refers back to some text that no longer exists. Also 'did not wish to be equal' could be read in the manuscript as 'wished to be equal'! The first question, however, is: when was the Chronicle written? A number of layers of material can be detected: some items have been derived from contemporary annals, some items have been added to the chronicle itself after it was composed, and some items could belong to the late twelfth century, when the chronicle was made part of a collection of historical pieces. Which layers do the opening items belong to? The account of the destruction of the Picts refers to the concept of 'equity' in association with law; this could indicate a legal vocabulary that might be unlikely in Scotland before the twelfth century. The idea that Cinaed was king of Dál Riata before becoming king of the Picts is difficult to assess without getting caught in a circular argument: if you are inclined to doubt the Scottish royal genealogy in which Cinaed is presented as a descendant of kings of Dál Riata, then you could argue that the notion of Cinaed as king of Dál Riata may have arisen from the concocted genealogy. Alternatively, if you accept the genealogy, you will see no need to doubt that Cinaed was king of Dál Riata. It is likely, however, that Dál Riata had been under Pictish control for nearly half a century by this stage. Also, the text calls Cinaed's kingdom 'Pictland': it does not use Alba as a term for a new 'united kingdom' of 'Pictland plus Dál Riata'. As for the idea of beginning with Cinaed, this could be a decision made by whoever initially created the Chronicle sometime around 960. This would have been at a time when Cinaed mac Alpín's descendants had achieved a monopoly of the kingship for more than a generation. It would have been natural, in this situation, to regard Cinaed as the kingship's founder. If so, this would be a direct reflection of mid-tenth-century realities, not of anything that may have been achieved by Cinaed himself. The view of Cinaed as founding the kingship is therefore likely to be an anachronism.

THE POTENTIAL OF PLACE-NAMES

Up to this point, the sources that have been put under the microscope have been concerned with important people and events. Not only is much of this inherently uncertain, but it can hardly claim to be the whole picture. What hope is there, however, of finding anything sensible to say about the development of society at large before 1100? It is true that written sources of the kind that have a direct bearing on such key issues as landholding and social relationships are almost wholly lacking. The documents that survive in ever greater numbers from the twelfth century onwards, nonetheless, contain within them a vital resource for the historian of pre-1100 society. This resource is place-names. It is very much to be regretted that the kind of thorough survey of documentary references to place-names that has been achieved in England and Northern Ireland is in its infancy in Scotland. There are a few excellent local surveys, it is true. By far the most significant for medievalists is the survey of Fife now being undertaken by Simon Taylor. If we want to glance at the distribution of a particular word in place-names, however, we still have to make do with Nicolaisen's pioneering maps, which are largely based on the Ordnance Survey.

The study of place-names (toponymics) is a discipline in its own right, of course. Not only does it have its own technical vocabulary, but it has an exciting range of methodological challenges, too. Taylor (1997) gives a remarkably lucid and full exposition of some key issues, and will repay repeated study. It is an essential springboard for what follows. One of the most significant of Nicolaisen's maps for the period 1100 is his map of places whose name begins with the element 'Pit-' (published in McNeill and MacQueen 1996, 51): for example, 'Pitlochry', 'Pitcarmick', 'Pitliver', 'Pittentaggart'. There are over two hundred examples in the Ordnance Survey Landranger series. In each case 'Pit-' is a Pictish word, *pett*, which is related to Modern Welsh *peth* (meaning 'thing', but also used of a 'bit' or 'portion' of something). It is also related (in a roundabout way) to the English word 'piece'. Its exact meaning in the context of these place-names is difficult to determine: it may denote a piece of a local unit of lordship, or simply a piece of land or a holding.

Because *pett* is a Pictish word, it has been natural to regard all 'Pit-' names as evidence of Pictish settlement. This appears to be confirmed by the distribution in Nicolaisen's map. If you look carefully, however, you will see that there are some examples south of the Forth beyond Pictish territory, and an absence in some areas that were Pictish, such as the far north. The absence could be due to uneven patterns of survival (remembering that the evidence for the map is modern). The presence of 'Pit-' names in non-Pictish territory in the south is much more difficult to explain. Could these southern examples have been coined later, after Pictland had become Alba and had begun to encroach on the south? But surely Pictish had died out by then?

The key to unlocking this puzzle is that almost all these names are, in fact, Gaelic. One way this can be seen is that, in all but a few cases, the part of the name that follows 'Pit-' is a Gaelic word. For example, in 'Pittentaggart' *pett* is followed by Gaelic *an t-sagairt*, meaning '*pett* of the priest'. This still leaves *pett*, of course. It has only recently been realised that this, too, became a Gaelic word, and has been found still in use in Lewis (Cox 1997). If *pett* was borrowed into Gaelic, and the section following 'Pit-' is Gaelic, then the simplest explanation is that the place-name was coined by Gaelic speakers. Only a handful have possible Pictish words after 'Pit-', so a few may have been coined by Pictish speakers. This means that 'Pit-' place-names probably began to be coined at the very end of the Pictish period, and were predominantly coined by the first generations of Gaelic-speakers in Pictland. This suggests that many belong to the tenth century.

But there is a problem. It is clear from Taylor 1997 that 'Pit-' names were not static: we should not imagine that most of the dots on Nicolaisen's map simply represent tenth-century names that survived until the nineteenth century, when the Ordnance Survey began to publish maps. *Pett* belongs to a class of place-name elements that could be used interchangeably with each other. There was even an option on whether to use it or not: for example, 'Pitliver' ('*pett* of the book': presumably 'book' here means 'Bible'), could be called simply 'Liver', however odd that may seem. This was presumably because *pett* (whatever it meant in this context) referred to something very common. It could, after all, have meant simply 'piece of land' or 'holding'.

Although we cannot be certain about what *pett* meant, some important conclusions can be drawn. One is that, although the word *pett* must have become very common, it only generated place-names shortly before Gaelic replaced Pictish, and for at least a couple of centuries afterwards. This suggests that there was a change in the structure of society that was experienced across the country that coincided with the switch from Pictish to Gaelic. Another conclusion is that for *pett* itself to have been borrowed from Pictish to Gaelic, it must presumably have stood for something that had no obvious Gaelic equivalent. Whatever the social change was, it was rooted in Pictish society, not imposed by invaders. This is consistent with other indications that the transition from Pictish to Gaelic was gradual (Barrow 1998): we should think of Picts changing language, rather than of Picts being wiped out by invading Gaels. This is all tantalisingly vague. There is a good chance, though, that the picture would become less fuzzy if an in-depth study of *pett* names was undertaken, providing it was sensitive to the behaviour of place-name elements in our sources discussed in Taylor (1997).

ALTERNATIVE PARADIGMS

When we add all this together, it is apparent that all the key elements of the standard account of Scotland's beginnings can be called into question. It is no surprise, given the lack of clear evidence, that recent attempts to create a narrative of the ninth century are so wildly divergent. A completely different story could be told: one in which Cinaed mac Alpín is a Pict, and the idea of Pictish kingship is boosted during the reign of his son Causantín; when Alba comes to prominence as the kingdom's name under Cinaed's grandsons, it is merely a Gaelicisation of 'Pictland'; and, in due course, once Gaelic has replaced Pictish, Cinaed's descendants are given a prestigious Gaelic pedigree; finally, although the king of Scots vindicated his claim to the south east at the battle of Carham (1018), it is at least a generation before Strathclyde is incorporated into his realm.

On the strength of your assessment of the sources you might like to join in and create your own narrative. Another approach to try is to consider the following questions when reading any secondary account of this period. In what ways have the gaps in the evidence been filled in order to create a narrative? Have the gaps been filled by using later material (such as Fordun) that is, strictly speaking, inadmissible as evidence for this purpose? To what extent is the narrative influenced by the old paradigm of the standard account of Scotland's beginnings? You will find that the old paradigm is astonishingly enduring. Even Anderson was influenced by it. In his famous compilations of translated extracts from sources, he accepted without question the idea that Mael Coluim II established his grandson, Donnchad, as king of Strathclyde after Owain, and that Owain the Bald who fought at Carham in 1018 was the same as Owain son of Dyfnwal who died in 1015 (Anderson 1908, 85 n.4, 82 n.3; and also Anderson 1922, i, 550 and n.2). Nobody knew the sources better than Anderson, and yet he did not spot that there was a problem: neither did anyone else, of course, until Archie Duncan's recent work.

There is clearly scope for a more fundamental change in direction than simply producing a range of possible narratives about Cinaed and so on. The traditional emphasis on a few notable 'events' can be seriously called into question. One alternative would be to use the sources, *not* for information about what may have happened, but as evidence for how people thought about their kingdom. This approach was adopted in discussing the Pictish king-list and to some extent also the Chronicle of the Kings of Alba. We can only gain access to the thinking of a small number of people, of course; but the texts typically belonged to important churches, and could well have reflected the aspirations of some, at least, of the political elite, and may in turn have exerted some influence in shaping these aspirations and establishing norms.

There is another approach to writing history that is free of the weakness inherent in an event-centred narrative. Its emphasis, rather, is on change as a process involving society at large. The attraction of this approach in trying to understand Scotland's origins is that debates about whether Cinaed mac Alpín was a Pict or a Gael, or about the political context of Gaelicisation, can largely be left to one side. Instead the focus is on trying to gauge when and how people's experience of living in different parts of Scotland changed so that they began to identify themselves, regardless of their regional affinities and ethnic origins, as 'Scots' living in a single country: 'Scotland'. The evidence (such as it is) suggests, however, that this point was not reached until the thirteenth century (Broun 1998b). If we wanted to understand the beginning of Scotland in these terms, then we would have to turn our attention to Scottish society in the generations before the Wars of Independence, beyond the scope of this chapter.

Finally, if we want to know more about social developments before there is a sufficient density of documentary record to shed light on the lives of most of Scotland's inhabitants, then we must look to place-names as our chief resource. This is true for the entire middle ages, not just the period before 1100. Unfortunately research into place-names is barely funded at all in Scotland (in sharp contrast to other countries in Britain and Ireland and Scandinavia). Until this situation changes there is little chance that place-names will yield their treasures.

REFERENCES TO BOOKS AND ARTICLES MENTIONED IN THE TEXT

Anderson, AO 1908 *Scottish Annals from English Chroniclers*. London. Reprinted 1991 with corrections by AO and MO Anderson. Stamford.

Anderson, AO 1922 *Early Sources of Scottish History, A.D.500–1286*, 2 vols. Edinburgh.

Anderson, AO 1940 *Prospects of the Advancement of Knowledge in Early Scottish History*, a lecture given to the Anthropological Section of the British Association on 1 September 1939. Dundee.

Bannerman, J 1999 'The Scottish Takeover of Pictland and the Relics of Columba', *in* Broun, D and Clancy, TO (eds), *Spes Scotorum, Hope of Scots. Saint Columba, Iona and Scotland*, Edinburgh, 71–94.

Barrow, GWS 1998 'The Uses of Place-Names and Scottish History: Pointers and Pitfalls', *in* Taylor, S (ed), *The Uses of Place-Names*, St. Andrews, 54–74.

Broun, D 1994 'The Origin of Scottish Identity in its European Context', *in* Crawford, BE (ed), *Scotland in Dark Age Europe*, St Andrews, 21–31.

Broun, D 1998a 'Pictish Kings, 761–839: Integration with Dál Riata or Separate Development', *in* Foster, S (ed), *The St Andrews Sarcophagus. A Pictish Masterpiece and its International Connections*, Dublin, 71–83.

Broun, D 1998b 'Defining Scotland and the Scots Before the Wars of Independence', *in* Broun, D, Finlay, RJ, and Lynch, M (eds), *Image and Identity: the Making and Remaking of Scotland through the Ages*, Edinburgh, 4–17.

Broun, D 1999 'Dunkeld and the Origin of Scottish Identity' *in* Broun, D and Clancy, TO (eds), *Spes Scotorum, Hope of Scots*, 95–111.

Broun, D 2004 'The Welsh Identity of the Kingdom of Strathclyde, *ca* 900–*ca* 1200', *Innes Review*, 55.

Broun, D (forthcoming) 'Alba: Pictish Homeland or Irish Offshoot', *in* O'Neill, P (ed), *Exile and Homecoming. Proceedings of the Fifth Australian Congress of Celtic Studies*. Sydney.

Campbell, E 1999 *Saints and Sea Kings: the First Kingdom of the Scots*. Edinburgh.

Cox, R 1997 'Modern Scottish Gaelic Reflexes of Two Pictish Words, **pett* and **lannerc*', *Nomina*, 20, 47–58.

Cowan, EJ 1981 'The Scottish Chronicle in the Poppleton Manuscript', *Innes Review*, 32, 3–21.

Dumville, DN 1997 *The Churches of North Britain in the First Viking-Age. The Fifth Whithorn Lecture, 14th September 1996*. Whithorn.

Dumville, DN 2000 'The Chronicle of the Kings of Alba', *in* Taylor, S (ed), *Kings, Clerics and Chronicles in Scotland, 500–1297. Essays in honour of Marjorie Anderson on the occasion of her ninetieth birthday*, Dublin, 73–86.

Dumville, DN 2002 'Ireland and North Britain in the Earlier Middle Ages: Contexts for *Míniugud Senchusa Fher nAlban*', *in* Colm Ó Baoill, C and McGuire, NR (eds), *Rannsachadh na Gàidhlig 2000*, Obar Dheathain (= Aberdeen), 185–212.

*Duncan, AAM 2002 *The Kingship of the Scots, 842–1292: Succession and Independence*. Edinburgh.

Herbert, M 2000 '*Rí Éirenn, Rí Alban*: Kingship and Identity in the Ninth and Tenth Centuries', *in* Taylor, S (ed), *Kings, Clerics and Chroniclers in Scotland, 500–1297*, Dublin, 62–72.

Hudson, BT 1994 *Kings of Celtic Scotland*. Westport CT.

Hudson, BT 1998 'The Scottish Chronicle', *Scottish Historical Review*, 77, 129–61.

Kirby, DP 1962 'Strathclyde and Cumbria: A Survey of Historical Development to 1092', *Transactions of the Cumberland and Westmorland Antiquarian and Archaeological Society*, new series 62, 71–94.

Kirby, DP 1971 'Britons and Angles', *in* Menzies, G (ed) *Who are the Scots?*, London, 80–89.

McNeill, PGB, and MacQueen, HL 1996 (eds), *Atlas of Scottish History to 1707*. Edinburgh.

Phythian-Adams, C 1996 *Land of Cumbrians. A Study in British Provincial Origins, A.D. 400–1200*. Aldershot.

Smyth, AP 1984 *Warlords and Holy Men: Scotland AD 80–1000*. London. Reprinted 1992, Edinburgh.

Taylor, S 1997 'Generic Element Variation, with Special Reference to Eastern Scotland', *Nomina*, 20, 5–22.

Wilson, PA 1966 'On the use of the terms 'Strathclyde' and 'Cumbria', *Transactions of the Cumberland and Westmorland Antiquarian and Archaeological Society*, new series 66, 57–92.

*Woolf, A 2001 'Birth of a Nation', *in* Menzies, G (ed), *In Search of Scotland*, Edinburgh, 24–45.

Woolf, A (unpublished) 'Event and Process in the Scottish Viking Age', paper delivered to the Society of Antiquaries of Scotland.

Wormald, P 1996 'The Emergence of the *Regnum Scottorum*: a Carolingian Hegemony?' *in* Crawford, BE (ed), *Scotland in Dark Age Britain*, St Andrews, 131–60.

FURTHER READING

The items above marked * are recommended for further reading, along with the following:

Clancy, TO and Crawford, BE 2001 'The Formation of the Scottish Kingdom', *in* Houston, RA, and Knox, WWJ (eds), *The New Penguin History of Scotland from the Earliest Times to the Present Day*, London, 28–95.

Crawford, BE 1996 (ed), *Scotland in Dark Age Britain*. St Andrews.

Driscoll, Stephen T 2002, *Alba: the Gaelic Kingdom of Scotland, AD 800-1124*. Edinburgh.

Foster, SM 2004 *Picts, Gaels and Scots*, 2nd edition, London. 1st edition 1996, London.

Taylor, S 1998 (ed), *The Uses of Place-Names*. St. Andrews.

Taylor, S 2000 (ed), *Kings, Clerics and Chronicles in Scotland, 500–1297. Essays in honour of Marjorie Anderson on the occasion of her ninetieth birthday*. Dublin.

CHAPTER TWO

The Anglo-Norman Impact, c.1100 – c.1286

Geoffrey Barrow

A kingdom of Scotland (Alba in the speech of the majority of its people) was firmly in existence from the early tenth century, ruled for over forty years (900–943) by a single king, Constantine son of Aed. Its geographical extent is uncertain, but we shall not be far wrong if we think of it as stretching from the Beauly Firth southward and eastward to the Firths of Clyde and Forth. Much of this territory had been ravaged time and again by armies of Scandinavian or mixed Norse-Gaelic composition originating in Ireland, the Isle of Man and the Scottish islands. Despite the slaughter, slave-taking and destruction inflicted by these raids, no substantial Scandinavian settlement of a permanent nature was ever established in Alba as defined here. It must be emphasized that a single, though ramified, dynasty held the kingship of this territory from the mid-ninth century to the mid-eleventh, while a single segment of the same dynasty ruled almost without a break from 1058 to 1286. Between c.950 and 1018 the kings of Scots extended their rule southward to the River Tweed.

If this kingdom of Alba or Scotland was to survive it had to accommodate itself within a northern Europe in which a relatively small number of distinct political entities were being formed – notably the kingdom of Germany under the Salian emperors, the slowly expanding kingdom of France under its long-lasting Capetian dynasty, the strategically placed kingdom of Denmark (less of a potential threat after the death of Cnut the Great in 1035), and, above all where Scotland was concerned, the kingdom of England, conquered (1066) and transformed by William the Bastard, duke of Normandy. The rise of these political entities was marked by substantial economic growth and the development of new military techniques.

In the two centuries from c.1050, military skills and techniques of warfare were of the utmost importance. There were lasting consequences for Christian Europe, east and west, arising from the battle of Manzikert (Malazgirt) in Armenia (1071), where the army of the Eastern Empire was annihilated by the Seljuk Turks and the emperor himself captured. The Turkish victory was contemporaneous with their conquest of Jerusalem in a war waged against their fellow Muslims, the Fatimid caliphs of Egypt. The menace of more intolerant rulers in the Holy Land stimulated western Christian powers – especially the Normans who were overrunning southern Italy and Sicily – to improve their skills in cavalry warfare and in the design and construction of fortifications.

Much of this military development is broadly associated with what historians for the past two centuries have called 'feudalism' or the 'feudal system'. This involved the creation by major rulers and their wealthiest subjects of estates whose holders ('tenants' or 'vassals') were required to perform relatively skilled, expensive military service involving possession of specially bred and trained horses (*destriers*) and elaborate protective clothing and equipment – in particular, the mail tunic or 'hauberk', cone-shaped helmet and kite-shaped shield.

Skill in horsemanship, in the use of weapons (especially lance, mace and sword), in the defence of simple 'motte and bailey' castles, was shared so widely throughout the aristocracy of north-west Europe that it gave rise to a freemasonry of knighthood in which kings, great magnates, middling nobles and simple knights could all join on a footing of something like equality. Kings and emperors were expected to be knighted, i.e. to undergo the elaborate, quasi-religious ceremonial by which a man was made a *chevalier*, *Ritter* or knight. Once knighted, he would not be, in that respect, superior to knights of lower social standing. Nothing in the written record of the twelfth and thirteenth centuries is more striking than, on the one hand, the prominence with which chroniclers record the knighting of kings and princes and, on the other hand, the manner in which in many thousands of formal documents the principals and witnesses are carefully given the title *dominus* (Sir) and the description *miles* (knight). At the battle of Hastings a Norman knight rushed to the body of King Harold of England as he lay dead and hacked at his thigh. This deed so shocked the victorious Duke William that he solemnly expelled its perpetrator from the order of knighthood – something which could not have happened in pre-Conquest England or in Scotland before the twelfth century (Mynors *et al* 1998–9).

This military freemasonry did not exist in England before 1066 or in Scotland before 1100. In England the 'housecarles' brought in by the Danish king, Cnut, formed a much smaller group than the post-Conquest knighthood. Although 'thegns', technically the noble class, were very numerous in eleventh-century England, they varied widely in wealth, status and functions. Above all, thegns formed hereditary castes, whereas knighthood never became hereditary in England or Scotland. Thegns in Scotland ('thanes' in modern usage) were more specialised than in England, serving as administrators or managers of the estates of kings or earls. They performed military service and might be responsible for organising the army service of able-bodied adult males. Only gradually, however, did individual Scottish thanes learn to perform the knight service on horseback judged to be essential by the twelfth century.

By the 1130s, two generations after the battle of Hastings, the rich kingdom of England was organized remarkably tightly for the purpose of providing an effective army in the king's service and maintaining castles as the up-to-date form of defence. Even as early as the later 1060s and during the 1070s the king, empowered by the harsh rule that every man who had fought in the English army at Hastings forfeited his lands, had granted out to his chief followers a great part of England south of the River Tees. More was given to favoured subjects by William II Rufus and his brother Henry I, yet the crown still retained a vast area scattered across the land as 'royal demesne'. Increasingly, in the period between Hastings and the 1150s, the expectation that a son – or a daughter if there were no sons – would inherit the father's estate hardened into an established rule. The overwhelming majority of the estates thus granted out and inherited, known as *feoda* (fiefs), were held of the crown in return for skilled, specialised military service.

It would have been impossible for the kingdom of Scotland, however determined its people might have been to cling to their ancient and customary ways, to ignore what was happening in England – now undoubtedly one of the richest and most powerful political units of western Europe. The Norman kings of England (1066–1135) showed no inclination to embark on the conquest or annexation of Scotland. They were content to obtain a series of submissions by which kings from Malcolm (Maelcoluim) III (1057–93) to David I (1124–53) acknowledged the English kings' superior lordship. That Anglo-Scottish relations were left in this relatively peaceful and civilised state was not due to any predilection on the part of the Normans to love the Scots. The hostility between Macbeth, king of Scots 1040–57, and Malcolm III who eventually supplanted him forced Malcolm to seek refuge at the court of Edward the Confessor (1042–66), last king of England of the old royal house of Wessex. When Malcolm took power in 1058 he was the first king of Scots to have spent any significant length of time in England, or to have personal knowledge of the English court. A series of quite extraordinary accidents of history brought about the situation that obtained in the early decades of the twelfth century, when three kings of Scotland in turn enjoyed exceptional peace at home and friendly relations with their more powerful neighbours to the south.

In the first place, the descendants of King Ethelred 'the Unready' (d. 1016) who had the best claim to the English throne in defiance of Danish or Norman conquerors returned to England from exile in Hungary in 1057. Within a decade, William Duke of Normandy had conquered England. Two years later the surviving West Saxon claimant, Edgar 'the Atheling', fled to Scotland with his mother and two sisters, the elder of whom, Margaret, became the second wife of the recently widowed King Malcolm III. Although theoretically Queen Margaret and her brother were opponents of the Norman conquerors, the Atheling was tolerated by William the Conqueror and his sons. The way was open for the elder daughter of Malcolm and Margaret – Edith (renamed Matilda by the Normans) to marry the youngest son, Henry, who followed his brother William Rufus on the throne and ruled for thirty-five years (1100–35), becoming known to posterity as Henry I, because his grandson was also called Henry.

Although Queen Matilda died in 1018 relations between her siblings on the Scottish throne and Henry I were good, and the only surviving child of Henry and Matilda – also Matilda (wife for fifteen years of the king of Germany, Emperor Henry V, 1106–25), was in close touch with her uncle King David I who, on Henry I's death in 1135, supported her claim to the English throne against her rival, Stephen of Blois. Relations between Malcolm III and William Rufus were not good (and were at their worst at the time of Malcolm's death in 1093). Nevertheless, we may see the Scottish royal house entering into a close relationship with the Norman rulers of England. In the person of David I it reached out further to establish friendship with the French monarchy in the reign of Louis VI (1108–37).

Given this Anglo-Scottish *rapprochement*, it would be surprising if certain defining features of post-Conquest England had not been copied in Scotland. In particular, we find that in the earlier decades of the twelfth century the 'motte and bailey' castle, imported into England from Normandy in 1066 and spread far across the country by 1100, was beginning to be introduced north of the border. Closely related to this development in the field of fortification was the introduction of the fief (*feudum* or estate, normally in land) held of the king in return for specialised military services. Many scores, if not hundreds, of such estates were created by kings and nobles from the time of Edgar (1097–1107) to the end of William the Lion's reign in 1214. Typically, these estates were held for the service of one knight, which could be performed in an actual campaign or in helping to garrison a royal castle. The greater lords, themselves holding estates in return for five or ten knights' service, imitated the crown, establishing knights' fees (*feuda* or *feoda militum*) within their own lordships. They also erected motte (or motte and bailey) castles, which their own knightly tenants would be organised to defend.

The knights and castle-builders came into Scotland from the continent – Flanders, Burgundy, Normandy, Brittany – and from England. The incomers were not always popular with the native inhabitants. In the 1120s a knight named Robert of Burgundy, to whom the king had granted the lands of Lochore in west Fife, infuriated the clergy serving the little church of St Serf on the island in Loch Leven by seizing the lands of Kirkness to which they had a strong claim. In 1154 two evidently native Scots named Arthur and Nes of Callendar plotted to kill the new king, David I's young grandson Malcolm IV, presumably because they feared the royal policy of encouraging foreign settlers. In 1168 some Scots 'treacherously' (as was alleged) slew an unmistakably Norman Raoul (Radulfus) Malchael and two of his companions as they rode through Scotland.

The most serious challenge to the innovative monarchy of the twelfth century came from the western fringe of Alba – the north-west Highlands and the Western Isles. In 1098 the King of Norway, Magnus Barelegs, made a treaty with Edgar king of Scots which provided that Norwegian sovereignty would be recognised not only over the Northern Isles (Orkney and Shetland) but also over the islands of Scotland's western seaboard (except, possibly, for Arran, Bute and the Cumbraes). For most of the twelfth century, government of this area by the Norwegian kings – mediated through the subordinate kings of Man – was relatively ineffectual, especially after the death of Olaf the Red, King of Man, in 1153. The islands between Skye and Kintyre, together with Argyll or Lorn, a mainland region which was part of the Scottish kingdom, fell under the domination of a family of Norse-Gaelic ancestry whose head was Somerled (Somhairle) son of Gillebrigde.

No contemporary source explains why Somerled took up arms against the kings David I and his grandson Malcolm IV. It is only a modern and possibly anachronistic interpretation which assumes that the motive must have been racial. It certainly cannot have been a simple matter of Celt *versus* Saxon, for Somerled's forces must have included many men whose ancestry was as much Norwegian as Gaelic, while the Scottish royal house was supported by 'Normans' (mixed Scandinavian and Romano-Frankish), Bretons (Celtic in ancestry and even in speech) and Flemings (Germanic in speech, but hardly Saxon). It might be nearer the mark if we surmised that Somerled's ambitions were simply territorial. In his last enterprise (1164) he brought a fleet and army up the Clyde to Renfrew, where he was defeated and killed.

The other champion to emerge from the western fringe of Scotland was Donald Mac William, grandson of King Duncan II (killed in 1094). Evidently brought up in a Gaelic-speaking *milieu*, his links with the north-west Highlands emerge clearly enough from the fact that his revolts prompted royal expeditions in the 1170s and 1180s to the country north west of Inverness. In Donald's case, the motive for revolt was undoubtedly dynastic. He aimed, so contemporaries relate, to seize the kingdom. Eventually hunted down and slain by King William's forces in 1187, Donald left descendants who persisted with dynastic claims and rebellions until the 1230s.

SOCIETY AND ECONOMY

Although one cannot put a figure to it, there can be no doubt that the population of Scotland expanded substantially between 1100 and 1300. The country produced wool, which was exported to the cloth towns of Flanders; the skins of sheep and lambs; the hides of cattle; hawks of various species for use in falconry; fish of many kinds, but especially salmon, herring and eels; pearls from the River Tay; gold from the Clydesdale hills; salt from the upper part of the Firth of Forth and coal from seams exposed along the shores of Fife and Lothian or simply dug from large cavities ('pots') that soon became hard to work, because of the lack of effective pumping equipment.

Agriculture and pastoralism easily prevailed over manufacture and the extractive industries. The characteristic grain grown was 'bere' (an old six-rowed variety of barley), oats and rye, but occasionally there is record of wheat and (from the thirteenth century) peas. In eastern Scotland 'open field' arable was normal – that is, the ground that could grow crops in each village or settlement was ploughed, cultivated and sown in a single continuous operation, the actual ploughing involving the use of a heavy wheel-less plough that normally required eight oxen to drag it along. In some settlements all the arable was concentrated in a single stretch of ground, peasants' holdings intermingling with those of their lord. In others there was segregation: Bond Nydie, the name of a habitation near St Andrews, commemorates the fact that here the cultivated land of the peasants (*bondi*) was separate from the part of Nydie held by the bishop. South of the Forth-Clyde isthmus the arable was characterised by a real measurement – the 'ploughgang' or 'ploughgate' – divisible into eight parts called 'oxgangs'. To the north, the land that was not waste, hill grazing or deer forest was composed of units of arable-with-pasture, to which the slightly puzzling term *dabhach* (davoch) was applied from early times. The word literally means 'vat' or 'tub', and its application to a sizeable piece of ground, possibly amounting to 150–200 acres, is not self-evidently appropriate. If the vat was filled with grain, that might refer to the seed corn required to plant a given area or perhaps to the tribute demanded by its lord. The term *dabhach* was in general use from the Firth of Forth northward to Sutherland and across to the Inner Hebrides; only in the Lennox (the district which includes Loch Lomond) was it replaced by the 'arachor', a term which certainly refers to ploughing.

Genuine towns (normally called 'burghs') multiplied and flourished, offering regular weekly markets or the occasional fair. Their inhabitants were mostly merchants and traders and their servants, but skilled craftsmen and industrial workers, for example fullers (Scots 'waulkers') and weavers (Scots 'websters'), might find a home in certain towns.

Urban development and activity added greatly to Scotland's prosperity and, since most of the larger or more important towns were established on royal demesne, much of this prosperity accrued to the crown. The well-known medieval saying 'town life makes free' points to another important contribution which burghs must have made to Scotland's social pattern – the opportunity that they could offer to the unfree (not necessarily absolute slaves) to emancipate themselves by evading recapture and dwelling in a burgh 'for a year and a day'.

A further contribution that town life made to Scottish social development was in the field of health care and provision for the old and infirm. Most of the hospitals for which there is medieval evidence were situated in or on the edge of towns and burghs. Those created explicitly for the segregation and care of lepers might be interpreted in a negative sense as no more than a measure of self-defence on behalf of the uninfected. But many hospitals were founded for the care of old people, and some may well have had a medical dimension – though the creation of a university chair of medicine would have to wait till the end of the fifteenth century, when one was established at Aberdeen. The point to be made here is that there would have been very few hospitals in Scotland had the country remained overwhelmingly rural. In the larger burghs such as Berwick upon Tweed, Edinburgh, Perth and Aberdeen the townspeople – burgesses and others – formed 'guilds' or associations to promote trade and protect privileges. Guilds took care of the sick and the elderly and were often founders and patrons of hospitals. It would be normal for a guild and its associated hospital or hospitals to seek protection and benefits from a chosen patron saint.

MONARCHY AND THE KINGDOM

Scotland was fortunate in having a royal dynasty which, with a brief break from 1093 to 1097, held the throne from 1058 to 1286. It did not hold the throne without opposition – rebellion was endemic in the medieval state. But from 1097, when Edgar drove his uncle, Domhnall Bán (Donald the Fair) off the throne, to 1286, when Alexander III met his death tragically on the Fife coast, there was no serious, let alone successful, attempt to block the succession of the senior male heir of the late king. This was demonstrated strikingly in 1153, when the twelve-year-old Malcolm

IV succeeded his grandfather; in 1214, when the eighteen-year-old Alexander II succeeded his elderly father William the Lion and, most remarkably of all, in 1249, when following the sudden death of King Alexander the leading nobles rallied in support of the not yet eight-year-old boy Alexander, to ensure that he was made king at Scone in the traditional manner. Indeed, the kingship was so firmly established that in 1284, after Alexander III's son (another Alexander) had tragically died at 21, the magnates were persuaded to recognise the king's infant granddaughter Margaret (daughter of the king of Norway) as heir to the Scottish throne.

The geographical kingdom in which this firmly established dynasty reigned grew in area steadily – sometimes dramatically – between 1124 and 1286. Although David I claimed royal dues from Argyll and Kintyre, his authority there was probably limited. He did, however, bring Moray (and possibly Ross) under his rule, a northward expansion of the Scottish kingdom consolidated and extended under his grandsons Malcolm IV (1153–65) and William the Lion (1165–1214). At the turn of the twelfth and thirteenth centuries the rebellious behaviour of the Earl of Caithness and Orkney, Harald Maddadsson, and the determination with which King William brought the earl to heel, enabled the Scottish crown to exercise a measure of control over the northern mainland, at least on the east side of the country. This control was evidently maintained through the next reign when the Earl and freeholders of Caithness were severely punished for the murder of their bishop, Adam of Melrose (1213–22). Thereafter a succession of earls seem to have been loyal to the Scottish monarchy until the first War of Independence.

There remained two regions of Scotland whose status was uncertain – Galloway in the south west and Argyll and the Western Isles. In the earlier twelfth century Galloway had been regarded (or at any rate regarded itself) as a kingdom, a dignity the kings of Scots wished to suppress. As late as 1200–1234 the lord of Galloway, Alan son of Lachlan, pursued a remarkably independent career, interfering freely in the affairs of northern Ireland and the Isle of Man, holding himself almost on equal terms with the king of Scots and hobnobbing with King John of England (Alan was the fifth layman, after four English earls, to be named as a sponsor for King John when he issued the famous Magna Carta at Runnymede in June, 1215). Although Alan married three times he had no legitimate son, and on his death in 1234 the men of Galloway petitioned the King of Scots to allow Alan's bastard son Thomas to inherit their province, under the king's immediate lordship and protection. King Alexander insisted on excluding Thomas and partitioning Galloway among Alan's three daughters, who had all married English barons. The Gallovidians rose in revolt and were suppressed with much savagery, northern magnates such as Walter Comyn Earl of Menteith and Farquhar Earl of Ross playing a leading role in the campaign of suppression. It has been said that the Gallovidians' readiness to turn to King Alexander on their lord's death 'confirms that Galloway was far less detached from the Scottish kingdom than it had been sixty years before' (Stringer 1993, 102). Nevertheless, Galloway remained in some ways distant or remote from Scotland until the fourteenth century or later.

Unlike Galloway, Argyll (with the peninsula of Kintyre) had been regarded as in some sense part of Scotland long before the twelfth century, even though it lay to the west of Drumalban, the 'spine of Alba', the hills from Ben Lomond to Loch Oich forming the watershed between Atlantic-flowing and North Sea-flowing rivers. Argyll was, after all, the 'shore of the Gael' or Scots, the cradle of the Scottish race. Even 'normanising' kings like David I or William the Lion were aware of the importance of Scotland's western approaches, which they protected with castles and military (feudal) lordships.

Twelfth-century Argyll shared one feature with contemporary Galloway: a ruling dynasty that claimed some quality of royalty. The origins of Argyll's dynasty are obscure. Biologically, they were a mixture of Gaelic and Norse, the second strain showing itself in their habitual use of the fast, lightly-built, oar-propelled galley or *birlinn*. The head of the dynasty in the middle of the twelfth century was Somerled (Norse *sumarlidi*, literally 'viking'), son of Gillebrigde. The monastic chroniclers of Furness and Melrose style Somerled *regulus*, 'petty king', of Argyll, a title which was probably meant to imply that although Somerled claimed kingly status, his kingship ought not to be equated with that of the kings of Scots or of England.

Somerled married more than once, but his chief wife was a daughter of Olaf the Red, king of Man and the Isles, who ruled the Hebrides, nominally on behalf of the king of Norway. In Olaf's lifetime, Somerled seems to have ruled peacefully, but in 1153, the year in which both King Olaf and King David I died, Somerled embarked on a long-drawn-out rebellion against the youthful king of Scots, Malcolm IV. The precise motive for this rebellion is unknown, but Somerled was in alliance with the sons of Malcolm Mac Aedh whose wife – presumably the sons' mother – was Somerled's sister. Malcolm was son of an Earl of Ross, Aedh, who had evidently incurred the wrath of David I and been deprived of his earldom. When Angus Earl of Moray, maternal grandson of Lulach who had been briefly king of Scots in 1057, rebelled against David I in 1130, Malcolm Mac Aedh was Angus's ally, but he was captured in 1134 and imprisoned in Roxburgh castle until 1157, when King Malcolm released him and gave him his father's earldom.

Somerled of Argyll does not seem to have been included in this reconciliation, but before Christmas 1160 he made peace with King Malcolm. He broke this peace four years later, leading a fleet and army up the River Clyde as far as Renfrew, where he was defeated and killed. Argyll remained at peace with the king of Scots till the 1220s, and it is arguable that the creation of a new diocese for Argyll in the 1190s (the region having previously been in Dunkeld diocese) was a friendly gesture on the part of the king of Scots.

The reign of Alexander II (1214-49) saw fundamental changes in the relations between the Scottish monarchy and the western seaboard. For the first time in almost a century, Norway had a strong king – Hakon IV Hakonsson – who ruled unchallenged for almost fifty years (1216–63). In Ewen (son of Duncan, son of Dubhgall (Dougal), son of Somerled) the two rulers – Alexander and Hakon – had to deal with a man of undoubted political and military ability who held firmly, for as long as he could, to his kingly title and his control over Mull, Morvern, Argyll proper and the islands of the Firth of Lorne. What proved too much for Ewen in the end was the determination of the kings of Scots, Alexander II and (after his minority) Alexander III (1249–86), to wrest the Western Isles from Norwegian possession and the equal determination of King Hakon to retain his sovereignty. It proved impossible for Ewen to be loyal to two masters, while independence for Argyll was out of the question.

With time on their side, the Scots could afford to wait till the summer of 1263 when King Hakon brought a large fleet first to the Northern then to the Western Isles. Hakon clearly wished to reaffirm Norwegian sovereignty and did not find his task easy. Ewen MacDougall of Argyll threw in his lot with the Scots, but could not prevent the Norwegian fleet sailing south round the Mull of Kintyre and into the Firth of Clyde. When on 2 October 1263 – partly because of a severe westerly gale – the Norwegians landed on the Scottish mainland at Largs, they were eventually beaten off by the local forces. Hakon died on the voyage home, and three years later the plenipotentiaries of the new king, Magnus the Lawmender, came to Perth and put their seals to a treaty with Scotland which proved of permanent effect. Norway acknowledged Scottish sovereignty in the Hebrides and Man, retaining only Orkney and Shetland. The Scots paid Norway 4,000 merks (one merk – a weight of silver, not a coin – was reckoned to be worth 13s. 4d. or two-thirds of a pound). They ought also to have paid a hundred merks annually in perpetuity, but payment of this 'annual' ceased in the fourteenth century – perhaps a perpetual liability was never meant to be taken seriously. Fifteen years after the Treaty of Perth, Alexander III's daughter Margaret married the king of Norway, Eric, and it was their only child (another Margaret) who was formally recognised as heir to the Scottish throne after the untimely death of King Alexander's sole surviving son. Although the little 'Maid of Norway' sadly died in 1290 on her way to Scotland, links between the two kingdoms remained close and not unfriendly for many generations.

GOVERNMENT

It remains to look at how the kingdom of Scotland was governed between the late eleventh and the late thirteenth centuries. At the top the king, solemnly inaugurated (not crowned) at Scone, ruled with a council, the membership of which was largely at his own discretion, although it would be hard for him to ignore the advice of certain senior bishops and religious (monks and canons-regular). Moreover, it was normal in the twelfth century for the kings to dignify certain household offices – in particular those of the steward, butler, constable, doorward and marischal – by making them hereditary. Once this had happened it would clearly be very difficult to exclude from the royal council a senior court officer who had inherited his office by royal grant: he could claim a position as of right. We may envisage a small 'inner council' of perhaps 10 or 15 members in regular attendance on the king. Four or five times a year, however, the king and his inner council would join a much larger assembly at which, in theory at least, every baron who claimed to hold his estate 'in chief' – i.e. directly – of the crown would be present. These larger and more solemn councils – sometimes called *colloquia* or parliaments – would customarily debate and decide solemn or 'national' business, including taxation (which was almost by definition extraordinary), foreign affairs and major legal or juridical business, including actual trials or civil lawsuits.

For the great bulk of the population (perhaps about half a million in the mid-thirteenth century) the king and his council would seem rather remote. The majority of inhabitants in rural areas were peasant farmers and their dependents. For them, matters of law and order were dealt with in the court held by, or at least on behalf of, their lord. If the lord had the rank of knight and held an estate which by c.1300 would be called a 'barony' he would have what in charters was called 'sake, soke, pit (i.e. ordeal pit) and gallows, and infangthief' – that is, a court which could deal with ordinary crime such as hot-blooded, open killing (not murder), theft, violence, drunkenness, disputes over tenancies and grazing rights etc. Murder (secret killing), rape, fire-raising (English 'arson') and raiding or rustling were all serious enough to be reserved for the higher courts held by sheriffs and justiciars. Treason could be dealt with only in the king's court, normally presided over by the justiciar, predecessor of the lord justice general. In Scotland, from approximately the Pentland Hills northward there were courts called 'couthal' or cuthill (derived from Gaelic *comhdál*, 'assembly'), where petty crimes and disputes could be settled. It is not known who would have convened or presided at these courts, but there were also lords' courts in northern Scotland with a higher jurisdiction than the 'couthal' courts. For example, the lords of Abernethy at the head of the Firth of Tay were entitled to hold one pit and gallows court at Abernethy for their tenants in Fife and Gowrie and another at Inverarity for their tenants in Angus.

Sheriffs were brought in gradually during the twelfth century. They were senior officers of the crown who held a wide responsibility in small regions, which came to be known as sheriffdoms or counties. A sheriff would normally have charge of the king's castle in the sheriffdom and would oversee the collection of revenues due to the crown. At regular intervals he would convene and preside over a meeting of the sheriffdom court (later simply the 'sheriff court') which had authority over men of baronial rank as well as substantial freeholders.

Above the sheriff court was the court held by the justiciars – one for Lothian, which normally comprised the whole country south of the Firths of Clyde and Forth, one for 'Scotia' which was understood to mean the whole of Scotland north of the Firths. From time to time, there might be a justiciar for Galloway, the geographical extent of which in this particular is nowhere stated. Sheriffs and justiciars must have been very busy men indeed. This may be demonstrated from abundant evidence, but one unpublished letter of King Malcolm IV (1153–1165) in favour of the Augustinian canons of Guisborough Priory in north Yorkshire shows clearly how much work might be loaded on to the shoulders of these indispensable officials. Apparently, Scots raiders were in the habit of travelling as far south as Yorkshire in search of prey, and if the Guisborough canons – who had presumably put a distinctive mark on their sheep and cattle – suspected that their beasts had been illegally driven north of the Border they could appeal for help to Scots law officers. The king gave leave to the priory's agents to search anywhere in Scotland for their stolen cattle. If they discovered them in Scotland north of the Forth, the local sheriff had to produce the beasts before the king's justiciar of Lothian or Teviotdale. If they were found in Lothian or Teviotdale then, in whichever sheriffdom they were found, the local sheriff had to see that full justice was done. One way or another a great deal of travelling and droving was envisaged here, with a heavy responsibility falling on Scottish justiciars and sheriffs.

The Anglo-Norman impact left an imperishable mark on Scotland and its history. Had England not been conquered by the Normans in 1066, and had England not been governed by two continental dynasties (Norman and Angevin) for three-and-a-half centuries, it is by no means far-fetched to imagine native English kings exerting pressure on the Scots, forcing them to surrender first Lothian and then perhaps Fife, Gowrie and Angus, or even the whole of Clydesdale. Instead, English kings hankered after continental territories and French became the official or court language of England until the end of the fourteenth century. Scots political spokesmen of the thirteenth and fourteenth centuries were not indulging in complete fantasy when they argued that their kings, descended from St Margaret, had better claims to England than the English dynasties had to Scotland, even though Henry of Anjou was St Margaret's great-grandson.

Twelfth-century Scotland inherited from its Scoto-Pictish past its kingship, sacred and tribal in character, strongly Christianised by the kings from Edgar onwards; its geographical or regional divisions with their rulers, *mórmaer* or earls; its thanedoms and popular courts; its ancient sacred places and shrines, such as Iona, Dunkeld, Abernethy and St Andrews; its languages, Gaelic, Cumbric, English and Norse. Between 1097 and 1214 many new features became part of the Scottish scene. We have seen how the crown insisted on an army of trained knights, prepared to fight on horseback, expensively mounted, armoured and equipped. Castles, many of which were remarkably simple affairs, were built right across southern Scotland from Berwick upon Tweed to Ayr and deep into Galloway, from Stirling northward to Aberdeen, Banff and along the Moray coastal plain to Inverness and beyond. A new kind of sheriff tightened the grip of the crown, not merely on royal demesne but on the country as a whole. Royal government introduced the charter (to record permanent grants) and the brieve or writ (to convey the king's immediate wishes or commands), both classes of document sealed with the king's seal impressed on wax, both classes totally innovatory. The kings encouraged the formation of privileged trading towns or burghs, occupying favourable localities often on or close to the coast, especially in the east. To facilitate trade, the kings from David I onward (1136) minted silver coins showing the king's name and head on the obverse side with the moneyer's name and (usually) a cross on the reverse. These coins were pennies, copied from the standard 'sterling' coin of England, weighing the 240th part of one pound of good quality silver.

Hand in hand with this development went a transformation in the character and constitution of the Christian church in Scotland. This involved enhancing the position and dignity of cathedrals and their bishops and the introduction of religious orders of men and women. Once again, as with castles, burghs and coinage, this ecclesiastical revolution was overwhelmingly the work of the royal house. There had been bishops in the Scottish church since at least the sixth century, but although a plurality of bishops may be guessed at or occasionally seen in the tenth and eleventh centuries, the Christian people of Scotland were not formally organized in a diocesan system. From the reign of Alexander I (1107–24) we can discern the beginnings of such a system which, though novel in itself, was respectful of ancient traditions and loyalties. Long before 1100, the bishop presiding at Kilrimund (i.e. St Andrews) had been styled *ardescop Alban* or 'high bishop of Scotland', implying lesser bishops. St Andrews remained the principal bishop's church or diocese of Scotland, but almost equal respect was accorded to Glasgow, famed for its shrine of St Kentigern or, affectionately, Mungo. Under these two leading churches there were, by 1200, eight lesser dioceses – Caithness, Ross, Moray, Aberdeen, Brechin, Dunkeld, Argyll and Dunblane – together with Galloway (also called *Candida Casa* or Whithorn), subject to York. Each diocese was divided into parishes, varying enormously in area, wealth and population. Between c.1100 and c.1250, the bishops of Scotland (most of whom were crown appointees) had created and consolidated the parish system. There could be friction between the crown and the church, but normally there was harmony, the church recognising on which side its bread was buttered. The Christian life of western Europe was thoroughly permeated throughout this period by monastic ideals that laid emphasis on withdrawal from the world, self-denial and charity. Many hundreds – indeed thousands – of religious houses for both men and women were founded across western Christendom. Scotland proved no exception in terms of variety among religious orders, but it is noteworthy that a remarkably high proportion of Scottish houses were founded by kings and queens or by members of the royal family. Monastic ideals had perhaps not struck such a deep chord among the population at large, and certainly if we compare the monastic situation in medieval England with that in Scotland we must agree that the southern kingdom was vastly more favourable to the acceptance and practice of monasticism.

Many of these innovations, even when their ancestry was Norman or continental (e.g. knights' fees and castles) were English in character, and their implementation was carried out by English men and women, in many cases reinforced by French, Flemings and Scandinavians. Compared with Scotland c.1100, mid thirteenth-century Scotland was a hotchpotch of races and even of languages. In the intervening century-and-a-half, the English language had made substantial gains, expanding from its five-centuries-old base in lower Tweeddale, the Merse and Midlothian and East Lothian to at least the towns and some rural areas of eastern Scotland north of Forth and Tay and as far north as the Moray Firth. Cumbric, the old Brittonic language of south-west Scotland, must have been virtually extinct by c.1250, while Gaelic seems to have retreated from Fife, lowland Angus and the Aberdeenshire and Moray littoral by, at latest, the middle decades of the fourteenth century. The position of French in Scotland, the language of incoming twelfth-century nobles and churchmen, was in sharp contrast with its predominance among the ruling class of midland and southern England. It must always have been a minority speech, although important in certain contexts. Linguistically, Scotland adhered much more closely to old and middle

English than England, as we can see from the following table where Scots usage is
shown in the left-hand column, English in the right-hand. OE stands for 'Old English',
ME for 'Middle English', Fr for 'French', Lat for 'Latin' and G for 'Gaelic'.

anent	OE	concerning	Fr +
doom	OE	judgement	Fr
doorward	OE	usher	Fr
eident	ME	diligent	Fr
flesher	OE	butcher	Fr
galluses	OE	braces	Fr
gar	ME	cause	Fr
girth	OE	sanctuary	Lat
greet	OE	cry	Fr
grieve	OE	bailiff	Fr
lith	OE	segment	Lat
manre(n)t	OE	homage	Fr
outwith	OE (northern)	outside	OE (southern)
thole, dree	OE	endure	Fr
threep (land)	OE	debatable (land)	Fr +
tocher	G	dowry	Fr
toun	OE	manor, village	Fr
weird	OE	fate Lat, fortune	Fr
wersh	ME	tasteless	Fr +

The older Scottish tongue, a form of Middle English, developed without a major
interruption into the Scots of modern times and reflects more fully than modern English
the speech of southern Britain before the Normans came. In the centuries covered by
this chapter, Scots was almost certainly becoming dominant everywhere south of Clyde
and Forth, save for the inland and western parishes of Galloway and Carrick. But even
in this southern region of Scotland there was a legacy of racial and linguistic mixture.
The East Lothian estate of Congalton had belonged to a man named after the famous
saint Comgall, of Bangor in northern Ireland and Tiree in the Hebrides. Not far from
Congalton are Aberlady (a purely Cumbric name) and Ballencrieff (purely Gaelic). In
Clydesdale the Gaelic-named Cormac had given his name to Cormiston. North of
Peebles, even within the twelfth century, an estate had begun as the probably Cumbric
Jacob's house (Penteiacob), changed into the toun of the presumably Gaelic-speaking
Gillemuire ('St Mary's servant') – Gillemurestun – and ended up as the toun of the
presumably Middle English-speaking Eadulf, now Eddleston – though they might have
been father and son. Further north, in eastern Perthshire, a presumably Gaelic-speaking
Gillegirig had given his name to 'Gillegirigestune' (now Kilgraston), while an incoming
neighbour Richard (French or English-speaking?) got the tenancy of 'Ricardestune',
now lost – though further south this same name, in three different localities, became
Riccarton. In Scotland between the 1090s and the 1290s there is plentiful evidence of
conservatism, but overwhelming evidence of radical change.

By no means all the peoples of western Europe organized themselves, or were organized, into distinct kingdoms or political unities before 1300. Scotland, which had succeeded in becoming a distinct kingdom by 1328 – perhaps even by 1266 – owed this result to a combination of self-awareness as a nation (achieved by 1286 if not sooner) and unusual military success (achieved between 1297 and the 1320s).

While this was the most important development in the history of the Scottish people between the eleventh and the fourteenth century, it was essentially a summing-up of a number of other developments which combined to give Scotland its distinctive identity and to fix its relationship with its neighbours and the wider world of western Christendom. First among these developments was the monarchy, preserved from ancient times but adapted to a political and social structure which embraced military feudalism and at least the beginnings of central government. Second among political and social developments was the formation of a hybrid nobility in which the dozen or so earls, superficially 'feudalised', represented continuity with Celtic Alba, while all but the wealthiest 'barons' – the class of lairds as they had become by the fifteenth century – formed a closely interrelated network of landowners in control of local government, filling the office of sheriff in almost 30 sheriffdoms, holding their own 'baron courts', and contributing to national defence by land and sea. Thirdly we have the phenomenon of urban growth, modest in terms of population increase but socially and economically significant. West-coast burghs traded with Irish seaports such as Dublin and Drogheda, east-coast burghs brought ships and merchants from northern France, Flanders, Germany and Norway. Finally we see that Scotland's identity was very much a matter of being recognised by her neighbours – France, not so remote as the map would suggest; Ireland, of old a major source of Scots culture, medievally a market for Scots military manpower; Norway, of old a predatory competitor, medievally an important trading partner; above all England, much richer and more populous, sometimes threatening invasion and the assertion of political hegemony, more often a peaceful source of trade, ideas and manpower. The achievement of all these developments owed much to the 'Anglo-Norman impact', beginning around 1095 and losing momentum during the early decades of the thirteenth century.

REFERENCES TO BOOKS AND ARTICLES MENTIONED IN THE TEXT

Mynors, R, Thomson, R and Winterbottom, M 1998–9 *Gesta Regum Anglorum*. Oxford.

Stringer, KJ 1993 'Periphery and core in thirteenth-century Scotland: Alan son of Roland, lord of Galloway and constable of Scotland', *in* Grant, A and Stringer, K (eds), *Medieval Scotland: Crown, Lordship and Community*, Edinburgh, 82–113.

FURTHER READING

The following are recommended for further reading:

Barrow, GWS 2003 *Kingship and Unity: Scotland, 1000-1306.* 2nd edn, Edinburgh.
Barrow, GWS 1980 *The Anglo-Norman Era in Scottish History.* Oxford.
Barrow, GWS 1985 *David I of Scotland: the balance of new and old.* Reading.
Davies, RR 1990 *Domination and Conquest: the Experience of Ireland, Scotland and Wales, 1100–1300.* Cambridge.
Duncan, AAM 1975 *Scotland: the Making of the Kingdom.* Edinburgh.
Frame, R 1990 *The Political Development of the British Isles, 1100–1400.* Oxford.
Ritchie, RLG 1954 *The Normans in Scotland.* Edinburgh.

CHAPTER THREE

The Wars of Independence

Fiona Watson

This chapter deals with one of the most emotionally-charged issues in Scottish history: the wars between Scotland and England. The period is certainly important, given that the nation was fighting for its very survival against a hostile takeover bid from its larger, wealthier southern neighbour. It has also provided Scotland with two of its greatest heroes: Sir William Wallace and King Robert Bruce. However, we must be particularly careful not to take our own prejudices and preconceptions with us into the past (especially if we have already seen the film *Braveheart*!). Though people in the thirteenth century may well have felt the same as we do about war and its associated traumas, beliefs about identity and political allegiance were rather different from today and must be examined critically and with reference to prevailing medieval ideas on such matters.

In December 1295, Edward I of England ordered the mobilisation of a great English army to muster at Newcastle on 1 March 1296. Its target was Scotland which, Edward suspected, was intending to conclude an alliance with England's greatest enemy, France. On the other side of the border, the Scots were well aware of the likelihood of invasion and decided to pre-empt it by ravaging the countryside around Carlisle at the end of March 1296. Within a few short months, the Scots had been soundly defeated in battle, the main trading centre at Berwick had seen many of its citizens slaughtered and the king, John Balliol, was en route south to imprisonment, along with many key members of the Scottish nobility. Edward was now master of Scotland and he would rule it as a province of England, just like Ireland and Wales.

Thus began a war that certainly did not end, as Edward initially believed, in the summer of 1296 but which dragged on, in some form or other, to within sight of the union of the Crowns of England and Scotland in 1603. Some people today believe that there can be little more to say about this most-raked over of subjects, but you might be surprised at just how far we are from a complete analysis of these wars within a broader context. As well as seeking to establish the facts about exactly what happened in the period from the death of Alexander III in 1286 onwards, historians have also focused on the extent and role of national identity as a motivating force for Scottish resistance to Edward I's imperial aims. Archie Duncan wrote over thirty years ago that: 'Scotland had evolved during the peaceful thirteenth century a political identity or nationhood'. Crucially, he asserts that this sense of national self was 'a cause, not a result, of the war for independence' (Duncan 1966, 184).

Most writers would agree with Duncan that a sense of national identity played a role in bringing about the wars with England, rather than resulting from them.

However, we can also trace changes in the way in which that identity manifested itself as the decades of war dragged on. As GWS Barrow notes, if the war had never broken out 'there would have been no occasion for the dark years of carnage and destruction, and the breeding of hatred between two nations who for the past century had been learning, not without success, to be friends' (Barrow 1988, 261). That deep-seated enmity has done much to condition a defensive Scottish identity, which still has resonances today (not least in the adoption as an unofficial national anthem of the song *Flower of Scotland*, with its rousing reminder that 'Proud Edward's army' was sent home 'to think again').

But there has certainly not been complete unanimity in the approach of Scottish historians to the wars of independence. Most obviously, commentators with union-ist sympathies have found dealing with the period rather problematic. Since they regarded the eventual incorporating union between Scotland and England in 1707 as a successful and beneficial arrangement, they could see some ultimate benefits in what might have happened three centuries earlier. Sir Walter Scott, in his popular rendering of Scottish history, *Tales of a Grandfather*, went so far as to say that:

> He [Edward I] proposed a marriage betwixt the Maiden of Norway, the young Queen of Scotland, and his own son, called Edward, after himself. A treaty was entered into for this purpose; and had the marriage been effected, and been followed by children, the union of England and Scotland might have taken place more than three hundred years sooner than it did, and an immeasurable quantity of money and bloodshed would probably have been saved. (Scott 1925, 41–2)

[handwritten margin note: modern opinion colours how the events played out, and their consequences]

A more recent writer brings a rather different emphasis to bear on the same event:

> Although the Scots agreed in March 1290 to go ahead with the marriage . . . alarm bells were clearly rung by Edward's interference that summer . . . In the final negotiations for the betrothal the Scots . . . were on their guard to protect Scottish independence under regnal union. (Penman 2002, 34–5)

There can be no doubt that a writer's personal perspective on the political position of post-Union Scotland, combined with the prevailing political climate of his or her own time, plays a fundamental role in how that individual evaluates the wars of independence. Having said that, any historian looking for academic credibility will make an effort to see events as those who took part in them might have done, rather than how they might appear to those of us living in a modern democracy. But it would be a brave historian indeed who could claim that he or she was totally uninfluenced by contemporary ideas about Scottish identity and the relationship with England.

Issues relating to nationalism and national identity are always problematic and liable to lead to the holding of polarised and deep-seated views. These issues are interesting but they can – and on this subject, often have – obscured other important aspects which historians have only recently begun to tackle. In particular, the propaganda produced on behalf of the usurper king, Robert I, still requires systematic unpicking in order for us to understand fully the complex internal Scottish political environment in which the war was fought. It is often said that history is written by its winners; Scottish history is no different. King Robert Bruce's enemies within Scotland – most notably the previous king, John Balliol, and Balliol's powerful backer, the former Guardian, John Comyn of Badenoch – have suffered for centuries, being either written off or written out of Scottish history. Robert Bruce's most eminent contemporary biographer maintains the following opinion about John Comyn, who was murdered by Bruce in 1306: 'His pedigree, connexions and career combine to make a brave story, but the harsh fact remains that he was an almost total failure' (Barrow 1988, 145). This ignores the fact that this same man had previously managed to force out his Bruce rival from the Guardianship that they shared by 1300, becoming sole Guardian himself a few years later. As the longest-standing leader of Scottish resistance to Edward I prior to Bruce himself, John Comyn succeeded in keeping Scottish armies in the field – though quite rightly, and importantly, they concentrated on harassing English forces rather than engaging them in combat after the defeat at Falkirk in 1298. He also presided over an administration that preserved links with the Continent, collected revenues essential to maintaining the war effort and, perhaps most importantly of all, was able to dispense justice on and for the people of Scotland, allowing them some semblance of a normal life. The fact that the above took place predominantly in that part of the country free from English occupation – that is, north of the Forth-Clyde line – does not make it any less important.

The wars of independence deserve to be treated as critically as any other period in Scottish history. As with any other period, the questions with which we have to deal also tend not to produce black and white answers, however much we might wish this were the case. Finally, just because Scotland faced an extremely grave threat from outside did not prevent more normal peacetime politics from playing a part in how the nation's leaders – or community of the realm, as these men were described collectively at the time – conducted themselves. Though this period produced two of Scotland's greatest heroes, we must still assess the wars of independence and its participants as subject to the usual frailties, complexities and contradictions of any other theatre of human activity.

THE OUTBREAK OF WAR AND ITS BACKGROUND

There is a presumption within most modern nations that their existence was always meant to be, and that any threat to that existence in the past was highly reprehensible, an arrogant challenge to the authority of destiny itself. In fact, history is littered with the remains of nations that never quite made it to a full-blown permanent acknowledgement of their status, but which nevertheless maintained the kind of cultural, social and political unity that otherwise might have qualified them for this. Brittany or Catalonia are obvious examples within a European context. On the other hand, most modern nations, certainly in the 'Old World', actually emerged out of a confluence of historical accidents, despite fundamental racial and other differences among the peoples encompassed within them.

Scotland and, indeed, England fall into this latter category. And if we admit that such circumstances can produce one nation, then there is no reason for that process to stop, especially within the confines of an island. The separate kingdoms of England and Scotland certainly made no particular geographical sense – the border between them demarcates a landscape of rolling hills and productive farmland on either side and arbitrarily split the Anglo-Saxons living there in the eleventh century between them. We should also remember that that same century could easily have seen the British Isles taken over completely by Scandinavian invaders – Cnut the Dane ruled England and various other Scandinavian rulers controlled Orkney, Shetland, the Western Isles, parts of northern and western mainland Scotland, the Isle of Man and Ireland. Only Wales and the Scottish kingdom (still known as Alba) remained in the hands of native dynasties, but the future remained hugely uncertain.

However, England and Scotland survived. In the meantime, there had been a number of occasions on which the armies of England had proved more powerful than those of Scotland, and the kings of Scots had been forced to acknowledge that fact. However, the arrival of the Normans to rule England from 1066 brought a new formality to these occasions. The swearing of homage and fealty was a very solemn acknowledgement of a superior by an inferior, but the kings of Scots seem to have felt no less royal for having performed it to the kings of England. It was essentially the price to be paid for being caught on the wrong side of the border, and made little difference to the Scottish desire to encroach on territory south of the Tweed that had once formed part of the old Anglo-Saxon kingdom of Northumbria.

Then, in 1174, William I of Scotland was defeated, captured and brought in chains before an irate Henry II of England for yet another attack on northern England. The Treaty of Falaise forced him to pay homage as usual and, more worryingly, to hand over a number of his southern castles as insurance for good behaviour. But it is unlikely that anyone in either kingdom seriously believed that Scotland was subject to the authority of England in any meaningful sense. And anyway, Henry's son, Richard the Lionheart, bought out the treaty for cash in the Quitclaim of Canterbury of 1189.

To add further complexity to the issue, pressure was also put on the English king by his Church, which claimed jurisdiction over parts of the Scottish church. And while the Scots could point to the papal bull of 1192, *cum universi*, which made the Scottish kirk a 'special daughter' of Rome 'no-one in between', the lack of an archbishop for the northern kingdom continued to make its position ambiguous. In 1250, the Pope denied the Scottish king the right to crowning and anointing – the ultimate symbol of divinely-ordained kingship – because of pressure from English churchmen in Rome, who reminded His Holiness of English claims to jurisdiction over Scotland. The status of the kingdom and its church were fundamentally intertwined and no categorical statement could be made about either without prompting a contradictory response from England.

By the middle of the thirteenth century, however, the main issue of contention –

Scottish claims to parts of the old Northumbria – had been settled by the Treaty of York (1230). From then on, both sides danced around what was becoming a complex legal issue. The Scottish king accepted that he must perform homage and fealty to the king of England for the lands that he held in the latter's kingdom, but by now he explicitly denied anyone's claims over the Scottish kingdom itself. The English king, on the other hand, took the view that the long-standing oaths given by the Scottish kings in the aftermath of military defeat implied that England was superior to Scotland in terms of feudal jurisdiction.

However, such debates were largely academic as the thirteenth century progressed. Finally, the two countries appeared to be settling down to a largely amicable relationship that reflected shared aristocratic values and the close intertwining of families, up to and including the royal houses, on both sides of the Tweed. As one historian wrote thirty years ago, in a statement that still finds agreement today: 'Whatever the technicalities of the relationship between the two realms the spirit of the relationship was one that left the Scots unaware of subordination' (Nicholson 1978, 33). And they might have continued in blissful ignorance were it not for one of those accidents of history that are quite unpredictable in terms of specific events, but entirely to be expected as a general phenomenon. In the end, we might also consider the view that even if the technical legal position was clear-cut in England's favour, the Scots were highly unlikely to 'have chosen not to go to war in defence of the actual independence of the kingdom' (Watson 2001, 92). The belief that Scotland was in reality an independent entity counted for far more than whatever was written on pieces of parchment.

THE PLIGHT OF A KINGLESS KINGDOM

On 19 March 1286, Alexander III, king of Scots, was thrown from his horse and killed. He had no male heir. His designated successor acknowledged, if reluctantly, by the Scottish nobility in 1284, was his young granddaughter, Margaret, currently growing up in Norway. However, this did not prevent the ageing Robert Bruce of Annandale from claiming that he was the rightful male heir through his mother, a daughter of David, earl of Huntingdon. Civil war, the greatest calamity that could ever befall a nation, loomed ominously on the horizon.

One of the greatest myths about the wars of independence revolves around the role of the Scottish nobility. There is a popular perception that these 'Anglo-Norman' ingrates failed Scotland in its hour of need through cowardice and blatant self-interest. Such views find some corroboration from closer to the time in which these events took place. The monastic chroniclers who wrote down the earliest histories of Scotland also felt exasperation towards the tendency of society's secular leaders to indulge in politics rather than getting on with the task of suppressing disorder (which monks hated even more than most!).

In response to more modern attitudes, it should be enough for us to examine what the nobility actually did in order to show that their role in leading the struggle for Scottish independence was absolutely essential. Admittedly certain individuals chose to side with Edward, but this does not alter the fundamental point that Scotland's natural leaders generally fulfilled their duty to those whom they were expected to protect. They did so despite the personal difficulties involved in siding against the English king who not only refused them access to their lands and family south of the border, but on occasions put them in prison and, eventually, had some of them executed.

With regard to the charge levelled at the Scottish nobility by the chroniclers – that they tended to get sidetracked by their own political squabbles instead of getting on with the job of protecting Scotland – there is perhaps some truth in this. It is becoming more clear that powerful factions – most notably the Bruces and their allies such as the Stewarts, and the Comyns, who backed the king, John Balliol – often put their personal agendas before the more immediate task of prosecuting the war against England. Indeed, it could be argued that the war was more effectively managed when one of these factions gained control of government, as happened when John Comyn of Badenoch ousted Robert Bruce, Earl of Carrick, from the Guardianship they shared around 1300 and, more obviously, when Bruce himself seized the throne after killing Comyn (though he then had a civil war to win as well).

There is no doubt that some of the antics of the Scottish nobility appear as little more than self-indulgent pub brawling. However, we should also remember that the abstract notion of loyalty to a country which we accept as natural today would have seemed very suspect indeed to a medieval lord brought up on the concept of personal loyalty. The oaths of homage and fealty which bound landowning society together were taken by individuals to individuals and honour was completely bound up with the necessity of being true to such oaths. Thus we should not underestimate the sincerity of the Earl of Strathearn who refused the usurper King Robert's demands for his homage in 1306, in part because he was currently at the allegiance of King Edward, with the assertion that his oath was not 'made of glass'. As a man of honour, he would stick with the choice that he had already made.

But when Alexander died in 1286, most Scottish nobles wanted above all to prevent a civil war and therefore to protect the succession of the Maid of Norway rather than put the ageing Robert Bruce on the throne. However, we should remember that the Comyns, who were no friends to the Bruces, were the dominant political faction at the time. Their interests and Scotland's interests, on this occasion, coincided perfectly, just as the interests of this Bruce's grandson, the future King Robert, would eventually become synonymous with those of his kingdom. We must be very careful not to judge against those whose personal priorities seem at odds with what we might deem to be the national interest, while passing no comment on those who saw advantage in pursuing a line which happened to coincide with it.

Ultimately, we should judge the Scottish political community as a whole by what it achieved, even if there were problems with certain individuals. In the aftermath of Alexander's death, they managed not only to stave off civil war, but to appoint an interim government which, among other difficulties, faced the task of negotiating for the Maid's future in Scotland. In this last respect, the six Guardians appointed to rule in the meantime found their greatest ally – and potential concern – in Margaret's great-uncle, the king of England. Nevertheless, the proposal that she should marry Edward I's son and heir, thereby implying a union of the crowns of Scotland and England, was generally regarded by those on both sides of the border as making the best of a bad situation. Sadly, the Maid died en route to her kingdom and the carefully-planned solution to the problem of a female monarch died with her. We will never know exactly when Edward I started to view the takeover of Scotland as more of a plan than an unforeseen opportunity. However, in the aftermath of Margaret's death, when civil war once more became an issue, there can be little doubt that his canny legal mind was already working overtime.

CHOOSING A NEW KING

The Scots were left with very few options open to them. Many seem to have already suspected Edward's motives towards the northern kingdom and may have been deeply concerned about the implications of his stated intention to preside over the legal process of deciding on the new king. However, unless that legal process was seen to be both neutral and authoritative, the kingdom would be torn apart by supporters of the two claimants to the throne, Robert Bruce and John Balliol.

The events surrounding the ultimate decision to award the crown of Scotland to John Balliol seem to get ever more complicated the more they are studied. The salient points remain that Balliol was regarded by the majority of the Scottish political community as the rightful heir, that Edward I paved the way to a strictly legalistic definition of restricted Scottish kingship under English claims of suzerainty during the long, drawn-out process of selection, and that Balliol himself, as Ranald Nicholson put it, 'set out to be no less a king than his predecessors' (Nicholson 1974, 44), whatever his subsequent, Bruce-induced, reputation might state. But within days of Balliol's inauguration in 1292, it became clear that Scottish and English views on his kingship were now fundamentally incompatible. It took another three years for the Scots to summon up the courage – and a treaty of mutual aid with England's enemy, France – to emphatically reassert their desire for an independent Scotland. If war was needed to bring that about, then so be it.

EDWARD I, RULER OF SCOTLAND

Despite the fact that most of the Scottish nobility had experienced little or no active service in war, they were remarkably gung ho in their approach to taking on the veteran commander, Edward I. The result was almost immediate defeat at Dunbar in April 1296 and the subsequent collapse of all armed resistance. By the end of the summer Edward had toured his new province taking homage and fealty from his new subjects, appointing officers of state and installing a new English government at Berwick. He returned south in September to the more important business of his imminent war with France, taking with him as prisoners King John and many prominent Scottish nobles.

If Edward had been as keen to ensure that the Scots experienced good government as he was to have them pay for it, then his administration might have achieved ultimate success. But within six months, the intensity of demands for taxation and the threat of military service against France for the 'middling sort' – respectable tenant farmers – led to spontaneous resistance. William Wallace first came to prominence during this largely uncoordinated rebellion and by the end of 1297 he had become leader of it. His victory, along with the northerner, Andrew Murray, in September at Stirling Bridge against Edward's lieutenant in Scotland, the Earl of Surrey, gave him an instantaneous reputation. To the Scots, he was the saviour for whom the nation had cried out in its hour of need. To the English he was nothing more than a thief, responsible for numerous barbarous acts against them. Both views have an element of truth in them, but are more generally wide of the mark.

As Guardian, Wallace oversaw the restoration of a Scottish administration in the name of the absent King John and the resurrection of a belief that full independence could be regained. But he did not do it alone. And when his army fell before Edward I at Falkirk in 1298, his mandate to lead the Scottish people, which had come to him as a result of military success, was no longer valid. Two nobles – John Comyn, younger, of Badenoch and Robert Bruce, Earl of Carrick – took over as Guardians, determined that, this time, Scottish resistance would continue in the face of defeat. A war of attrition dragged on, the Scots having finally learned to say no to battles. England struggled to put armies in the field year after year, and Edward suffered the frustration of Scottish diplomatic success in the courts of Rome and France which ultimately won King John his release. *[handwritten marginal note: more political savvy than military victory.]*

But Scotland had little political clout on its own terms in European politics. The considerable diplomatic successes achieved by the nation's representatives were derived from Scotland's usefulness as an enemy of England situated on the latter's northern border. When the priorities of the great European powers – most particularly the Pope, Boniface VIII, and Philip IV of France – shifted, so did their loyalty to the Scottish cause. By the end of 1302, in a complete reversal of the previous position, Scotland came under papal pressure to acquiesce to English demands, a situation that they could not ignore forever. *[handwritten marginal note: Scotland was a pawn]*

However, the Scots contemplated submitting to Edward I only once an English army had crossed the River Forth and pushed into northern Scotland for the first time since 1297. This was the heartland of Scottish government and it would now be almost impossible to maintain an effective enough administration to prosecute the war. After eight years of fighting, the Scottish nobility, led by the Guardian, John Comyn, sued for peace. Edward was prepared to be magnanimous, so long as the Scots were sufficiently humble, a tacit acknowledgement of the effectiveness of Scottish resistance against him. However, not everyone could be forgiven and, in August 1305, immediately before a parliament at Westminster met to discuss the final details of the settlement of Scotland, Sir William Wallace was executed for treason.

THE REIGN OF KING ROBERT BRUCE

The Bruce family was remarkably consistent in its approach to the wars with England: they sided with whoever was most likely to bring them the throne which had been denied to them by the decision to give it to Balliol in 1292. Thus the young Robert Bruce, Earl of Carrick, grandson of Balliol's rival, actually became a Guardian of Scotland on behalf of King John. He did so not because he had come to accept that Balliol had won, but because the latter was now in prison and the Bruces needed to play a role in Scottish politics to counterbalance the influence of the Comyns. However, the younger Robert's position was made so difficult by Sir John Comyn that he could wield little effective power as Guardian and gave up the role. By 1302, as rumours reached Scotland that King John was about to return with a French army, the advantage now lay in making peace with Edward I, which he promptly did. However, once Comyn was also restored to Edward's peace after the submissions of 1304, the Earl of Carrick found himself sidelined once again. The English king had no desire to give encouragement to any latent Bruce ambitions to be king of Scots and anyway, he now had the most powerful man in Scotland (Comyn) to work with.

In 1305, at the age of only thirty-three, Robert Bruce was faced with the prospect of life in a political wilderness. He found such a future quite unacceptable. We know that he had made an unspecified agreement of mutual cooperation with the Bishop of St Andrews, William Lamberton, in 1304, presumably as a means of canvassing for support for a bid for the throne, when the time was right. We can also assume that Lamberton was not the only senior Scottish figure that Bruce talked to. Unfortunately it is not entirely clear why he arranged to meet with John Comyn in the Greyfriars Church in Dumfries on 10 February 1306. The most likely explanation is that Bruce wished to discuss the conditions under which Comyn would accept him as king, but Sir John presumably refused to contemplate the idea, their old antagonisms rushed to the surface and Bruce reached for his dagger.

With Comyn dead, there was only one course of action: he had to make his bid for the throne now. Six weeks later, Bruce was inaugurated as king at the traditional site at Scone. Support for him was hardly overwhelming: only the Bishops of Glasgow and St Andrews (the latter perhaps under duress) and two or three earls turned up. Edward I could hardly believe the rumours of this new insurrection, but once they were confirmed, his anger was truly terrible. This was a personal betrayal and quite unforgivable; Bruce and anyone who dared to support him would be shown no mercy.

The new king faced a daunting set of challenges. Edward was not in good health and perhaps unlikely to last too much longer. But while he was alive, the homage and fealties so recently sworn to him by the Scottish nobility meant that many, even if they might ultimately have wished to see Bruce take the throne of Scotland, could not honestly break their oaths. Then there was the small matter of the murder of Sir John at the high altar of a church. For the Comyns and their friends, the backbone of Scottish resistance before 1304, Bruce's actions gave them no choice but to side with the English king against this murderous usurper. The community of the realm of Scotland was utterly divided and we must not forget that, for many, the morally right course of action could not mean supporting the new king. Nicholson says, 'The eventual success of Bruce's bid for the throne cannot disguise the fact that it was, at the time, rash, self-willed and premature, and occurred in dismal circumstances' (Nicholson 1974, 71).

The reign of King Robert I is perhaps one of the most difficult to analyse objectively, simply because it started so inauspiciously and ended in almost unbelievable success. He was also blessed with extremely effective propagandists whose writings have been taken at face value for a very long time. Indeed, the following words written by Bruce's most eminent modern biographer perhaps sum up best the difficulties faced by the historian in dealing with the hero king:

> The story of how Robert Bruce returned to Scotland, of how after many disasters and setbacks he slowly won the initiative, of how by a wonderful mixture of patience, sagacity and daring he made himself master of all but one of the great fortresses held by the English, until he was powerful enough at last to meet the challenge of a full-scale invasion led by the King of England in person, is the story of one of the great heroic enterprises of history. (Barrow 1988, 165)

There is no doubt that Bruce's dramatic return to Scotland in 1307, the beginnings of his later startling military victories compounded by the death of Edward I, was an incredible achievement. Only a man of unusual fortitude, ability and luck could have turned such a dreadful start around. But to depict it purely as a heroic enterprise underplays the complexity of the situation that Scotland found itself in. Indeed, the above extract is entirely misleading in mentioning only 'the great fortresses held by the English' – the backbone of resistance to Bruce as Edward II began to turn his back on a coherent strategy for Scotland lay with other Scots. To suggest that heroism is an attribute that can be ascribed solely to those who struggled with Bruce does a disservice to those who had very good reasons indeed for siding against him. This does not excuse the English, and Edward I in particular, for the viciousness of their treatment of Bruce's supporters, but we should remember that the Comyns and their allies did not start the civil war. King Robert alone bears responsibility for that. As Chris Brown puts it, in his recent work on the second wars of independence: 'Opposition to the Bruce dynasty tends to be seen as support for the English occupation. It was the aim of the Bruce party propaganda that it should be seen in that light, and that aim was achieved more than adequately' (Brown 2002).

However, this should not detract from the significance of Bruce's achievements. Indeed, recognising the extent of the difficulties he faced surely enhances them. The new king had to win support through success and that success came with a custom-built military strategy that contrasted his own speed and mobility with the general ineffectiveness of his many opponents. As Edward II returned home for his coronation, Bruce and his lieutenants took the war across the length and breadth of the country until most of his irreconcilable enemies were forced into exile. By

[handwritten margin note: History written by the winners. and the betrayed]

1309, the king could call his first parliament, which turned its attention to the international scene. As a result, the first major piece of propaganda from Bruce's chancery (responsible for producing government documents) was sent to the pope, ostensibly by the Scottish clergy, arguing for the new king's legitimacy. This was necessary not least because they had been arguing equally vehemently for the legitimacy of another king who was still alive (Balliol) less than a decade earlier.

Such documents are as much a part of the prosecution of this war as sieges and military campaigns. Bruce could (and did) remove Edward II's garrisons from almost all of Scotland, his writ might hold sway across the land, but this was not enough. With his Queen in captivity from 1307, his only offspring was a daughter, Marjory. All his brothers except one (Edward) had been executed. For the Bruce dynasty to survive, he needed not only a son, but a stable political environment to facilitate the transition to the new king after his death. And only an acknowledgement of Scotland's independence and his own right to rule could bring that about. The question was how to persuade Edward II to make it.

Bruce tried everything. Raiding into the north of England began to increase in effectiveness and organisation from 1311, providing a valuable form of involuntary taxation to fill the Scottish king's war chest. But Edward II lived too far south to care much about the plight of his northern subjects. English politics had so far rendered the English king unwilling or unable to do much to thwart King Robert's reconquest. But in 1313, the judicial murder of Edward's favourite, Piers Gaveston, left most of the English nobility looking for a project that would allow them to rally around their king. A campaign against the Scots fitted the bill admirably, not least because one of Scotland's most strategic castles, Stirling, was due to fall to King Robert if not relieved by midsummer 1314.

The battle of Bannockburn has gone down in legend as the archetypal victory of David over Goliath. In a way it epitomises this phase of the war as a whole: the Scots under Bruce planned carefully and effectively, adapting their tactics to make best use of the terrain; the English threw away all the advantages normally enjoyed by their impressive military machine through sheer arrogance and lack of effective leadership; the Scots won the day. God had shown his hand in giving King Robert the victory. Many of the Scottish nobility who had hitherto sat on the fence were thus persuaded to come down on Bruce's side. The plethora of high-class prisoners not only brought unimaginable riches to individual Scots but also purchased the freedom of Bruce's wife and daughter. Yet the Scots still had not won the war.

It has been argued that the period after the Scottish victory at Bannockburn, followed in the next year by Bruce's most audacious venture yet – the invasion of Ireland (a province of England at that time) – and continuing forays into northern England 'saw an unparalleled Scottish military hegemony in Britain' (McNamee 1997, 74). Such a situation – normally assumed to belong to the English as a matter of course - is an extraordinary tribute to King Robert's qualities of leadership and the discipline and loyalty of the men who fought for him. Unfortunately, the pursuit of military pre-eminence remained dedicated to the securing of an apparently unattainable goal – English acknowledgement of Scottish independence. The campaigns in Ireland, designed, like the raids into England, to try to persuade Edward II to give up on Scotland as a financial and political liability, finally brought Bruce to the limits of his strategic abilities. Unfortunately these campaigns were launched at the start of a three-year period of European-wide harvest failure and cattle disease, making it extremely difficult to maintain an army in the field. The Gaelic Irish, who had supposedly chosen Edward Bruce, the Scottish king's brother and heir, as High King, began to resent the Scots as much as the English. The Bruces, who almost certainly spoke Gaelic and seem to have been comfortable within the politics of western Scotland, may have misjudged the complexity of native Irish politics and there is good reason to suppose that they 'had their sights fixed firmly on their own aggrandisement' rather than a genuine pan-Celtic alliance (McNamee 1997, 192).

war for selfish reasons – Ireland used as a pawn

The Irish venture proved that King Robert, who campaigned personally with his brother, was not militarily invincible and by 1318 the Scottish parliament was forced to legislate against those who spoke against the king. In the same year, Edward Bruce was killed. The future of the Bruce dynasty now rested with Marjory Bruce's tiny son, Robert Stewart, or the ability of the king himself to father an heir. To add to Bruce's difficulties, the pope demanded that the Scots and English stop fighting each other and divert their energies into a new Crusade against the Infidel. Unfortunately, the Scottish king ploughed ahead with the recapture of Berwick, the last Edwardian-held castle, but his disregard for a direct papal request was certain to bring a sentence of excommunication on himself and interdict on the whole country.

Edward II may have proved himself entirely unable to manage the military side of Scottish affairs, but he had other cards to play. In 1320, as King Robert's propagandists began work on a document designed to persuade the pope of the strength of noble support for Bruce's royal duty to expel the English from Scotland (otherwise known as the Declaration of Arbroath), a young man arrived at the English court. This was Edward Balliol, eldest son of King John, and his presence in England was designed to provide a focus for those members of the Scottish nobility who still remembered how Bruce had seized the throne. King Edward's plan almost worked: in 1320, an assassination plot, which almost certainly aimed at restoring the Balliol line to the Scottish throne, was uncovered and its conspirators dealt with most severely. Though the very idea of replacing Robert Bruce might seem the height of ingratitude given all that he had endured and accomplished, the question marks over his legitimacy as king would never stop feelings of genuine misgiving in some quarters.

The conspiracy seems to have taught Bruce a lesson, too, and he began to look more closely at the issue of patronage, a key royal duty. Up until then, his land grants had been concentrated on the royal family and the very closest of Bruce supporters; now the king looked to prove to his nobility more generally that loyalty would be rewarded. Reality was also catching up with him in other ways. There was no sign of an heir and the king's health – never that good since the dark first days of his reign – made a long minority look highly likely (in 1320 Robert Stewart, the heir, was only three). Bowing to the inevitable, in 1323 King Robert began negotiating with King

Edward for a thirteen-year truce, binding, most crucially, in the event of either monarch's death. This was the best that Bruce could guarantee for the future of his family and his country.

AN UNEXPECTED PEACE

But if King Robert had one thing on his side at crucial moments, it was luck. A year after the truce of 1323, his son, David, was born. Though Edward still would not contemplate a final peace, English politics were beginning to unravel, leading ultimately to the king's deposition and murder in 1326/7. Bruce seized the moment. Despite the agreement that the 13-year truce should remain in place, he launched an attack from Ireland in February 1327, followed closely by an invasion of the north of England a few months later. Though the Scottish king was in desperate health, the strength of his will saw him through. The unpopular English regency government led by the Queen Mother on behalf of her son, Edward III, decided that Scotland was a problem they could do without. Negotiations for a final peace were concluded at Edinburgh on 17 March 1328 and ratified by an English parliament at Northampton two months later, much to the fury of the English generally and their youthful king in particular.

For King Robert, however, it was the document he so desperately needed to let him die in peace. Other affairs of state were now dealt with, most particularly the naming of his nephew and wise commander, Thomas Randolph, Earl of Moray, as Guardian during the inevitable minority of his son. Bruce could do nothing more and on 7 June 1329 he died, surely as one of Scotland's greatest kings and most exceptional of men.

THE WAR RUMBLES ON

The treaty of Edinburgh–Northampton lasted a mere four years. Edward III continued to act according to the letter, if not the spirit, of the agreement, covertly encouraging the disinherited – those Scots who had lost land and titles siding against Bruce – to fight for their birthrights. Their leaders were Edward Balliol and Henry Beaumont, heir to the Comyn earldom of Buchan. Unfortunately for Scotland, the Guardian who faced this new threat of an invading army was not Randolph, who died in 1332, but the Earl of Mar, who had spent much of his time in England as a friend of Edward II. Within a year of David II's coronation, Scone witnessed that of Edward Balliol, restored to his father's throne in September 1332. Unfortunately, and unlike his father, this Balliol owed everything to the English king and was prepared to reward him with the annexation of much of southern Scotland to the English crown.

By now Edward III was directly involved and, as the war dragged on, the full power of the English military machine was brought to bear once more against Scotland. The Bruce commanders provided a less than impressive showing and the young King David was whisked off to France for safety in 1334. Fresh hope of competent leadership came to the Bruce camp with the ransoming of Andrew Murray, son of Wallace's fellow commander at Stirling Bridge, in the same year. However, the upper hand still lay with Edward III, who succeeded in bringing most of the Scottish nobility, including David Bruce's heir, Robert Stewart, to his peace in 1335. But the Guardian, Sir Andrew Murray, was still at large and capable of inflicting defeat on pro-Balliol supporters. Edward III was frustrated in his aim of securing Scotland once and for all so that, just like his grandfather, he could turn to more rewarding enterprises against France. By 1337 command of English forces in Scotland was handed over to Thomas Beauchamp, Earl of Warwick. Four years later the situation was stable enough to warrant the return of King David.

The dreadful conditions inflicted on the inhabitants of Scotland by these long years of war can be underestimated simply because we know that Edward III did finally give up on any active interest in Scotland in preference for his participation in what eventually became known as the Hundred Years War. Even the capture of King David during a Scottish raid into northern England in 1346 made little difference to the overall prosecution of the war. His nephew and heir, Robert Stewart, was appointed Guardian and began the creation of a personal political following that was to cause King David considerable difficulties in enforcing his own will on the political community after his eventual return to Scotland in 1357. But such internal family wranglings underline the fact that, though Anglo-Scottish hostilities continued as a recurring theme, they were no longer a way of life. The English kings continued to assert their superior rights over the Crown of Scotland until well into the sixteenth century, resulting in occasional campaigns and the encouragement of cross-border raiding by both governments. Although these military endeavours resulted in the capture of one king of Scots (James I) and the deaths, directly or indirectly, of three more (Jameses II, IV and V), the reality, nevertheless, of an independent Scotland underpinned British politics and, to a lesser extent, European politics too.

SOME FINAL THOUGHTS ON THE WARS OF INDEPENDENCE

Many modern Scots have looked to the great heroes of the wars of independence to inspire a sense of national pride that was perhaps less easily found in twentieth-century Scotland at least. It will be interesting to see how later historians analyse the development of attitudes to this iconic period in the nation's history in the aftermath of devolution. However, it should be stating the obvious to assert that a twenty-first century democracy has little in common with its predecessor of seven hundred years ago. For a start, the idea of a nation-at-arms was fundamental to the medieval Scottish identity. As Carol Edington has noted, medieval 'Scots frequently viewed their entire history as one of protracted warfare', provoking considerable pride in the belief that they 'have bene xviii hundreth yeire inconquest [unconquered]' (Edington 1998, 69). Modern Scots no longer identify directly with such martial sentiments, however much the bitter resentment and xenophobia towards the English that stemmed from these wars still play a part in the national psyche.

ditto between England and France !

However, the historian has the unenviable task of unpicking the emotional legacy of a war of potential conquest. Most particularly, the civil wars that formed an integral part of the wider Anglo-Scottish theatre of engagement must be analysed without falling into the trap of ascribing the moral high ground automatically to one side simply because it was able to assume the mantle of being 'patriotic'. The wars of independence were many things, but they certainly were not black and white.

REFERENCES TO BOOKS AND ARTICLES MENTIONED IN THE TEXT

*Barrow, GWS 1988 *Robert Bruce and the Community of the Realm of Scotland*. Edinburgh.

Brown, C 2002 *The Second Scottish Wars of Independence, 1332–1363*. Stroud.

Duncan, AAM 1966 'The Community of the Realm of Scotland and Robert Bruce: a review', *Scottish Historical Review*, 45, 184–201.

Edington, C 1998 'Paragons and Patriots: National Identity and the Chivalric Ideal in Late-Medieval Scotland', *in* Broun, D, Finlay, RJ and Lynch, M (eds), *Image and Identity. The Making and Re-making of Scotland through the Ages*, Edinburgh, 69–81.

McNamee, C 1997 *The Wars of the Bruces. Scotland, England and Ireland, 1306–1328*. East Linton.

*Nicholson, R 1978 *Scotland: The Later Middle Ages*. Edinburgh.

*Penman, M 2002 *The Scottish Civil War: The Bruces and the Balliols and the War for Control of Scotland, 1286–1356*. Stroud.

Scott, Sir Walter 1925 *Tales of a Grandfather, being the History of Scotland from the earliest period to the Union of Scotland and England*, abridged by Elsie M Lang. London.

*Watson, F 1998 *Under the Hammer: Edward the First and Scotland*. East Linton.

Watson, F 2001. *Scotland. A History*. Stroud.

FURTHER READING

The items above marked * are recommended for further reading, along with the following:

Boardman, S 1996 *The Early Stewart Kings, Robert II and Robert III 1371–1406*. East Linton.

Davies, RR 1990 *Domination and Conquest: The Experience of Ireland, Scotland and Wales, 1100–1300*. Cambridge.

Duffy, S 1991 'The Bruce Brothers and the Irish Sea World, 1306–1329', *Cambridge Medieval Celtic Studies*, 21, 1306–29.

Ferguson, W 1994 *Scotland's Relations with England. A Survey to 1707*. Edinburgh.

Fisher, A 2002 *William Wallace*. Edinburgh.

Frame, R 1995 *The Political Development of the British Isles*. Oxford.

Goldstein, RJ 1993 *The Matter of Scotland: Historical Narrative in Medieval Scotland*. Lincoln; London.

*Grant, A 1991 *Independence and Nationhood, Scotland, 1306–1469*. Edinburgh.

MacDonald, R Andrew 1997 *The Kingdom of the Isles. Scotland's Western Seaboard, c.1100–c.1336*. East Linton.

Paterson, RC 1996 *For the Lion: A History of the Scottish Wars of Independence*. Edinburgh.

*Prestwich, M 2003 *The Three Edwards: War and State in England, 1272–1377*. London.
Prestwich, M 1997 *Edward I*. New Haven, Conn.; London.
*Prestwich, M 1987 'Colonial Scotland: The English in Scotland under Edward I', *in* Mason R
    (ed), *Scotland and England, 1286–1815*, Edinburgh, 6–17.
Young, A 1997 *Robert the Bruce's Rivals: The Comyns, 1212–1314*. East Linton.

Both sides fought for what they believed to be theirs. Whether Scottish or English, Bruce or Balliol, everyone had an agenda. They all thought the throne was theirs. There is no mention of the people in any of this. In all this war, how did any of the rulers treat the people? Did they fight for the greater good, or like children squabbling over a toy? Neither side is clean but, in war you can't be. At some point everyone seems to have been used as a pawn in some grander scheme. Everyone had their own goal, their own wish to rule something. It was war, but ultimately it was bargaining, no different to modern politics. Only now there are fewer executions and a lot more ink. It's still negotiation. It's still posturing.

CHAPTER FOUR

Stewart Monarchy, (1371–1513)

Michael Brown

The 142 years from the accession of the first Stewart king – Robert II – in 1371 to the death of his descendant – James IV – in 1513 represented a period of particular significance in the political development of Scotland. By comparison with the wars of independence that preceded it and the upheavals of the mid-sixteenth century that followed, the reigns of the first six Stewart monarchs witnessed an era of dynastic stability and external security, during which Scotland was recognised as a full participant in the European states system. Internally, the later middle ages were a crucial period for Scotland. Between the later fourteenth and early sixteenth centuries Scotland developed its own character and structures as a polity, a separate political society. The distinctive rules and institutions of Scottish government were produced or further solidified in a period when the Scottish political class was consciously mistrustful of external, particularly English, influences.

This chapter's focus on monarchy is a reflection of the view Scots, and most other European polities, had of both the ideals and realities of government. As a figure whose special authority was built on long-standing tradition and was understood to derive from rights of blood, the acclamation of his subjects and from divine sanction, the kings of Scots had the right to rule and order their realm. Their exercise of power was not beyond the rules of political society. The oaths sworn by the teenage James II and by his subjects in 1445 provide an indication of this, albeit in unusually limited terms. The king's subjects were bound to serve and support him against all other people with all their resources. In return, James swore to protect them as the three estates of the realm (the term can be read as those attending parliament but also is the fifteenth-century equivalent of the community of the realm) and to uphold and not alter the laws of the kingdom without securing their consent. In practice, Scots expected their king to exercise justice over them, maintaining the peace and order of the land, and to ensure their protection from external foes. In return they owed the king obedience to his will, certain financial obligations and limited military service. The king's character and policies were one of the major influences on the political life of Scotland.

Particular attention will be given in this chapter to the recent debates amongst historians about this period. Many of these debates have focused on the political stability of Scotland under the Stewarts. There has been a traditional view of the period, certainly up to the 1490s, that effective kingship involved a degree of conflict with the crown's subjects and that such conflicts were the principal characteristic of

Scottish political life. More recently greater stress has been placed on the normal cooperation that existed between crown and nobility, resting on shared interests. In the same way questions have also been raised about the way Scottish government worked. Perceptions that the government of Scotland was limited in scope and effectiveness and backward in character have been challenged in more recent approaches, which have emphasised its positive aspects and demonstrated its greater effectiveness. In essence, such debates revolve around the cohesion and character of the late medieval realm (Wormald 1985b; M Brown 1994b).

As the introduction above suggests, the question of relations between kings and subjects during the late medieval period has been dominated by the dealings of the crown with the Scottish nobility. The nobility was not simply a collection of wealthy and socially significant individuals. They formed a group which was the accepted source of political direction beneath the king, with whom the crown had to work in the government of the kingdom. The greatest nobles, the earls and leading barons, were themselves leaders of localities. In these roles, such magnates had formal powers of jurisdiction and less formal bonds of lordship which allowed them to call on lesser nobles and commoners for political and even military support. Discussion of the changing composition, expectations and resources of the nobility goes hand in hand with general debates about the way Scotland operated as a kingdom.

EARLY STEWART KINGSHIP, (1371 – 1424)

The first half-century of Stewart government witnessed both the establishment of the new dynasty on the throne and a distinctive era of kingship. Between 1371 and 1420 Scotland had three rulers – two crowned and one uncrowned. Along with Robert II and his eldest son, who took the throne as Robert III, was also Robert Earl of Fife and Duke of Albany (here referred to as Albany). Albany was Robert II's second surviving son and for much of the period from 1388 until 1420 ruled Scotland as the lieutenant of, first his father, then his brother and finally his nephew, James I. The transfer of royal authority to a deputy, which occurred five times between 1371 and 1424, and what that reveals about the state of the kingdom has been one of the major issues arising from this period. The frequency with which such delegation occurred has produced divergent views of this period amongst historians. The traditional view was that such transfers of power were indicative of political failure and that this was the principal characteristic of Scottish politics during the period. The contrast between the forceful and centrally-based kingship of Robert II's predecessor, David II (Bruce) and the apparently ineffective rule of the first two Stewart kings has been used to demonstrate this (Nicholson 1974). However, more recent studies have emphasised instead the relative stability of the period up to 1424 and argued that Robert II was largely successful in securing his dynasty and that he and his sons avoided major internal conflict (Grant 1984; Boardman 1996a).

Robert II's rule certainly has to be taken in context. As a king from a new royal line and with a long and chequered career as a magnate behind him, Robert lacked the political credibility to continue the style of kingship pursued by David II. This style had depended on displays of personal authority over his greatest subjects (including Robert), the maintenance of a large and expensive royal entourage and large-scale financial contributions from the three estates (Penman 2004). Instead Robert's aim was to entrench the Stewarts in both royal and aristocratic circles. He used royal powers over the distribution of lands and titles to confirm or settle extensive lands on his five legitimate sons. This was the completion of a long-term process of Stewart aggrandizement, but it meant that by the end of his reign these princes held eight out of fifteen Scottish earldoms. Robert was equally keen to avoid challenges to his rule from outside the Stewart family. The demonstration by the great southern magnate, William Earl of Douglas, before Robert's accession was a warning to the new king. Douglas was placated with pensions, offices and by a marriage between his son and Robert's daughter. Similar acts of patronage drew powerful supporters of David II into the new king's circle. Unlike David, Robert II used royal resources to extend his familial connections and broaden acceptance of his kingship rather than to provide the means to establish a dominant and demanding royal administration.

The private patronage diverted to the king's sons was also part of Robert's approach to public authority. By the early 1380s (when Robert was in his sixties) he also used his sons as deputies. His third son, Alexander Lord of Badenoch, had been the king's lieutenant in northern Scotland since 1372, while his second son, Robert of Albany, acted as chamberlain, the chief financial officer of the crown after 1382. From 1380 the king's eldest son and heir, John Earl of Carrick was named lieutenant in the marches. The creation of regional lieutenancies was based on earlier approaches and reflected a growing recognition that continuing war with England in the south and the increasing problems of local violence and disorder associated with the Gaelic communities of the Highlands required special responses. However, such delegation of powers over justice, diplomacy and war to his sons are also emblematic of Robert's limited personal involvement in certain aspects of his office. The limited political and financial demands of his kingship avoided conflict but may also have reduced his personal prestige, removing the 'raddour' (ability to inspire obedience through fear, which was part of David II's rule). By contrast Robert was dependent on the goodwill and unity of the family nexus that he had built up.

The breakdown of the unity of the royal family was the prime reason for the political difficulties faced by Robert II and Robert III between 1384 and 1406. Robert II's delegation of wide-ranging powers to his sons had given them a share in the authority of the crown. The development of rivalries and ambitions, perhaps allied to individual failings, may be regarded as an essential factor in bringing about a series of changes of management in the kingdom. The first of these in 1384 can be seen as the natural impatience of a middle-aged heir. Robert II was made to surrender power over justice to Carrick who was named lieutenant of the kingdom by 1388 (Boardman 2004). However, at the end of that year, the defence of the realm and the maintenance of the law were removed from Carrick and given to his younger brother, Albany. Albany remained lieutenant until 1393, despite Carrick's succession to the throne as Robert III in 1390. Robert III never possessed the full authority of kingship and in 1399 the powers of lieutenancy were given to his twenty-one-year-old son, David duke of Rothesay. In late 1401 he was arrested and replaced by his uncle, Albany, who, as lieutenant and then governor, was effective ruler of Scotland until his death in 1420.

These changes in the control of royal policy clearly indicate rivalries within Robert II's family. Yet coups followed set rules. The office of lieutenant itself had developed during the wars to provide leadership in the absence of a king. Its revival from the 1380s was justified by reference to 'mysgovernance' and, as Rothesay's appointment in 1399 expressly stated, the new lieutenant was expected to reform past failings. Consent for appointments was secured by meetings of the estates in parliament or the less formal general council. Though such changes were confined to the royal family, they were not divorced from wider concerns. Statements about misgovernment were not simply political window-dressing. The appointment of a series of lieutenants was a product of the perceived failures of early Stewart rulers which created pressure for change. In 1384 Carrick's appointment can be linked to the concerns of regional communities. In the south, nobles, led by the new earl of Douglas, sought royal sponsorship for renewed war with England. In the north there was dissatisfaction with the actions of the lieutenant, the king's third son, Alexander. Complaints about his misuse of his office and support for Gaelic kindreds had been ignored by the king. Carrick's appointment was expected to satisfy both constituencies. His fall in 1388 was a result of his failure to improve things in the north and the death of his ally, Douglas, in battle with the English. As the role of the Douglas earls in every change of lieutenant from 1384 to 1402 showed, royal politics could not be separated from regional politics. (M Brown 1998).

While difficulties clearly existed, there was no breakdown in political order in the early Stewart period. Yet tensions were clearly generated by these shifts in government. These were revealed in particular by the lieutenancy of Rothesay. Rothesay's appointment was different from those of previous lieutenants. He was assigned a council of advisors and given a three-year term, both fitting for a young prince being trained for kingship. Yet when his term ended, Rothesay was removed in a coup which involved his death in the custody of Albany. Though contemporaries hedged between disease and starvation as the cause of his demise and denounced Rothesay as a dissolute and irresponsible playboy, the prince's real crime was to pursue an active agenda, rejecting conciliar restraint and seeking extended power. The alliance of Albany, Douglas and others which secured his removal was a determined assertion of the early Stewart status quo in which kingship was a limited political force.

As ruler of Scotland for the next eighteen years, Albany represented the continuation of the political environment established in the 1370s. When Robert III died in 1406, two weeks after the capture of his heir, James, by the English, the senior royal line had disappeared from Scotland. The response of the estates was to raise Albany to be their governor. With an experienced regent, personal kingship had a reduced significance. The ease with which Albany established his pre-eminence after 1402 was due to the lack of obvious alternatives and to his unparalleled ability to play the system. His rule as governor was limited in scope. Albany held no full parliaments and sought no taxation. His gestures towards full royal status were not sufficient to offend his peers. Most importantly his management of politics rested on the distribution of authority. The Earl of Douglas was allowed to exert extensive personal lordship and hold numerous offices in the south, while in the north east Albany's nephew, the Earl of Mar, was appointed lieutenant with wide powers over justice and generous grants of money. Like his father, Albany sought to satisfy aristocratic ambitions and avoid conflict. His bond (private alliance) with Douglas in 1409 probably followed a period of conflict between the two magnates. This bound them to mutual support and to the resolution of conflict between their followers in customary terms (Wormald 1985a). As an agreement between the governor of the kingdom and the greatest southern lord, however, it represents the use of private agreements in place of the exertion of the public power of the crown.

The verdict on Albany's governorship has been positive. His interventions were generally effective and, despite his delegation of power, he held the balance of power with ease. However the experience of his son, Murdoch, who succeeded as governor in 1420, shows the personal nature of this type of rule. Without the ideological weight of kingship or his father's accumulated skill and connections, Murdoch was unable to maintain his position for more than a few years. This vulnerability recalls the events of the 1380s and 1390s and suggests that the early Stewart approach to rule avoided conflict at a price. Though it is right to emphasise the general stability of Scotland in these years, the delegation of authority and the satisfaction of regional interests reduced the practical authority and disposable resources of the crown, allowing the consolidation of aristocratic pretensions and identities by magnates like the earls of Douglas and the lords of the Isles. That such families claimed special rights and effectively ran their own foreign policies from 1400 is a mark of royal failure not success (M Brown 1997).

KINGS AND MIGHTY LORDS, (1424 – 1455)

The three decades that followed the end of the Albany governorship raise very different questions about royal authority and its place in Scotland. It is much harder to suggest that these years were characterised by a low-key approach to politics. The period between James I's return from captivity in 1424 and his son James II's defeat of the Earl of Douglas in 1455 was overshadowed by spectacular conflicts at the top of political society. Just over a year after his return to Scotland, James I engineered the execution of Murdoch Duke of Albany, eliminating the family that had dominated recent politics. James's reign ended with an even more shocking event. The murder of the king by a group of his subjects was an act without precedent in three centuries of Scottish history. It meant that the throne passed to James's young son and for the next dozen years there was, once again, no adult king to head the government. The assumption of power by James II heralded a new period of conflict. Between 1450 and 1455 the king initiated a series of attacks on the earls of Douglas, defeating them only at the third attempt.

Recent arguments have rightly stressed the exceptional nature of these conflicts (Grant 1984; Wormald 1985b). However it is possible to regard the neutralisation of the houses of Albany and Douglas and the assassination of James I as extreme expressions of a more general political atmosphere that had a considerable effect on the character of Scottish political society. One sign of this may be the extreme alterations that occurred amongst the higher nobility. In this thirty-year period, fifteen Scottish earldoms passed temporarily or permanently into the crown's control, including ancient estates like Fife, Strathearn, Mar and March. Leading noble families like the Black Douglases, the Dunbars, and all the Stewart magnates descended from Robert II became extinct through natural or violent means. Such a turnover matches that of the wars of independence and suggests a degree of instability. Yet the fifteenth century witnessed no external threat or dynastic crisis, so how can this be explained?

It is hard not to find an answer to this question in the ambitions of James I. His return to Scotland was presented as a deliberate break with the recent past. He denounced the 'neglectful government' of his cousin, Duke Murdoch and set out to establish a very different style of rule. James was undoubtedly influenced by his experiences of monarchy in England and France where the dignity and resources of the royal office clearly impressed him (M Brown 1994). He also had Scottish precedents. Many of his laws and his approach to government borrowed from the kingship of David II. James was quick to state his intentions. Following his coronation, James held the first full parliament for a generation. At the parliament statutes were issued which form a statement about James's position. Laws against private feuds and rebellion, for the curtailing of aristocratic retinues and to ensure that royal officers allowed 'the kingis commonis' access to the law show that James was presenting himself as the source of peace and order for his whole people. Unlike previous rulers, he would not accept aristocratic misrule and posed as protector of his weak subjects against the strong. Alongside such potent claims to public authority, James also issued statutes seeking to recover the lands and revenues of the crown and asking for a grant of taxation. This grant was to pay the king's ransom to the English, but together these acts were a warning that a more potent monarchy was also likely to be more financially demanding (Tanner 2001).

James's rule would be more politically demanding as well. The execution of his heir and chief vassal, Duke Murdoch, in 1425 displayed the new extent of royal authority and broke the patterns of early Stewart politics. Rather than avoid conflict, James initiated it. Faced by no real challenge from Murdoch, James probably acted to remove a family which had been a check on the crown and to increase his own resources in land and lordship by annexing the Albany estates. It was a sign of an increasingly general policy in which the king acted in conflict with individual nobles. Other great magnates, the Lord of the Isles, the Earl of Douglas and the Earl of March suffered arrest, imprisonment and the loss of some or all of their lands, while in several cases James intervened to deny the rights of claimants to property and secure land for the crown. When James did make land grants, often they were only for life, ensuring eventual reversion to the crown. The king's handling of his nobility had a strong financial element that pervaded his rule in other ways. While early Stewart rulers kept their demands to a minimum, James sought to maximise them. His request for funds to pay his ransom led to taxes being levied in 1424 and 1426, but growing reluctance by his subjects encouraged James to cease payment in 1428. He kept the money raised however, spending it on the trappings of kingship (Duncan 1984). The resulting mistrust engendered resistance to future requests for taxes in 1431 and 1436 and, to maintain his level of expenditure, James employed other methods. Acquisition of land was part of this, but he also raised loans from his subjects, worked the judicial system for profit and increased income from the customs. The funds raised allowed James to portray himself and his court as a prestigious and sophisticated centre for the realm – another contrast with his father.

The methods and aims of James's rule clearly divided contemporaries. The chronicler Walter Bower, writing in the 1440s, shared the ideals of his kingship in upholding justice and proclaimed James 'our lawgiver king'. However, he also had doubts about the means used (M Brown 2000). His account of the execution of Murdoch, for example, which in one version reads as a straight description of kingly authority, was altered by Bower to lament the deaths of the 'noble' duke and his family. Bower similarly hints at reservations about James's financial policies and these criticisms chime with more extreme comments in a work found in English manuscripts from the period (Connolly 1992). This contained accusations of tyranny against James for killing Albany and impoverishing his people. For two very different works to raise similar complaints suggests that the king had provoked hostility. The arrests of a series of lords at court also suggests a degree of mistrust, which proved to be well-founded. The murder of James at Perth in February 1437 was not a result of broadly-based opposition. The conspiracy involved die-hard Albany partisans, backed by men close to the king who mistrusted James's intentions (M Brown 1992). Their decision to act may have been encouraged by general grievances about royal policy.

The round-up and execution of the conspirators in six weeks has led many to conclude that James's killers badly misjudged Scottish attitudes. The king may not have been loved but his death was an unnatural crime (Grant 1984). Yet the conspirators had lost a short civil war in which most Scots remained neutral, while Bower's condemnation of the deed was coloured by politics after 1437. That James was betrayed by his household steward suggests that his style of rule had not convinced those closest to him. The murder is proof that the authority which James exercised had shaky foundations: that many may have regarded his policies as breaching normal political rules without plotting his death.

The impact of James's rule was worked out in the year after his death and the minority of James II (from 1437 to 1449) appears to have been a period of exceptional disorder. The removal of so many of the magnate families by extinction or forfeiture had left many localities without an obvious source of leadership. The result could be violent local competition for this leading role as in the north-east, where the Gordons and Lindsays waged war to establish regional pre-eminence.

There were similar feuds in Berwickshire, Ayrshire and the Lennox. This disorder was also a product of the lack of an adult king. James I had developed the crown as a source of justice throughout Scotland and also as a direct landlord in many regions. Unlike 1406, when the absence of a king mattered little with many alternative sources of leadership, in 1437 it left a large gap in the polity. Though the Earl of Douglas acted as lieutenant in the traditional manner, on his death in 1439 he was not replaced. The way royal government was maintained also reflected the old king's achievements. Leading figures after 1439 owed their influence to positions as royal officers not private lordship. Middling barons like William Crichton, Alexander Livingston and James Douglas of Abercorn neutralised obvious figures of authority, like the queen mother and the new earl of Douglas. Though Douglas and his son reduced their conciliar role in favour of establishing their rights over the Douglas earldom, Crichton and Livingston remained primarily royal councillors (McGladdery 1990; Dunlop 1950; M Brown 1998).

The period of minority had apparently contradictory effects on royal authority. The direct authority of the king was obviously removed and there seem to have been deliberate attempts to reverse some of James I's judgements. The oath sworn by James II in 1445 suggests that a limited view of the crown's prerogatives was being advanced. However at the same time the oaths sworn to the king show that minority regimes were seeking to deploy royal authority as a means of securing shaky legitimacy (Tanner 2001; M Brown 2004). The use of James II's person to present opponents as rebels suggests confidence in the prestige of monarchy. In this and in the importance of royal office-holding the legacy of James I's efforts was apparent.

This legacy was even more obvious when James II reached adulthood. The adoption of a style of kingship that forcefully sought increased political and financial resources and challenged structures of lordship that restricted these ambitions, shows the influence of James I. They led James II into even greater difficulties. A series of conflicts with the earls of Douglas tested the position of the crown fully. Royal confiscation of Douglas property in 1450 ended in the king restoring Earl William Douglas and, when the latter refused to aid the king against rebellions in the north in February 1452, James and his courtiers killed the earl. This precipitated a conflict that saw the Douglases burn Stirling and the king campaign in the south, but which ended in a compromise. Three years of wary cooperation ended in 1455 with a sustained royal offensive that lasted six months and drove the Douglases into exile.

This five-year period marked the crisis of the late medieval monarchy. In particular James II's killing of Earl William in 1452 asks major questions about the position of the crown. The slaying of a great subject by the king's hand was a crime for which James had to seek exoneration from parliament. It can be argued that these events showed the strength of the monarchy. James had committed an unlawful act but, unlike his father's killers, escaped its consequences. His exoneration from guilt revealed that, despite the personal behaviour of the king, the dignity and function of his office required that he be freed from stigma. The bulk of the political class needed royal leadership and recognised this by supporting James in 1452 (J Brown 1977). The contemporary *Auchinleck Chronicle* contrasted the

Douglases' 600 men at Stirling with the 30,000 men who were supposed to have served with James in the south (McGladdery 1990). However the events of that year were not one-sided. That James was powerless to prevent the burning of Stirling in March suggests that support was slow to gather around the king. The attitude of the Auchinleck account was also lukewarm towards James, and records criticisms of the king. It hints that the parliament which exonerated James and the campaign that followed were not triumphs of communal support, but partisan and limited in success. The settlement of the conflict was a compromise, which suggests a stalemate. The events of 1452 clearly showed the limits to royal power and the possibility of effective resistance to it. If James had fallen into his enemies' hands it is hard to see him escaping his father's fate, and more likely that the Douglases would have prospered. The ultimate success of James II in 1455 certainly was a demonstration of the material resources of the crown in politics and warfare, but the need for a six-month civil war to prove this ascendancy indicates the resilience of other traditions of lordship in Scotland.

NEW MONARCHY, (1455 – 1513)

The fall of the Douglas earls removed the last great magnate house from the heartlands of royal Scotland, and inaugurated a new era of kingship. There remained no single lord with the resources to curtail the authority of the king, and the territorial possessions of the crown were far beyond the greatest subject. The result was a heightened consciousness of royal status after 1455. In ideological terms, stress was placed on the supreme jurisdiction of the crown throughout its territory, ruling as an emperor in his kingdom. This authority was symbolised by the adoption of the closed, imperial crown under James III (Mason 1999). Such claims mirrored contemporary European practice as well as being a natural extension of statements about royalty under James I and II, but they also expressed a new reality. The statute of 1457 that spoke of one king and one law universal in Scotland reflected the recognition by the political class that the crown and its institutions were the natural focus of activity. Such an attitude did not remove tensions. The territorial and political dominance of the crown made the actions of the king even more significant. General complaints about royal justice and finance became a regular feature of political life but within a structure in which a ruler of moderate sense held all the advantages.

This was clear in the late 1450s. Fresh from victory over the Douglases, James II largely enjoyed a free hand. He waged a sustained war with England and postured ineffectively in diplomatic circles. He also imposed his will in disputes over lands, annexing the earldoms of Moray and Mar for the crown. James's concern to restock the depleted ranks of the higher nobility led to the creation of several earls and numerous lords of parliament without the distribution of major patronage (Grant 1984; McGladdery 1990). Significantly, the king reserved such patronage for his family. His three younger sons were each given earldoms acquired by the crown since 1424, while his half-brother received a fourth grant. Along with the sizeable portion assigned to his queen, Mary of Guelders, such generosity was part of a political debate. In 1455 parliament had ordained that a body of lands be permanently annexed to the crown. This Act of Annexation was designed to prevent the weakening of royal resources and avoid the kind of forceful seizures of property seen under James II and his father. It also recognised that a well-provided monarchy was a source of stability but it is clear that the initiative for the act came from the estates and balanced James's grants to his family. Such moderate restraint was also present in a statute from 1458 praising the king for success against 'rebellys' but asking him 'with all humilite' to keep justice and execute the laws.

Up to the king's accidental death in war in 1460, this tone of loyal advice and cooperation from the estates for royal policy marks the transformation from the early 1450s. The removal of the king did not break this atmosphere. By comparison with the troubled 1440s, the minority of James III was a period of limited tensions. Disputes over the leadership of the young king's council did occur, between the queen mother and Bishop Kennedy of St Andrews, and then with the ascendancy of the Boyd family. However, there were no violent arrests or executions of rivals and no upsurge of local feuding. The offices of state remained in the same hands, suggesting limited swings of power and, though James III punished the Boyds on his assumption of power in 1469, his action enjoyed wide support and threatened no wider conflict.

It is against this background that the disastrous personal reign of James III has to be explained. During the decade from 1469, James's kingship provoked growing criticism and complaint from his subjects on a range of issues. Between 1479 and 1482 the failure of the policies of the crown led to the collapse of the king's authority, his imprisonment and discussions about his removal from power. Despite surviving this crisis, James III continued to arouse opposition and in 1488 a faction of lords under the nominal leadership of the king's eldest son took up arms against him. In a five-month civil war, James III proved unable to raise steady support and was killed in battle near Stirling in June 1488. The hostility that James experienced and his imprisonment and death at the hands of his own subjects may suggest that the crown's authority and status remained limited and subject to challenge. However, while it is certainly the case that royal government depended on cooperation and support from the wider polity, the events of the 1470s and 1480s do not necessarily indicate major institutional limitations as much as the dependence of late medieval monarchy on the personal abilities and performance of the ruler. A king who failed to work with his subjects and respond to complaints would create problems in the system of government (Macdougall 1982).

James III's kingship generated criticism on a number of counts. His dealings with neighbouring realms upset established interests and identities. He pursued a policy of peace with England which led to a treaty in 1474 and a series of unfulfilled marriage agreements. This new approach was a response to the end of Anglo-French warfare and had obvious potential benefits, but it went against established traditions, especially in the Borders, and did not prevent English aggression in the early 1480s. The king's financial policies also aroused complaint. Six requests for taxation produced small returns and James looked to other means of money-raising. As well as making new seizures of land, he paid his debts with debased coinage and hoarded 'good' money of purer metal. The longest-running complaints concerned justice. Parliament repeatedly asked James to hold his justice ayres, personally travelling through Scotland to oversee the courts, and in 1478 linked this request to the existence of feuds in many parts of Scotland. The king was similarly asked not to allow criminals to purchase remissions releasing them from punishment in return for payment to the crown. It can be argued that such complaints obscure James's real intentions. His foreign policy was a reasonable response to new circumstances designed to ensure peace. Equally, financial measures were necessary to increase the still limited income of the crown. In justice too, James was not simply lazy and greedy but an innovator. His use of central courts of appeal or sessions sitting semi-permanently suggests a desire to provide a fixed focus for justice in Edinburgh and James certainly regarded the burgh as his principal seat of government (MacFarlane 1985).

Whatever James's ideas about his office, it was his inability to retain the support of his subjects that would be crucial. He lacked the personal qualities that made for an effective king. His untrustworthiness was reminiscent of his grandfather, but was not balanced by James I's ability to win respect. He was accused of favouritism, yet failed to reward service and lost the sympathy of his natural allies. His attempts to centralise government were regarded with suspicion; failure to perform the duties of his office and his elevated view of kingship were not balanced by displays of royal wealth and status. In addition, James faced the difficulty of having adult brothers whose ambitions had to be accommodated. The crisis of 1482 stemmed from a combination of one of these brothers, (Alexander Duke of Albany), an English invasion and the arrest of James by his own lords who had gathered to meet the invasion. James was imprisoned for several months and escaped only because of his enemies' inability to agree. The vengeance taken by James after release showed a king who had learned nothing. In 1488 a new rebellion broke out involving many who had previously been loyal to the king. James's son joined the rebels and the king lost support by agreeing and then breaking terms with his opponents. Unlike James II in 1455 who used royal powers to raise troops and isolated his enemies, James III ended up weaker than his opponents and was killed in a brief, one-sided clash.

The glaring, personal failings of James III are highlighted by the next reign. Unlike his father, James IV showed an ability to use the strengths that the crown had developed by providing the kind of monarchy acceptable to his subjects (Macdougall 1989). However, in many ways his policies were similar to those of the old king. Like his father, James IV pursued an ambitious foreign policy, which involved a peace treaty with England. He also sought a greatly increased royal income from a variety of sources, which threatened criticism. Amongst these was the attempt to make large profits by granting remissions for serious crimes, a practice that was seen as undermining justice. However, though James IV used similar methods to his father he was a shrewder judge of his subjects and a superior political manager. For example, he balanced peace with England with continued friendship to France, while the selling of remissions was set against the king's personal participation in judicial matters. Unlike his father, he undertook justice ayres in person, hearing cases throughout Scotland and appearing in person to quell outbreaks of local disorder. Such a king could not be, and was not, accused of failing in his duties. In financial matters too, James's requests for taxation, his enforcement of the feudal rights of the crown and his exploitation of crown lands, although occasionally provoking complaint, did not fuel simmering tensions of the kind found in the 1470s and 1480s (Madden 1976a, 1976b). What is striking about the two decades from the mid 1490s is the absence of major political events in Lowland Scotland.

This indicated James's success as a king in forestalling problems and managing his polity. While he enjoyed an element of luck, much of the king's success was down to his exercise of kingship. Unlike his father, James was a lavish spender who made his court the centre of entertainments, display and culture as well as a place of business in which the king took an active part. Such a centre drew in and impressed the king's greatest subjects and James's relations with his nobility were far easier than any of his Stewart forebears. He avoided favouring individual families unduly, even those, like the Hepburns, upon whom he relied. James distributed patronage widely and, even more importantly, did not alienate magnates against whom he had taken action, thus giving them the chance of recovery. A good case study is provided by Archibald Earl of Angus. Angus, an ambitious magnate with important southern lands, had been a major problem for James III and had played a dubious role in the opening years of James IV's reign. The king clearly distrusted him. He kept him in custody for several years and, in 1510, the earl was charged with failing to pay proper relief, the sum due on inheritance, and asked for forty-five years' worth of rents. Though allowed to pay a fraction of this sum, Angus had clearly been targeted. However, James's actions had no political comeback. The earl returned to the council, was allowed access to the king, and his family gave loyal service until the end of the reign. Good general relations prevented individual grievances from developing into discontent. James also showed an awareness of this by choosing to summon parliament infrequently. By avoiding the forum in which collective grievances might be aired, the king probably felt he was maintaining personal initiative in domestic politics (Macdougall 2004). Even the disastrous end of the reign at the battle of Flodden in 1513 was testament to James's political achievements. Along with the king, the dead in the battle included nine earls and fourteen barons, an indication of the unity of purpose that James had achieved.

CROWN AND NOBILITY

The narrative of kingship in late medieval Scotland perhaps encourages the view that tensions between the crown and nobility were the dominant feature of political life. The Stewart and Douglas magnates certainly created enormous problems for the first four Stewart kings, and the nobility as a group remained a demanding constituency able to articulate criticism of the crown and expecting its interests to be served. However, beneath the obvious crises was a political structure that rested on relatively stable relationships between crown and nobility (Grant 1987; Wormald 1985b). These relationships transcended crises – however serious – though major clashes certainly left their mark on the shape of the nobility as a group (Grant 1978). Only the king (directly or through a lieutenant) possessed the authority to run the realm, to mobilise the army in its defence, or to maintain internal peace by settling disputes amongst its leading families. Scottish writers, citing the disasters of the late thirteenth century, portrayed the crown as the guarantor of Scotland's stability. However, to perform this role the crown required the active participation of its nobility. At the centre, the principal offices of state and positions on the king's council continued to be held by nobles, but this interdependence was clearest at a local level.

Working with limited resources, Scottish kings had little paid bureaucracy and relied on local lords as the agents of government. Magnates and barons acted as justiciars and sheriffs and used their own resources and connections to perform key functions at local level. They enforced royal justice by holding their courts and, in the case of sheriffs, raised revenues. Though such royal officers combined private interests with their official duties, were rooted in local politics and, in the case of some sheriffs, even had a heritable right to their posts, this did not necessarily lead to a dangerously unbalanced and localised system of administration. It did, however, limit the level of centralised control, not necessarily a bad thing as comparison with contemporary English government suggests (Grant 1987). There were, moreover, several hundred earldoms, lordships and baronies that acted as private jurisdictions. The role of royal government here was to oversee the judgements of these courts of barony or regality. In normal circumstances this system worked adequately, but it restricted the king's political choices and made it essential for him to cooperate with local interests. When a king interfered too strongly – as James III did in Berwickshire – he could generate local opposition.

The view that, without royal control, the nobility would revert to anarchic and violent feuding suggested in some older works (Balfour Melville 1936; Dunlop 1950) also needs serious modification. Examples of major private conflict, like that associated with Alexander Stewart of Badenoch in the 1380s and 1390s or the feud between the Lindsays and the Gordons in the 1440s, were significant but exceptional in scale (Boardman 1996b; Grant 1992). They show what happened when structures of regional or local lordship broke down. Normally though, such structures provided a relatively stable focus for political life. The private and public roles of magnates like Alexander Earl of Mar or the earls of Douglas provided political leadership and local government for regions and, while the Douglases' lordship was dismantled by James II, this hardly spelt the end of similar, more confined structures of aristocratic influence, more acceptable to the crown (M Brown 1997; M Brown 1998). The 1409 bond between Albany and Douglas demonstrates the regulatory role played by magnates. The agreement was designed to prevent friction and dispute, not simply between the principals but also between their followers, resolving such clashes by arbitration. On a smaller scale, similar bonds can be found regulating relations amongst the nobility, promising protection and reward and settling disputes, without open reference to the royal government (Wormald 1985a).

PARLIAMENT

The century from 1371 also witnessed the full development of the Scottish parliament. The traditional view criticised the institution as an inferior version of the English parliament, which largely endorsed royal decisions (Rait 1924). It is true that parliament developed as a royal institution, called by the king and acting as the final court of his justice. However, recent study has demonstrated the effectiveness of parliament as a forum for complaint, as well as support, which kings found difficult to manipulate and yet felt obliged to summon on an almost annual basis between 1424 and 1496 (Tanner 2001). Parliament comprised three estates: the clergy, nobility and burgesses, all sitting in a single chamber. By the late fourteenth century it had developed a range of roles. It was the highest law court in the realm, the body which tried tenants-in-chief for treason. More obviously it had a legislative function, producing statutes dealing with a huge range of issues. Gatherings of the estates also represented the means to gain popular consent for major decisions. Grants of taxation could be obtained only with its consent and both changes to the royal succession, as in 1371, and appointments of lieutenants, like that of Rothesay, were also issued during meetings of the estates.

Relations between kings and their subjects in parliament varied according to the wider political context. The parliament of 1424, held after James I's coronation, was a display of the king's authority. In a very different way, the parliament of July 1452, held by James II amidst the crisis with the Douglases also sought to augment his personal position. It was a partisan gathering of royal adherents rather than a meeting of the community. It cleared the king's name, witnessed his patronage and prepared for the attack on his enemies. These enemies were outside parliament, demonstrating their scorn for the gathering.

The crown developed methods to limit discussion, amongst them the delegation of much of parliament's function to a smaller body, the lords of the articles (Tanner 2000a). However, the effect of this can be exaggerated and all kings found parliament to be a focus for criticism of their policies. The complaints levelled at James III's failure to perform the justice ayres in 1478 were one example of this. In particular, after 1424, such criticism was associated with royal requests for taxation. Most parliaments were summoned with the aim of securing funds from the estates and regular requests led to growing complaint. In 1431 James I was granted taxation only if its expenditure was controlled by representatives of parliament, and in 1436 a further request for a contribution led to an attempt to arrest the king. Such control of the king's policy or person was attempted on occasion. In 1398, Rothesay's actions as lieutenant were to be supervised by the general council (an informal meeting of the estates) and in 1482 James III resisted parliamentary efforts to appoint his brother as his lieutenant (Tanner 2000b).

Such politically significant events indicate the political standing accorded to meetings of the estates. Parliaments and general councils acted as sources of legitimacy and authority, especially during royal minorities. The 1445 parliament, for example, was effectively the resolution of a civil war with oaths sworn by king and estates and rewards and punishments handed out. While such meetings were part of royal government, the decision of James IV to cease summoning full parliaments is striking. A financially well-provided ruler saw the political role of parliament as a threat, and delegated its other powers to less formal bodies (Macdougall 2004).

ROYAL RESOURCES

One way of tracing the development of royal power between 1371 and 1424 is through the issue of finance. As has been shown above, the crown's resources were regularly a matter of political debate. In particular, royal demands for taxation often led to debates about royal policy. This was because communal consent was required for taxation to be levied and in Scotland such consent was often hard to achieve. The estates were anxious to avoid the almost annual grants of taxation secured by English kings, and approved grants of money only in certain circumstances. Even when considered legitimate, as in paying for James I's ransom, the estates quickly grew reluctant to agreeing to annual taxes which they felt impoverished the kingdom. From the crown's perspective, however, taxation remained the best means of raising large sums from their subjects. The readiness of rulers to brave political problems for cash was a measure of their relative ambitions. The early Stewart kings and governors asked for taxation very rarely, avoiding further criticism of their rule, and later minority regimes tended to do likewise. However, from James I onwards, the crown made regular requests for money, despite the likelihood of opposition.

For the kings from James I to James IV it was vital to augment the normal income of the crown if they were to develop the status of their office. This ordinary revenue was drawn from a number of sources: the rents paid by burghs; the customs charged on exported wool and hides; the lands of the crown and feudal duties known as casualties charged on their vassals. The early Stewarts lived off this income, taking advantage of high wool prices to collect large sums from the customs, but this did not last beyond the 1390s and it was hard to boost revenue from either burgh rents or customs. Income from crown lands clearly did grow. The annexations of James I and II quadrupled the size of the royal demesne, which was regarded by 1455 as a reliable source of income. However, much of it was consumed by the running of the lands and the surplus remained static until the 1500s. This was addressed by James IV's introduction of feu-farming into royal lands, giving tenants longer-term leases (and thus greater security) but also charging much higher rents. Though causing hardship and armed resistance from some tenants, it saw massive increases in royal income. In Fife income doubled and in Ettrick Forest it rose from over £500 to over £2,500. James IV also pursued lords for feudal casualties. Angus was charged £45,000 for neglecting to pay the relief or succession duty on Kirriemuir, but allowed to settle for about £1,300, while the Earl of Rothes was pursued by the crown for a payment of over £2,000. The greater vigour of James IV's methods was a measure of his security and neither feuing nor casualties caused the level of collective disquiet created by taxation. The king's policies led to the crown drawing an annual income of nearly £45,000 by 1510, perhaps twenty times the royal income in the 1420s.

However, James IV did not live within this income but exceeded it in the display and expenditure associated with the crown. Starting with James I, Scottish kings were determined to develop an image of monarchy that depended on the lavish outlay of money. The development of purpose-built royal residences at Linlithgow, Falkland, Dunfermline and Stirling provided the settings for both formal and informal contact between king and political elite. Expenditure on clothing and decoration ensured the image of the crown within these residences would impress both subjects and visitors. Similarly the money laid out on weapons of war was as much about prestige as practical power. The artillery trains possessed by the fifteenth-century rulers and the huge sums spent by James IV on his fleet (one ship alone, the *Michael*, cost up to £30,000) created the impression of wealth and power (Macdougall 1989). Kings who used income to buy support, like Robert II, or who hoarded it, like James III, enjoyed less respect from their subjects. Though tensions could arise from the search for greater wealth, increasing the crown's income was integrally linked in the eyes of Stewart kings to the increase of their authority.

REFERENCES TO BOOKS AND ARTICLES MENTIONED IN THE TEXT

Items marked * are recommended for further reading.

Balfour Melville, EWM 1936 *James I King of Scots*. London.
*Boardman, S 1996a *The Early Stewart Kings: Robert II and Robert III*. East Linton.
Boardman, S 1996b 'Lordship in the north-east: the Badenoch Stewarts 1: Alexander Stewart Earl of Buchan', *Northern Scotland*, 16, 1–30.
Boardman, S 2004 'Coronations, Kings and Guardians: Politics, Parliaments and General Councils, 1371–1406', *in* Brown, KM and Tanner, RJ (eds), *Parliament and Politics in Scotland, 1235–1560*, Edinburgh, 102–122.
*Brown, J 1977 'The Exercise of Power' *in* Brown, J (ed), *Scottish Society in the Fifteenth Century*, London, 33–65.
Brown, M 1992 'That old serpent and ancient of evil days': Walter Earl of Atholl and the death of James I', *Scottish Historical Review*, 71, 23–45.
*Brown, M 1994a *James I*. Edinburgh.
*Brown, M 1994b 'Scotland Tamed: Kings and Magnates in Late Medieval Scotland: A review of recent work', *Innes Review*, 45, 120–46.
Brown, M 1996 'Regional lordship in north-east Scotland: the Badenoch Stewarts 2: Alexander Stewart Earl of Mar', *Northern Scotland*, 16, 31–54.
*Brown, M 1997 'Rejoice to hear of Douglas': The house of Douglas and the presentation of magnate power in late Medieval Scotland', *Scottish Historical Review*, 76, 161–184.
Brown, M 1998 *The Black Douglases*. East Linton.

Brown, M 2000 'Vile Times': Bower's last book and the minority of James II', *Scottish Historical Review*, 79, 165–188.

Brown, M 2004 'Public authority and factional conflict: crown, parliament and polity, 1424–1455' *in* Brown, KM and Tanner, RJ (eds), *Parliament and Politics in Scotland, 1235–1560*, Edinburgh, 123–144.

Connolly, M 1992 '*The Dethe of the Kynge of Scotis* : a new edition', *Scottish Historical Review*, 71, 46–69.

Duncan, AAM 1984 *James I, King of Scots, 1424–1437*. Glasgow.

Dunlop, AI 1950 *The Life and Times of James Kennedy Bishop of St Andrews*. Edinburgh.

Grant, A 1978 'The Development of the Scottish Peerage', *Scottish Historical Review*, 57, 1–27.

Grant, A 1984 *Independence and Nationhood, Scotland, 1306–1469*. London.

*Grant, A 1987 'Crown and Nobility in Late Medieval Britain', *in* R Mason (ed), *Scotland and England, 1286–1815*, Edinburgh, 34–59.

Grant, A 1992 'The Wolf of Badenoch', *in* Sellar, WDH (ed), *Moray, Province and People*, Inverness, 143–161.

*Macdougall, NAT 1982 *James III: a political study*. Edinburgh.

*Macdougall, NAT 1989 *James IV*. Edinburgh.

Macdougall, NAT 2004 'The estates in eclipse: politics and parliament in the reign of James IV', *in* Brown, KM and Tanner, RJ (eds), *Parliament and Politics in Scotland, 1235–1560*, Edinburgh, 145–59.

Macfarlane, LM 1985 *William Elphinstone and the Kingdom of Scotland, 1431–1514*. Aberdeen.

*McGladdery, CA 1990 *James II*. Edinburgh.

Madden, C 1976, 'Royal treatment of feudal casualties in late Medieval Scotland', *Scottish Historical Review*, 55, 172–194.

Madden, C 1976b 'The Feuing of Ettrick Forest', *Innes Review*, 27, 70–84.

Mason, R 1999 'This realm of Scotland is an empire? Imperial ideas and iconography in Renaissance Scotland', *in* Crawford, BE (ed), *Church, Chronicle and Learning in late Medieval and early Modern Scotland*, Edinburgh, 73–85.

*Nicholson, R 1974 *Scotland: The Later Middle Ages*. Edinburgh.

Penman, M 2004 *David II*. East Linton.

Rait, RS 1924 *The Parliaments of Scotland*. Glasgow.

Tanner, RJ 2000a 'The Lords of the Articles before 1540: a reassessment', *Scottish Historical Review*, 79, 189–212.

Tanner, RJ 2000b 'I arest you sir, in the name of the thre astattes in perlement': the Scottish Parliament and resistance to the crown in the fifteenth century', *in* Thornton, T (ed), *Social attitudes and political structures in the fifteenth century*, Stroud, 101–17.

Tanner, RJ 2001 *The Late Medieval Scottish Parliament*. East Linton.

Wormald, JM 1985a *Lords and Men in Scotland: Bonds of Manrent, 1442–1603*. Edinburgh.

*Wormald, JM 1985b 'Taming the Magnates?', *in* Stringer KJ (ed), *Essays on the Nobility of Medieval Scotland*, Edinburgh, 270–80.

CHAPTER FIVE

The Western *Gàidhealtachd* in the Middle Ages

R Andrew McDonald

The Scottish chronicler John of Fordun, who composed his *Cronica Gentis Scotorum* or *History of the Scottish Nation* in the 1370s and early 1380s, included in this work the earliest literary description of that motif that dominates so much of our thinking about Scottish history: the division between Highlands and Lowlands, Gaelic speakers and Scots speakers. 'The manners and customs of the Scots vary with the diversity of their speech,' he writes:

> For two languages are spoken amongst them, the Scottish [i.e. Gaelic] and the Teutonic [i.e. Scots]; the latter of which is the language of those who occupy the seaboard and the plains, while the race of Scottish speech inhabits the highlands and outlying islands. The people of the coast are of domestic and civilized habits, trusty, patient, and urbane, decent in their attire, affable, and peaceful . . . The highlanders and people of the islands, on the other hand, are a savage and untamed nation, rude and independent, given to rapine, ease-loving, of a docile and warm disposition, comely in person, but unsightly in dress, hostile to the English people and language, and . . . exceedingly cruel. (Skene 1872, 38)

While many subsequent medieval and early modern writers described the inhabitants of the Highlands in similar terms, it was not until the nineteenth century that prejudice, neglect, or (from the eighteenth century) Romantic musings gave way to serious scholarly investigations of the Highlands (Cowan 2000). Among the nineteenth-century pioneers of the history of the Highlands and Gaelic-speaking Scotland (the *Gàidhealtachd*) was William Forbes Skene, whose great work on *Celtic Scotland* (1876–80) 'cannot be ignored by anyone investigating the first millennium and a half of Scottish history' (Cowan 2000, 4), although the works of Donald Gregory (1836) and EW Robertson (1862) also proved influential. By the time of Skene's death in 1892, the Highlands had been rediscovered as a subject for serious investigation, and the decades since the 1980s have witnessed a proliferation of works concerned with the Highlands and Gaelic-speaking Scotland. Indeed, where once this subject suffered from neglect, it is now possible for one recent commentator to remark that it represents 'an aspect of Scottish history which has received a considerable, some would say disproportionate, amount of scholarly attention in recent years' (Lynch 2001, 291).

LAND, PEOPLE, TRAVEL AND TRANSPORTATION

What, then, are the Highlands? For Fordun, as for many subsequent writers, the Highlands could be conceived in topographical terms, as a rugged, mountainous region (see Map 1.The Highlands c.1400). The Highlands in fact constitute approximately fifty per cent of the total land area of Scotland and about twenty per cent of the total of Britain. It is common to associate the Highlands with the north of Scotland and the Lowlands with the south, but an alternative and more accurate distinction is between east and west: the so-called 'Highland line' actually runs approximately south west to north east, stretching from near Dumbarton on the Clyde north-eastwards to Stonehaven on the east coast before curling back westwards and northwards into Ross and Sutherland. Fordun captured the nature of much of this region when he wrote that, 'lofty mountains stretch through the midst of [Scotland], from end to end, as do the tall Alps through Europe' (Skene 1872, 36). The English chronicler Matthew Paris, whose early map of the British Isles (c. 1250) otherwise displays gaps in its knowledge of north Britain, was aware of the difficult nature of Highland terrain. He described the central and northern Highlands as 'a mountainous and woody region,' and Argyll as 'a maritime district' (Brown 1891, map following introduction).

The Highlands, then, did possess unity based upon physical environment. Yet within that environment are important variations, and we must not press too far the homogeneous nature of the region. The mountains of *Drumalban*, 'the spine of Britain', divide the eastern and central Highlands from the western, while the great mountain mass known in the middle ages as the Mounth (modern Grampians) stretches from the east coast near Stonehaven to the west, creating an important barrier north of the Forth. The Northern and Western Isles display a diverse topography, from the mountains of Skye and Rum to the flat fertile land of Tiree; some islands like Islay, Jura, Arran and Bute might be said to have more in common with the Lowlands than with the Highlands. Like the Highlands, the Lowlands themselves were also far from homogeneous, divided as they were in the medieval period by marshes in the Forth valley, and by the firths of Forth and Tay (Webster 1997). On Matthew Paris's map, the Forth and Clyde estuaries slice so deeply into Scotland as to render northern Scotland virtually an island, warranting the legend 'Scocia Ultra Marina' or 'Scotland Beyond the Sea' (Brown 1891, map following introduction). And of course, much of what is often described as 'Lowlands' in fact consists of hilly upland terrain. Thus, as Barrow remarks, any division of Scotland into north/Highlands and south/Lowlands is facile: 'Scotland north of the Mounth was certainly not what we should call the Highlands, any more than Scotland south of the Mounth was the Lowlands; both included Highland and Lowland territory.' (Barrow 1973d, 366).

Fordun observed of the Scottish mountains that, 'Impassable as they are on horseback, save in very few places, they can hardly be crossed even on foot' (Skene 1872 36), and there has been a tendency to regard the Highlands as a world apart, primarily because of the difficulties of travel both to and within the region. But just

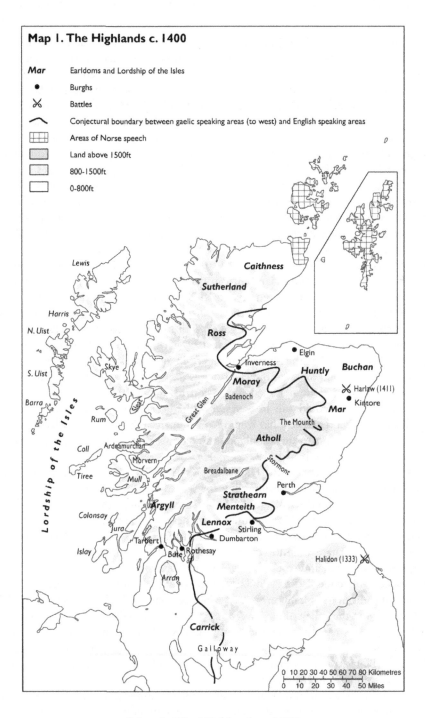

Map 1. The Highlands c.1400

how impassable were the Highlands in the middle ages? Though roads were few and travel was challenging in the pre-modern period, movement was of course not impossible (Barrow 1984). From at least the middle of the fourteenth century a series of drove roads facilitated the driving of cattle to markets in the Lowlands and England from the Highlands and the Isles (Haldane 1952). In the west, with its deeply indented coastline of sea-lochs and islands, the waterways constituted a sea-road rather than a hindrance to transportation and communication, and the west highland galley was important to life here. Few Scottish kings can have known the Highlands better than Robert I (1306–29), whose itinerary demonstrates that the 'Highland line' was no barrier to travel. Bruce's path to exile in 1306 took him through Argyll and Kintyre into the Isles, while his wife was sent across the Mounth to Kildrummy. Soon after his return in 1307, Bruce spent 1308 and 1309 sub-jugating foes in the north and west: his campaigns against the MacDougalls of Argyll involved action up and down the west coast from Loch Broom (where one of his acts is dated: Duncan 1988, no 9) to Dunstaffnage. In 1315, as part of an expedition to the Isles and Ireland, Bruce even had himself hauled across the narrow isthmus of land between Knapdale and Kintyre, from East Loch Tarbert to West Loch Tarbert (the place-name Tarbert (*tairm-bert*) itself means an isthmus over which ships could be dragged) in a galley with sails hoisted (a move calculated to impress the Highland chieftains) (Duncan 1997). This was a mode of transportation perhaps also utilized by the Norwegian ruler Magnus Barelegs in 1098, when he laid claim to Kintyre and many of the Hebrides as part of an agreement with the king of Scots whereby Magnus obtained possession of all the islands off the west coast around which he could sail in a vessel with the rudder set. The author of the *Orkneyinga Saga* remarked that Kintyre 'juts out from the west of Scotland, and the isthmus connecting it to the mainland is so narrow that ships are regularly hauled across'(Pálsson and Edwards 1978, ch. 41).

Another characteristic of the Highlands, also perceived by Fordun, was the poor quality of the soil and its unsuitability for settled agriculture, as compared to the more fertile and productive lands of the east. Although the study of medieval Scottish rural life is largely in its infancy, modern scholars like Barrow, Dodgshon and Grant have tended to play down the contrast between Highlands and Lowlands in this regard. There was, for example, a pastoral element in the economy of all regions of Scotland, and stock-raising was significant in the Lowlands as well as the Highlands (Haldane 1952). Similarly, land could be cultivated wherever it was practicable, even in upland terrain. At Melrose abbey, founded by David I (1124–53) in 1136 in the valley of the Tweed, the Cistercian monks derived a considerable amount of their revenue from the pasturing of stock (Haldane 1952), while in the later thirteenth century, John Comyn, Lord of Badenoch, permitted his men of Invertilt (Blair Atholl) to take from the local woodlands materials with which to construct ploughs, harrows, and carts (Barrow 1973d; see also 1973b). Similarly, landlords in some Lowland farming communities acquired grazings in upland areas: townships in the Merse used grazings in the Lammermuirs, for example, and landlords in Aberdeenshire acquired grazings on the edge of the Cairngorms (Dixon

2002). Regional variations within the Western Isles should also be noted. Even in the poor climatic conditions of the sixteenth century, the Archdeacon of the Isles, Donald Monro, whose *Description of the Western Islands of Scotland* of 1549 is an important source for the political, social, and economic situation in the Western Isles, commented upon the fertility of many islands. Of Tiree, for example, he wrote that, 'Na cuntrie may be mair fertile of corn . . .' (Munro 1961, 65). In contrast, the thirteenth-century Manx chronicle remarked upon the 'mountainous (sic) and rocky, and . . . almost completely untilled' nature of Lewis, adding that this land 'in no way sufficed to sustain' the Manx prince to whom it was given in the early thirteenth century (Broderick 1995, f 41 v).

Another problem is assessing the extent to which settlement patterns in the High-lands and Lowlands differed. While it is true that different terms seem to have been applied to settlements in each region (*clachan* or *baile* in the Highlands and *fermtoun* in the Lowlands), Roger Dodgshon (1980) has argued that the differences are not clear-cut, with *clachan* sometimes used in the Lowlands and *toun* (if not *fermtoun*) also used in the Highlands. Similarly, it is difficult to establish a firm association of settlement morphology with topography. As Dodgshon puts it, 'a loose distinction can be drawn between a minority of settlements which possessed a semblance of order and the majority which did not. The latter formed the typical toun in both the Highlands and Lowlands. In it, dwellings, byres and kailyards were disposed as irregularly shaped clusters.' (Dodgshon 1980, 63). Clearly, what is most significant about medieval settlement patterns is not any distinction between Highlands and Lowlands, but rather the overwhelmingly rural distribution of the population in small communities, widely scattered across the country. These settlements were grouped together into broader units known as multiple estates; essentially units of lordship, multiple estates were geared towards the extraction of labour services, dues and payments in kind from tenants to the landlord (who might be the king, a chieftain, a baron, or an ecclesiastical institution or individual like a bishop). Multiple estates in Scotland are found in different cultural contexts (e.g. Pictish, Norse, Anglian) and, though best known from the shires and thanages of the east and south-east, Dodgshon has made a compelling argument based on a variety of circumstantial evidence for their existence throughout the north and west as well (1981, ch. 3).

When considering rural life in the medieval period, then, differences between Highlands and Lowlands can be exaggerated. The majority of Scots in the middle ages lived in the countryside, in small scattered communities devoid of planned organization and devoted to some form of agriculture; most rendered labour services, payments and dues to landlords. While some broad distinctions might be made between arable and pastoral economies and between ordered settlements and irregular ones, such distinctions must not be regarded as absolute, with local variation playing a significant role across Scotland. Finally, where population distribution was concerned, the distinction between Highlands and Lowlands seems to have been almost meaningless in the middle ages: the medieval population was much more evenly dispersed than is the case today (Houston and Knox 2001).

In one very important manner, however, the development of Highlands and

Lowlands did diverge in the medieval period, for the former did not directly share in one of the major socio-economic transformations of the twelfth and thirteenth centuries: the development of burghs (towns). Whatever their origins, the development of burghs as jurisdictionally, commercially, and tenurially privileged communities in the twelfth century was largely limited to the eastern side of the country. Of the forty or so in existence by about 1214 the majority were situated in the east, and burghs were markedly absent from the Highlands. Yet it would be dangerous to suppose that this lack of burghs denotes a concomitant lack of trade and commerce, even if we must not paint too rosy a picture of the medieval economy here. Droving is attested from at least the mid-fourteenth century and demonstrates one manner in which Highlands and Lowlands interacted commercially in the late medieval and early modern period, with cattle being driven from Skye, Argyll and the North to markets in the Lowlands and in England (Haldane 1952). Similarly, burghs that were situated on the edge of the Highlands provided opportunities for interaction. Dumbarton, founded in 1222 by Alexander II (1214–49), and granted a fair in 1226, seems to have developed as a port of communication and commerce between the east and west of Scotland. In 1275, for example, the men of Dumbarton were ordered not to trouble the Bishop of Glasgow's men going to and returning from Argyll with merchandise. In the same year, some of Alexander of Argyll's men were arrested with their vessel and goods in Bristol on suspicion of piracy; the value of the goods was stated to have been 160 marks (£106 13s 4d) but their nature was, unfortunately, not mentioned (Bain 1881, II, no. 55, 63). And in 1292 the west-coast potentates Alexander of Argyll, Angus the son of Donald, his son Alexander, and their merchants, were granted license to trade in Ireland (Bain 1881, II, no. 635). Caldwell and Ewart have made a compelling argument from an archaeological perspective that Finlaggan on Islay, the centre of the Lordship of the Isles in the fourteenth and fifteenth centuries (see below), could be regarded as a proto-urban centre, 'with a sizeable population, offering the facilities available elsewhere in burghs' (1993, 161) – but there is little evidence for the existence of other similar centers in the West Highlands and Islands in this period.

One commodity that was certainly exported from the West Highlands in the middle ages was people: from the mid-thirteenth century Irish sources make reference to the galloglasses (*gallóclaig*), mercenary warriors more famous from the later medieval and early modern periods in Irish and Hebridean history. Several of the ruling kindreds in the Hebrides were involved in the business of supplying these formidable mercenary troops, principally to Ireland. By the fourteenth century, some families like the MacSweens had established Galloglass dynasties there, and mercenary activity was an important connector between Gaelic Scotland and Gaelic Ireland (McKerral 1951; Lydon 1992).

'DAPPLED SAILS'

Hundreds of years of travel, trade, and warfare in the Highlands are symbolized by the West Highland galley, which became a cultural icon of the region in the middle ages (Rixson 1998). In the maritime environment of the west, chieftains from Somerled in the twelfth century to Donald Dubh in the sixteenth commanded fleets of galleys (or birlinns) that could be used for military purposes or for engaging in peaceful pursuits such as trade. Representations of these sleek vessels, direct descendants of the Viking longship, can still be seen on carved stones at places like Iona, Kilmory, and Oronsay today (Steer and Bannerman 1977), and graffiti carvings of them are to be found at the old parish church at Kilchattan, Luing. The galley also formed a prominent motif on the seals of West Highland and Island potentates like Angus Óg of Islay, whose well-preserved thirteenth-century seal depicts a lovely birlinn with sail furled. These vessels were clinker built, with symmetrical high stems and sterns, and were powered by oar and sail; unlike their Viking ancestors, they had stern rudders. Evidence for the West Highland galley becomes more plentiful from the time of the wars of independence, in which sea-power played an important role (Reid 1960). A Gaelic poem preserved in the *Book of the Dean of Lismore*, for example, recounts the 'Tryst of a fleet against Castle Sween,' an event that likely belongs to the Scottish civil war of the early fourteenth century (c.1310): 'They have a straight stern-wind behind them . . . their dappled sails are bulging, foam rises to vessels' sides' (Watson 1937, 11). In the mid-sixteenth century Donald Monro frequently remarked on harbours suitable for 'hieland galeis', and as late as 1605 the Scottish Crown complained that: 'ane of the cheife and principall causses quhich procurit the rebellion and disobedience of the Ilismen [in Lewis] is the number of galleyes . . . within the Ilis' (Hill Burton 1887, VII, 84–85). To date, no West Highland *Mary Rose* or Oseberg ship has been recovered, but a good deal has been learned from the *Aileach*, a forty-foot replica vessel built in 1991 and maintained by the Lord of the Isles Trust, a charitable organization that promotes knowledge of the maritime history of Celtic Scotland (Clark 1993; www.mallaigheritage.org.uk/aileach/aileach1.htm).

LANGUAGE

Fordun was the first Scottish chronicler to conceive of the Highlands as a region distinct in linguistic terms. Broadly speaking, Gaelic reached its greatest extent in the early twelfth century, when it was in widespread use in Scotland north of the Forth; it was also widely spoken in Galloway, where it did not die out until the fifteenth century. South of the Forth, Scots (akin to English) was already established by the twelfth century, but it was the expansion and consolidation of this language from around 1100 that had a particularly pervasive influence: Barrow (1989) has remarked that the spread of Middle English may well be the most enduring legacy of the so-called 'Norman conquest' of Scotland in the twelfth century. Certainly by the time Fordun was writing, Gaelic was becoming restricted to many upland parishes in eastern Scotland, with similar developments taking place around Stirling and Dumbarton, while in regions like Fife it was probably almost extinct as a vernacular by Fordun's day (Barrow 1973d). In the later middle ages, then, the divide between Gaelic speaking regions and Scots speaking regions began to coalesce with the geographic distinction between Highlands and Lowlands: 'The Highlands and Islands were now synonymous, as they had not previously been, with the Gaidhealtachd ... while the Lowlands ... became the country of the Sasunnach, the people who (whatever their racial origin) spoke and wrote a variant of the English tongue' (Barrow 1973d, 363; see also Bannerman 1990).

On the other hand, some parts of the Highlands were not Gaelic-speaking in Fordun's lifetime or for centuries thereafter (see Map 2. Linguistic Changes). In regions settled by the Vikings, for example (particularly in the north and west and in the islands), the Norse language was widely spoken. A Scandinavian dialect called Norn remained the common speech in Orkney throughout the sixteenth century, and even longer in Shetland; its replacement by Scots has been called 'negligible' until after 1379 (Wainwright 1962, 121). The Western Isles, on the other hand, have been regarded as bilingual Gaelic-Norse until at least the thirteenth century before undergoing a gradual process of re-Gaelicization (McLeod 2004). Still other regions outside the geographical Highlands, like Galloway, remained Gaelic speaking until the fifteenth century, while Gaelic survived in some Lowland regions into the nineteenth century (Newton 2000). Finally, it is significant that Latin remained the universal language of church and education in Highlands and Lowlands alike (as throughout the rest of Europe) in the middle ages (Watt 1981). Michael Newton has thus cautioned against equating the term *Gàidhealtachd* with the Highlands in the medieval period, arguing that this term originally referred to a cultural space (Gaelic speakers and the areas inhabited by them) rather than a geographical zone, and suggesting that 'only in recent times has the equation of Highlands and Gaelic-speakers, and Lowlands and Lallans-speakers, become fixed in both Gaelic and English tradition' (Newton 2000, 235). Similarly, Barrow's seminal study of the 'Lost Gàidhealtachd of medieval Scotland' (1989) reveals, through methodical sifting of a wide range of evidence, that Gaelic only gradually receded from much of eastern Scotland, and that the later middle ages were in fact a time of linguistic coexistence and slow change rather than of black-and-white dichotomies. Despite the retreat of Gaelic, it was not until the very end of the middle ages that its social status began to decline vis-à-vis Scots, which, by the fifteenth century, was the language of court, government, and nobility in Scotland. Gaelic may have been disparaged by some later medieval writers like the author of the allegorical *Buke of the Howlat* (c. 1450), whose grotesque Gaelic-speaking bard recites gibberish (Bawcutt and Riddy 1987, 76), but the late middle ages were certainly not a time of universal decay for that language. Alexander Grant (1984) has pointed out that James IV (1488–1513) thought Gaelic worth learning in the 1490s, and the so-called 'Renaissance' of Gaelic culture associated with the Lordship of the Isles is considered in more detail below. Similarly, John Bannerman, in his seminal study of the Beaton medical kindred (1986), has reminded us that Gaelic was one of only four languages (apart from Arabic, Latin, and Greek) in which learned tracts of medieval Europe were written in our period. The Gaelic medical manuscripts of the fourteenth to sixteenth centuries that belonged to the MacBeths or Beatons (hereditary physicians to the Lords of the Isles), and the O'Conachers or MacConachers (a family of doctors in Lorn) are well known and display considerable learning, quoting all the authorities familiar to medieval medicine, including Hippocrates, Euclid and Galen (Bannerman 1986; Grant and Cheape 1987). Finally, there must be a certain irony in the fact that Scottish kingship and identity in the high middle ages were ineluctably bound up with Scotland's Gaelic heritage. When Alexander III (1249–86) was inaugurated as king of Scots in 1249, part of the ceremony, described by the later chronicler Walter Bower, involved a Highland bard reciting Alexander's genealogy (in Gaelic) right back to the first Scot: 'Though a wild highlander he [the bard] was honourably attired after his own fashion, clad in a scarlet robe. Bending his knee in a scrupulously correct manner and inclining his head, he greeted the king in his mother tongue, saying courteously, 'God bless the king of Albany, Alexander mac Alexander, mac William, mac Henry, mac David . . .' (Watt 1990, v, 294–5). A suitable reminder, if one is needed, that Gaelic traditions lay at the heart of the medieval Scottish kingdom, monarchy, and identity: 'Alexander's genealogy, as represented at his coronation [inauguration], associated him with the founding myth of Scotland and the Gaelic highlands.' (Moll 2002, 132).

POWER AND POLITICS: FROM SOMERLED TO THE LORDS OF THE ISLES, C.1100–1500

The history of the West Highlands in our period begins with the rise to power of the mighty Somerled (d.1164), who dominated the mainland and islands from the Mull of Kintyre northward to Skye. Arguably of even greater significance, however, is his role as the progenitor of several kindreds that dominated political and cultural life in the region for four hundred years. Of mixed Gaelic and Norse ancestry, Somerled carved out his insular and mainland kingdom in an era when both Scottish and Norwegian power in the Isles was weak. His main rivals were neither the Scottish nor Norwegian rulers but rather, initially, another Scandinavian dynasty that had established itself in the Isle of Man in the late eleventh century. In 1156 Somerled vanquished one of these Manx sea kings, Godfrey, in a naval battle, and he won another victory in 1158, after which Godfrey fled to Norway (Broderick 1995, f. 37 v). Somerled is principally famous for his conflicts with the kings of Scots from the early 1150s, which culminated in his 1164 invasion of the Clyde estuary with a massive fleet of ships, filled with warriors from the Hebrides, Kintyre, and Dublin. In the ensuing conflict near Renfrew, Somerled was slain (Clancy 1998, 212–14). The motivations behind this invasion remain problematic, although the claims of generations of historians from the late middle ages onwards that he sought the kingship for himself must be dismissed; more likely, he was concerned with the intrusion of Scottish royal authority into the eastern frontiers of his sea-girt kingdom, an interpretation that might be borne out by the site of the battle at Renfrew, near the legal centre of the recently

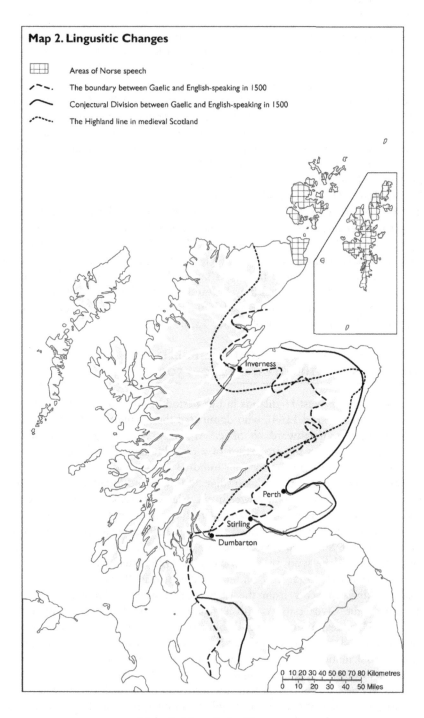

Map 2. Lingusitic Changes

Areas of Norse speech

The boundary between Gaelic and English-speaking in 1500

Conjectural Division between Gaelic and English-speaking in 1500

The Highland line in medieval Scotland

Inverness

Perth

Stirling

Dumbarton

0 10 20 30 40 50 60 70 80 Kilometres

0   10   20   30   40   50 Miles

Map 2. Linguistic Changes

established Stewart lordship in the west of Scotland (McDonald 2003a). Whatever the case might have been, by engaging in conflict with the Scottish kings, Somerled established a pattern that would play itself out more fully over the next three centuries of Highland history.

In recent years, the view of Somerled as a dependent subject or underking has given way to an interpretation of him as a largely if not entirely autonomous ruler, in an age when kingships in north Britain were still relative and multiple kingships were not quite a thing of the past (Frame 1990). The use of terms by Scottish chroniclers describing Somerled's subordinate status (e.g. *regulus*, *princeps*) is likely more indicative of the perspective of those writing rather than the reality, and a clearer indication of Somerled's place in a Hebridean context is provided by Irish annalists, who described him as *rí Innse Gall & Cind tire* (ruler of the Hebrides and Kintyre) on his death in 1164 (Stokes 1898, 195; McDonald 1997). Unquestionably, however, one of Somerled's legacies to the history of the Highlands was this regnal status, which was inherited by his descendants and ultimately lay behind the title *dominus insularum* (Lord of the Isles) adopted by the later rulers of the region (see below).

Whatever unity Somerled had imposed over his sea-girt kingdom was shattered with his death and not restored until the establishment of the Lordship of the Isles in the early fourteenth century. In fact, the century from the death of Somerled to the cession of the Hebrides to Scotland in 1266 was a time of intense competition and conflict, as Somerled's descendants, the Manx kings and, increasingly, Scottish and Norwegian rulers jockeyed for power and territory. One legacy of the period was the fragmentation of Somerled's kingdom and its division among his descendants, known broadly as the MacSorleys but by the thirteenth century divided into three principal kindreds: MacDougalls, MacDonalds and MacRuairis (see below). Competition among them was fierce, and this opened the door for the Manx dynasty to re-establish itself, which is precisely what happened when Godfrey, who had been displaced by Somerled, returned to power shortly after 1164. Until the death of the last Manx king in 1265, these rulers controlled, in theory at least, much of the northern Hebrides, including Skye, Lewis, Harris, the Uists and Barra – a little-known Manx factor in the history of medieval Scotland.

It was not until the first decades of the thirteenth century that the Scottish kings began to get serious about subduing the west and annexing it to the Scottish kingdom. This was accomplished both through diplomatic/military avenues and more gradual, almost imperceptible, processes of assimilation, and it is important to note that while much of the initiative for military action came from the Scottish crown, much of the impetus for assimilation seems to have come from the magnates themselves. Major military expeditions were mounted under Alexander II in 1221 and/or 1222 (the sources are unclear), and a second, in 1249, directed against a great-grandson of Somerled named Ewen of Argyll, reached the island of Kerrera before the king's death brought it to a premature conclusion. The intensification of Scottish royal authority provoked a response from the newly resurgent Norwegian monarchy, and in 1230 King Hákon IV (1217–63) dispatched a fleet of his own; it attacked Bute before disbanding, but left the MacSorleys firmly entrenched in power. It was not until the 1260s that the final incorporation of the region into the Scottish kingdom occurred. A Scottish expedition to Skye in 1262 provoked Hákon IV to gather a massive fleet, and the ensuing series of skirmishes known rather grandly as the Battle of Largs, fought on the Ayrshire coast between 30 September and 3 October 1263, was hailed as a victory by both sides. Subsequent diplomatic initiatives produced the Treaty of Perth in 1266, by which the western islands were ceded to Scotland from Norway (Donaldson 1974, 34). Historians have extensively discussed these events over the past twenty years (Barrow 1981; Donaldson 1990; Cowan 1990; McDonald 1997), and appropriately so, since they were an important step in what one historian has called the 'winning of the west' for the Scottish kingdom (Barrow 1981).

Although scholars have tended to concentrate upon political and military events like those outlined above, these would undoubtedly have been less successful had not other, more subtle and gradual processes of cultural assimilation been drawing West Highland chieftains toward the centre of the Scottish kingdom for some time. Recent scholarship has begun to recognize the significance of these processes (Davies 1990; Bartlett 1993), and it is striking that many of Somerled's descendants were accommodating themselves to aspects of Scottish society from the next generation after Somerled himself. We can see this through not only shifting patterns of matrimonial alliances among West Highland chieftains in the thirteenth century, as they began to marry into eastern families, but also through the entry of Lowland names into West Highland families like the MacDougalls and MacDonalds which had hitherto been dominated by Gaelic and Norse names. That these shifts should occur at precisely the moment when Scottish royal authority was intensifying in the region can hardly be coincidence, and indicates the drawing of West Highland chieftains in from the margins (McDonald 1999). Similarly, it is possible to document the penetration of the broader European influences that were taking root within the Scottish kingdom as a whole among Hebridean and West Highland chieftains from this time. Thus, we find members of the MacSorleys (and other prominent West Highland families too) utilizing Latin documents to record land grants and seals to authenticate these documents, and we also find scattered references to the adoption of contemporary fashions of knighthood and chivalry among the families of the region. Finally, many of the remarkable stone castles that are still to be seen scattered throughout the West Highlands and Islands today date from this period (Dunstaffnage Castle, north of Oban, is a good example) (Dunbar 1981). Some of these things (e.g. knight service, castles) have come to be associated with that particular medieval European military-political system known as feudalism (Ganshof 1964; Barrow 1973c), and it remains common to speak of the penetration of feudalism into the Highlands from this time (Grant and Cheape 1987). What is important to recognize, whether we choose to use the term feudalism or not, is that the impetus for change often initiated with the West Highland ruling élite themselves rather than being imposed from outside, and, moreover, that the result was the development of a 'hybrid' society that fused aspects of traditional Gaelic-Norse culture with new European impulses and therefore mirrored the broader development of the medieval Scottish kingdom itself (Grant 1988; McDonald 1999). This hybrid society is nicely encapsulated in the seal said to have been used by Ranald, son of Somerled, in the early thirteenth century, of which a description survives although the seal does not: on one side Ranald was depicted as a knight, with suitable accoutrements, while the other side of the seal bore an impression of a Highland galley (McDonald 1995). The formidable Ferchar Maccintsacairt of Ross provides another example of a Highland magnate who moved effortlessly between two worlds. Of obscure but indubitably Gaelic origin, he quashed an insurrection in Moray and Ross in 1215, was rewarded with knighthood, and eventually rose to the top ranks of the Scottish nobility in the thirteenth century when he attained the title earl of Ross c. 1226 (McDonald 2003b).

Twenty years after the Treaty of Perth, Somerled's descendants remained dominant in the west. The MacDougall lords of Argyll claimed descent from Dugald, possibly the eldest son of Somerled, but otherwise an obscure figure. Dugald's grandson, Ewen, was a key figure in the monumental events of the two decades between the 1240s and 1260s, and his son and grandson, Alexander and John, were prominent in the west for some forty years until their respective deaths in 1311 and 1317. As lords of Argyll, the MacDougalls controlled a vast insular and mainland territory comprising Lorn, Benderloch, Lismore, northern Jura, Mull, the Treshnish Isles, Coll and Tiree. The MacDonald lords of Islay were descended from Donald, son of Ranald, another of Somerled's sons; Donald was probably dead by the 1260s, when his son, Angus Mór, was active. He, too, was a powerful figure, whose predatory activities in the Irish Sea and the Hebrides were the subject of celebration in a Gaelic praise poem (Clancy 1998, 288–91). His sons were Alexander and Angus Óg, the latter of whom seems to have played a significant role in the wars of independence (see below). As lords of Islay, they controlled Kintyre, Islay, south Jura, and probably Colonsay and Oronsay. The third kindred descended from Somerled, and perhaps the least known, was the MacRuairi Lords of Garmoran. Descended from Ruairi, son of Ranald, son of Somerled, they were represented in the 1260s by Dugald MacRuairi, who was noteworthy for his freebooting activities in the Irish Sea and his steadfast Norwegian allegiance in the wake of the cession of the west to Scotland; but his brother, Alan, and his sons Ruairi and Lachlan, and his daughter Christiana, were also prominent figures in the later thirteenth and early fourteenth century. Their far-flung lordship encompassed Moidart, Arisaig, Morar, Knoydart, Rhum and Eigg (probably) and possibly Barra, the Uists, and Harris. By the late thirteenth century, thanks to both royal policy and subtle cultural processes, these descendants of Somerled found themselves firmly assimilated into the Scottish kingdom: a document of 1284 included the heads of the three major MacSorley kindreds – 'Alex de Ergadia', 'Anegus filius Douenaldi' and 'Alanus filius Rotherici'– among the 'barons of the realm of Scotland' (Thomson 1814, I, 424).

Although MacDonalds, MacDougalls and MacRuairis formed a ruling élite in West Highland society, in the twelfth to fourteenth centuries many other kindreds emerge into the historical record, lending credibility to the characterization of this period in the Highlands as the 'age of the clans' (Dodgshon 2002). Among those that occupied prominent positions from the thirteenth century were the MacSweens in Cowal and Knapdale (Sellar 1971), the MacGilchrists in Glassary (Moncreiffe 1967), and the MacNaughtons around Loch Awe (McPhail 1914; Moncreiffe 1967). Much ink has, of course, been spilt on the subject of the so-called Highland clans, yet the very term can be misleading (Munro 1981). The Highland line was no barrier to landownership, and many kindreds associated with the Highlands controlled much broader power bases: at its height in the thirteenth century, the Comyn lordship embraced lands from Roxburghshire to Badenoch and Lochaber, including a vast bloc of territory in the north that stretched from Buchan in the east to Loch Linnhe on the west coast (Young 1997). In some respects, then, the 'Highland clans' so beloved of writers are nothing more than a romantic creation: how, for example, should we categorize a family like the Comyns? Finally, many clans traced lineages back to eponymous ancestors who were not of Gaelic stock. Somerled was of mixed Gaelic and Norse ancestry, but other kindreds claimed descent from Scandinavian figures: behind the MacLeods and McCorquodales, for example, are the Old Norse names Liotr and Thorketill respectively (Moncreiffe 1967). Similarly, other clans, like the Campbells (discussed further below) descended from Brittonic or Norman ancestors (Sellar 1973), while still others, like the Stewarts (another family with both Lowland and Highland holdings), trace their lineages to twelfth-century immigrants from the Continent (Moncreiffe 1967). What the origins and development of the 'Highland clans' really illustrate is not only the multi-ethnic nature of the medieval Scottish kingdom, but also its hybrid nature, in which Gaelic, Brittonic, Scandinavian, English and Continental elements interacted and mingled. In this respect as in so many others, broader themes in medieval Scottish history are mirrored in the history of the Highlands (Grant 1988).

THE WARS OF INDEPENDENCE

The dynastic and civil conflicts of the late thirteenth and fourteenth centuries, commonly known as the Wars of Independence, had a profound impact on power politics in the west. On the one hand, the involvement of West Highland and Island rulers in these conflicts illustrates the extent to which the region had become an integral part of the Scottish kingdom. MacDonald support for Robert Bruce, like MacDougall enmity for his cause, is well known (Lamont 1981). In the pages of John Barbour's late fourteenth-century epic poem *The Bruce*, Angus Óg of Islay is depicted as a steadfast supporter who aided Bruce in his darkest hour, while the MacDougalls, particularly John of Lorn, are implacable foes, by virtue of the marriage alliance between MacDougalls and Comyns; indeed, it was John Mac-Dougall of Argyll who dealt Bruce one of the two key defeats of 1306 that led to his temporary exile from Scotland (Duncan 1997). But contemporary documents from the 1290s show that MacDonalds and MacDougalls were already at odds with one another over Lismore, and that both changed sides several times through the later 1290s, so that the 'national' conflict was superimposed over pre-existing local rivalries in the west (McDonald 1997). What is clear, however, is that, as Evan

Barron so convincingly demonstrated nearly a century ago (1914), distinctions between Highlands and Lowlands are meaningless where the civil and dynastic conflicts of the late thirteenth and early fourteenth century are concerned.

Bruce's ultimate triumph in the Scottish civil war had a profound impact on the balance of power in West Highland society. Bruce defeated his implacable foes the MacDougalls of Argyll in a campaign or series of campaigns in 1308–09, and, while both Alexander and his son John escaped and lived the rest of their lives in exile in England and Ireland, like other rivals of Bruce, they saw their lands forfeited and redistributed to loyalists. The principal beneficiaries were the MacDonalds, who acquired the Comyn lordship of Lochaber and neighbouring Morvern, while Mull and Tiree were gained from the MacDougalls (Barrow 1988, 291). But the MacDonalds were not the only kindred to benefit from the downfall of the MacDougalls and Comyns. One family that greatly prospered under the new regime was the Campbells, whose origins are obscure but whose greatness certainly dates from the reign of Robert I (Barrow 1988, 289; Sellar 1973). Under King Robert, various members of the Campbell kindred made significant gains at the expense of the MacDougalls, acquiring or being confirmed in many territories in the west, including parts of Benderloch, as well as the MacDougall strongholds of Dunollie and Dunstaffnage (Barrow 1988, 289–90). This was also the era when MacRuairi power reached its greatest extent, with the family well-entrenched in the 'archipe-lagic lordship' (Barrow 1988, 291) of Garmoran. Lachlan and Ruairi MacRuairi have been regarded as predatory troublemakers in the region, but MacRuairi support for Robert Bruce ensured the (short-lived) success of this branch of Somerled's descendants. Christiana MacRuairi, in fact, emerges as one of the few West Highland women of whom much can be said for this period: daughter and heiress of Alan MacRuairi of Garmoran, she married Duncan, son of Earl Donald I of Mar, and appears to have been an early and steadfast supporter of Bruce, no doubt because of Bruce's own connections to the Mar kindred. She controlled a considerable bloc of insular and mainland territory including Knoydart, Moidart, Arisaig, Rum, Eigg, Uist, Barra and Gigha, and she is certainly the 'Christiana of the Isles' who, according to John of Fordun (Skene 1872, 335), aided Bruce during his flight from Scotland. Clearly a formidable Highland lady, Christiana's place in history remains largely uninvestigated and would certainly repay further careful study.

AN AGE OF PROSPERITY FOR THE HIGHLANDS?
THE LORDSHIP OF THE ISLES

The Lordship of the Isles was Gaelic Scotland's most impressive creation and perhaps its most characteristic institution (see Map 3. The Lordship of the Isles). For a century and a half, four MacDonald Lords of the Isles – John (1336–87), Donald (1387–1423), Alexander (1423–49), and John (1449–93), each the son of his predecessor – presided over what is regarded in the Scottish Gaelic tradition as *Linn an Àigh*, the age of joy (or prosperity) (McLeod 2004).

By the middle of the fourteenth century, Angus Óg's son John of Islay, the first Lord of the Isles, had established himself in a position of considerable strength. Building upon the foundation of Robert I's grants to his father, John acquired further grants from both Edward Balliol and David II (1329-71) by fishing in the troubled waters of the second Scottish civil war of the 1330s and 1340s. His marriage in 1346 to Amy MacRuairi, the heiress to the MacRuairi lordship of Garmoran, brought these expansive territories into his control as well (though the MacRuairis were absorbed into the MacDonald kindred), and by the time of his death in 1387 he controlled the entire Hebrides from Islay to Lewis – excluding Skye – and most of the mainland from Kintyre to Glenelg: a virtual recreation of the vast insular and mainland lordship of Somerled. The Latin title *dominus Insularum* (Lord of the Isles), the earliest use of which by John occurs in a document of 1336 (Munro and Munro 1986, no. 3), also points to another continuity with the past. Steer and Bannerman (1977) believe this title is derived from the Gaelic *rí Innse Gall*, ruler of the Isles, and therefore in direct line from Somerled. It is noteworthy that the title was self-styled, and modern historians have been inclined to regard the Lords of the Isles as possessing virtual sovereignty within their territories, ruling, as it were, a 'kingdom within a kingdom' (MacKenzie 1949, 93). This continuity in title as well as territory is significant because 'the area in part or in whole had a continuous history as a political entity at least from the 12th century' (Steer and Bannerman 1977, 201).

John's son Donald, by his second wife, Margaret Stewart, a daughter of Robert Stewart (future Robert II, 1371–90), succeeded as Lord of the Isles upon the death of his father in 1387, and continued the territorial aggrandizement of the Lordship. Described as 'one of the most spirited men of the nation in his time' (McPhail 1914, 34), Donald aspired to secure the earldom of Ross in right of his wife, Mary (or Mariota) Leslie, resulting in the famous battle of Harlaw near Aberdeen in 1411. Few events in Highland history have been as mythologized as Harlaw, which has come to be regarded as a clash between Highlands and Lowlands. In fact, Highlanders were present on both sides, and the conflict is now largely interpreted as a contest over the vacant earldom of Ross between families that were related by intermarriage (MacKenzie 1949). Nicholson (1974) has argued that the true significance of Harlaw lies in its *perception* as a conflict between Highlands and Lowlands, signalling increasing antagonism between the two regions in the fourteenth century.

By the early fifteenth century, when Alexander succeeded Donald, the dynamic that had fuelled the rise to ascendancy of the Lords of the Isles was already changing. Although on the one hand the Lords had emerged as the leading power in the Highlands, a position they would hold until the end of the century, on the other hand their increasing involvement in the politics of the kingdom (a result of their claims to Ross) left them more vulnerable to a resurgent Stewart monarchy determined to impose its power over the entire kingdom. Thus, although Alexander was eventually recognized as earl of Ross in 1437, a title he and his son held until 1475, the early years of his lordship were marked by conflict with James I (1406–37), resulting in a

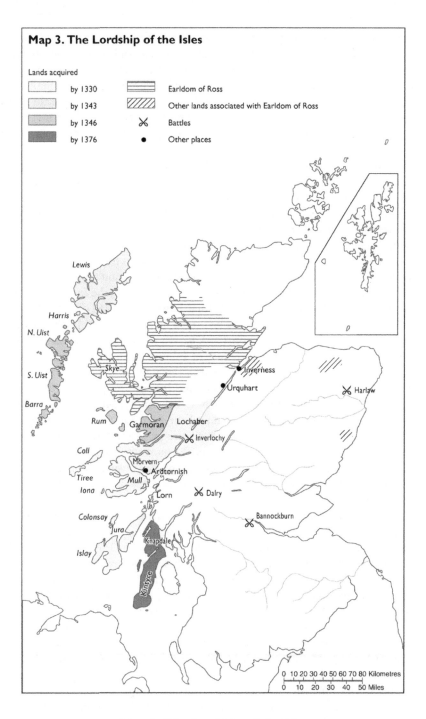

Map 3. The Lordship of the Isles

Lands acquired

by 1330	
by 1343	
by 1346	
by 1376	

Earldom of Ross

Other lands associated with Earldom of Ross

✂ Battles

● Other places

Lewis

Harris

N. Uist

S. Uist

Skye

Barra

Rum

Garmoran

Lochaber

Inverness

Urquhart

✂ Harlaw

✂ Inverlochy

Coll

Morvern

Ardtornish

Tiree

Mull

Iona

Lorn

✂ Dalry

Colonsay

Jura

Bannockburn

✂

Islay

Knapdale

Kintyre

0 10 20 30 40 50 60 70 80 Kilometres

0 10 20 30 40 50 Miles

Map 3. The Lordship of the Isles

humiliating submission and brief imprisonment at Tantallon castle (1431). Alexander, who lived until 1449, has been regarded by modern historians as a powerful magnate, but was remembered in later MacDonald tradition as 'a man born to much trouble in his lifetime' (McPhail 1914, 34). This expression might equally characterize his son, John, the last Lord of the Isles, of whom it has been said that he 'managed to quarrel with his wife, his son and his king and to lose both his earldom and his lordship' (Munro 1981, 29) before dying in 1503 as a pensioner of the crown.

What brought about the downfall of the mighty Lords of the Isles? Historians have argued that their demise was dependent upon two factors, both of which led them into conflict with the crown. First, expansion eastward into Ross drew the Lords into the turbulent nexus of Scottish politics, making them into mainland magnates as well as insular princes (Munro and Munro 1986; Grant 1988); for this reason, Ross has been regarded as the 'Achilles' heel' of the Lordship (MacDougall 2000). In the shorter term, however, it was the dealings of the Lords with the kings of England that cost them dear, while internal problems simultaneously weakened the unity of the Lordship (Steer and Bannerman 1977). John, the fourth Lord, made a secret treaty in 1462 with the English King Edward IV (1461–70, 1471–83), by which the kingdom of Scotland would be carved up among John, James the Earl of Douglas, and Edward IV (Donaldson 1974, 82–4); when this treaty was discovered by the crown, it led to the first forfeiture of John in 1475, but he was eventually restored to his territories, except Ross, which remained in crown hands. Within a few years, internal struggles between John and his son, Angus (who defeated his father at the famous Battle of Bloody Bay, near Tobermory, Mull, c. 1481), and then his nephew, Alexander of Lochalsh, reduced the Lordship to disorder (Nicholson 1974), leading to the second and final forfeiture in 1493. A series of attempts to restore the Lordship over the next fifty years, the most serious of them led by John's grandson, Donald Dubh, in 1544/45, ultimately proved unsuccessful, leaving Gaelic poets to lament the passing of the golden age while a new round of power struggles erupted in the Highlands.

Writing within living memory of the demise of the Lordship, Donald Monro observed in 1549 that 'In thair [i.e. Lords of the Isles] time thair was great peace and welth in the Iles throw the ministration of justice' (Munro 1961, 57), and modern historians have concurred with this emphasis on the order and stability imposed by the Lords of the Isles. How was this accomplished? One of the key pieces of governmental machinery within the Lordship was the Council of the Isles (Consilium Insularum) (Bannerman 1977, 221). Comprised of 'fourteen of the Iles best Barons' from the leading kindreds as well as the bishop of the Isles and the abbot of Iona, the Council traditionally met at Finlaggan on Islay (Munro 1961, 57), the centre of Clan Donald power, but it was also peripatetic and it is known to have met on Eigg, Mull, and Oronsay, as well as at Dingwall and Inverness during the period when the Lord of the Isles was also Earl of Ross (Munro and Munro 1986). The Council's jurisdiction was wide-ranging and seems to have embraced diplomacy, marriage and inheritance, finance, and law; it also played a role in the election of a successor to the Lord of the Isles within the kin-based society, and was concerned with the inauguration of the Lords (of which several, later, accounts survive) (Bannerman 1977; Munro and Munro 1986). Further evidence of a sophisticated apparatus of government and administration is provided by references to various officials within the Lordship, including secretaries, clerks, scribes, chamberlains, chaplains, stewards, bailies, constables, and lawmen; a chancellor is also known (the chancellor supervised the chancery or writing office and was responsible for the seal of the Lord of the Isles, several examples of which survive) (Munro and Munro 1986). MacDuffie of Colonsay 'kept the records of the Isles' (McPhail 1914, 25), and the corpus of Latin charters issued by the chancery of the Lords of the Isles, in addition to providing a wealth of important details on the history of the Lordship, serves as a further reminder of a relatively sophisticated administration (Munro and Munro 1986). In contrast to the numerous Latin charters of the Lordship, only a single Gaelic charter, from 1408, survives. This is a grant by Donald to Brian Vicar Mackay of lands in Islay (Lamont 1960; Munro and Munro 1986 no. 16), which scholars have regarded as fitting into a continuing oral tradition of Gaelic law (Bannerman 1977, 228).

In addition to imposing a remarkable degree of order and stability over their territories, the Lords also presided over an astonishing array of cultural accomplishments, contributing further to the notion of a golden age under the Lordship. It is well known that Gaelic society embraced a professional class known as the *aes dána*, or 'folk of gifts,' who included poets, genealogists, historians, lawmen, physicians, and musicians as well as craftsmen like sculptors, and who were accorded a very high social status (Thomson 1968; Bannerman 1977). The Lords of the Isles patronized such learned families. Pride of place went to the MacMhuirich family of poets, one of whom, Lachlan Mór MacMhuirich, composed the famous 'Incitement to Battle' before the battle of Harlaw; a similar prestige was clearly enjoyed by the Beatons or MacBeths, whose fame as the principal physicians in the Isles has already been noted, and whose length of service surpassed even the MacMhuirich poets. Among other learned families must be included the MacIlshenaich (MacShannon) family of harpists, and there is some evidence for a family practising law on a hereditary basis as well (Thomson 1968; Bannerman 1977). Historians have observed a close correspondence with Gaelic Ireland where many of these learned orders are concerned, particularly with regard to their organization, and there was certainly movement back and forth across the North Channel (Thomson 1968). Little wonder that scholars like Kenneth Jackson (1951) have argued that, until at least the end of the sixteenth century, Ireland and the Highlands formed one culture province of the 'sea-divided Gael,' a paradigm that has proven influential but continues to be refined and adjusted (McLeod 2004). It is perhaps particularly important to bear in mind that the clergy and monastic orders constituted not only another element within the learned orders of Highland society, but one of a universal nature in medieval European society (Watt 1981).

An astonishing array of carved stones still stands in mute testimony to the cultural accomplishments of the Lordship. Scattered from the Mull of Kintyre to Knoydart and from Islay to Lewis, and concentrated at specific sites such as Iona, Oronsay, Kilmichael and Kilmartin, over six hundred monumental sculptures survive: decorated grave slabs, effigies, and crosses in a distinctive west Highland style, with representations of foliage, figures, animals and objects from contemporary life. Most of these date to the fourteenth to sixteenth centuries, and there is evidence for four or five different bodies of craftsmen (loosely termed 'schools') operating in Iona, Oronsay, Kintyre and around Loch Awe and Loch Sween. These carved stones, which have been the subject of a thorough and fascinating study by Steer and Bannerman (1977), possess historical, genealogical and linguistic significance, providing as they do not only representations of costume, weapons, armour, tools and other objects from daily use but also inscriptions that can be of great value to the historian and genealogist. On those stones decorated with figures, we come face to face with some of the medieval inhabitants of the western Highlands and isles: chieftains outfitted for war, with armour (often of a distinctive quilted type known as an aketon), helmets, swords (a favourite motif, appearing on crosses and slabs without human figures as well), and shields (often emblazoned with a galley), or churchmen and monks in vestments and habits (there are several fine tomb effigies of Iona abbots). More rarely, we glimpse men in civil dress, or women in either civil or ecclesiastical garb (Prioress Anna MacLean of Iona is represented on a particularly fine tomb slab). Sometimes we are privy to extraordinary vignettes of everyday life, as on the famous tomb of Alexander MacLeod (died c. 1547) at Rodel, Harris, with its depiction of a hunting scene: Alexander, in full armour, with sword and long-handled axe (hardly appropriate hunting attire!), precedes two gillies (attendants) in civil dress, holding hounds on leashes; their quarry, three noble stags, is depicted on an adjacent panel (Steer and Bannerman 1977, plate no. 32). Other carvings depict a variety of implements and utensils: shears, caskets, chalices, eating and drinking utensils, combs, and tools. Musical instruments are rare, but include two depictions of a harp. One is very worn, but the other can be identified as a distinct type of Hiberno-Scottish instrument known as a clarsach (bagpipes do not appear as they did not become the dominant instrument in the region until a later period). Taken altogether, these remarkable carved stones provide not only a remarkable glimpse into everyday life and objects of the period, but also serve as mute reminders of the dynamism and vitality of cultural life under the Lordship.

CONCLUSIONS

What then, are the Highlands? As we have seen, this question can be answered, at least for the medieval period, in several different manners: topographically; linguistically; and politically and socially. To these answers should perhaps be added one more: the Highlands as a scholarly construct originating in the late medieval period and developing throughout the modern era. Thus, as we have seen, although the Highlands do possess topographical unity, it is a mistake to regard the Highland zone as uniformly harsh and impenetrable; similarly, in linguistic terms, at least five different languages were in use throughout the Highlands in our period (Gaelic,

Norse, Middle English, French and Latin). In political and social terms, the Highland line proved no barrier to medieval landownership and lordship or to the influx of foreign influences, although politically the west Highlands were among the last regions to be incorporated into the Scottish kingdom.

So to what extent were the Highlands a distinct society? This motif is so ingrained in our historical thinking about the region that it proves difficult to discard. Certainly every medieval writer after Fordun thought of Highlanders as barbarians and the stereotype of the 'wild Scot' in opposition to the civil Scots of the Lowlands is well-known (Smout 1969). Interestingly, however, Gaelic Scotland seems to have developed no such stereotype of the Lowlands in our period (McLeod 2004), and scholars like Alexander Grant (1984) have demonstrated how many of the trouble-makers in the Highlands were actually members of Lowland kindreds. The Wolf of Badenoch provides a good example: in Smout's words, 'a son of the king and a royally appointed Earl of Buchan, he gathered the tribal hosts around him to fight the king's sheriffs, destroy his castles, and plunder far into the Lowlands' (1969, 40) in the late fourteenth century.

Yet, as I have attempted to show, such black and white distinctions between Highlands and Lowlands may be more a hindrance than a help in understanding the complex historical processes at work in the Highlands in the middle ages. As should be clear from much of the foregoing discussion, the notion of the Highlands as a distinct and somehow purely Gaelic society, socially conservative, politically char-acterized by the age-old conflict between Celtic and feudal societies, fails to bear up under closer scrutiny. The cultural inheritance of West Highland society was in fact as complex as that of the rest of the Scottish kingdom itself, so that many of the broader themes of Scottish history in the high middle ages played out on a West Highland stage in the same period. To take but one example, the interaction and balance between old and new forms a prominent theme in Scottish history of the twelfth and thirteenth centuries as English and Continental influences, ideas, and individuals found their way north into Scotland (Barrow 1980). The Highland line, however, was no barrier to the infiltration of these influences, and they affected West Highland society as profoundly as the rest of the Scottish kingdom. Thus, although we are often told that Highland society was opposed to and vigorously resisted the onslaught of feudalism as represented by the use of written instruments of land ownership and entitlement, the ruling elite here was hardly inimical to the use of such documents; the Lords of the Isles, as we have seen, embraced 'charter lordship,' issuing many Latin documents that in form and content prove to be little different from those issued by Scottish kings and Lowland magnates (Bannerman 1977 227-8); the same is true of the late medieval Campbell lordship, which has been examined by Steve Boardman (2003). West Highland society struck its own balance between old and new in the later middle ages, but it was responding to the same impulses and influences that shaped the rest of the Scottish kingdom. It remains doubtful whether we can sustain for much longer the notion of the Highlands as a land apart.

On the other hand, however, archaeologists like Caldwell and Ewart (1993) have argued that, in terms of material culture, the West Highlands *do* demonstrate uniqueness, and they have identified several important traits: the absence of money; the tradition of boat-building; a distinct type of hand-made pottery; and the distribution of West Highland sculpture. As they remark, 'no other region of Scotland can be so clearly distinguished by its material culture as the Lordship of the Isles' (1993, 164). If all of this seems rather paradoxical and unsatisfactory by way of conclusion, then one solution might be that historical and archaeological investigators will often provide differing answers to the same questions. Whatever the case may be, scholarship continues to move forward, and as historians and archaeologists persist in their investigations, black-and-white dichotomies will continue to dissolve and give way to more sophisticated and nuanced interpretations of what is undoubtedly one of the most fascinating topics in medieval Scottish history.

REFERENCES TO BOOKS AND ARTICLES MENTIONED IN THE TEXT

Items marked * are recommended for further reading.

Bain, J et al (eds) 1881–88 *Calendar of Documents Relating to Scotland Preserved in Her Majesty's Public Record Office, London.* 4 vols. Edinburgh.

*Bannerman, J 1977 'The Lordship of the Isles' *in* Brown, J (ed), *Scottish Society in the Fifteenth Century*, London, 209–40.

Bannerman, J 1986 *The Beatons: A medical kindred in the classical Gaelic tradition.* Edinburgh.

Bannerman, J 1990 'The Scots Language and the Kin-based Society', *in* Thomson, D (ed), *Gaelic and Scots in Harmony. Proceedings of the Second International Conference on the Languages of Scotland* (University of Glasgow, 1988), Glasgow, 1–19.

Barron, EM 1914 *The Scottish War of Independence.* London.

Barrow, GWS 1973a 'Pre-feudal Scotland: shires and thanes', *in* his *The Kingdom of the Scots. Government, Church and Society from the eleventh to the fourteenth century*, London, 7–68.

Barrow, GWS 1973b 'Rural settlement in central and eastern Scotland' in *idem, The Kingdom of the Scots*, 257–78.

Barrow, GWS 1973c 'The beginnings of military feudalism' in *idem, The Kingdom of the Scots*, 279–314.

*Barrow, GWS 1973d 'The Highlands in the lifetime of Robert the Bruce' in *idem, The Kingdom of the Scots*, 362–83.

Barrow, GWS 1980 *The Anglo-Norman Era in Scottish History.* Oxford.

Barrow, GWS 1981 *Kingship and Unity: Scotland 1000-1306.* London.

Barrow, GWS 1984 'Land Routes: The Medieval Evidence', *in* Fenton, A and Stell, G (eds), *Loads and Roads in Scotland and Beyond: Land Transport Over 6000 Years*, Edinburgh, 49–66.

Barrow, GWS 1988 *Robert Bruce and the Community of the Realm of Scotland.* 3rd edn. Edinburgh.

Barrow, GWS 1989 'The lost Gàidhealtachd of medieval Scotland', *in* Gillies, W (ed), *Gaelic and Scotland. Alba Agus A' Ghàidhlig*, Edinburgh, 67–88.

Bartlett, R 1993 *The Making of Europe: Conquest Colonization and Cultural Change, 950–1350.* London.

Bawcutt, P and Riddy, F (eds) 1987 *Longer Scottish Poems Volume One: 1375–1650*, Edinburgh, 43–84.

Boardman, S 2003 'The Campbells and charter lordship in medieval Argyll', *in* Boardman, S and Ross, A (eds), *The Exercise of Power in Medieval Scotland c. 1200–1500*, Dublin 95–117.

Broderick, G (ed/trans) 1995 *Cronica Regum Mannie et Insularum. Chronicles of the Kings of Man and the Isles. BL Cotton Julius A vii.* 2nd ed, repr. 1996. Douglas.

Broun, D 1990 'A New Look at *Gesta Annalia* attributed to John of Fordun', *in* Crawford, B (ed), *Church, Chronicle and Learning in Medieval and Early Renaissance Scotland*, Edinburgh, 9–30.

Brown, P H (ed) 1891 *Early Travellers in Scotland*. Edinburgh.

Burton, JH and Masson, D (eds) 1877–98 *Register of the Privy Council of Scotland*. 1st series, 14 vols. Edinburgh.

Caldwell, DH and Ewart, G 1993 'Finlaggan and the Lordship of the Isles: An Archaeological Approach', *Scottish Historical Review*, 72, 146–66.

Clancy, TO (ed) 1998 *The Triumph Tree: Scotland's Earliest Poetry AD 550–1350*. Edinburgh.

Clark, W 1993 *The Lord of the Isles' Voyage. Western Ireland to the Scottish Hebrides in a 16th century Galley*. Naas, Co. Kildare.

Cowan, EJ 1990 'Norwegian Sunset – Scottish Dawn', *in* Reid, NH (ed), *Scotland in the Reign of Alexander III, 1249–1286*, Edinburgh, 103–132.

*Cowan, EJ and McDonald, RA (eds) 2000 *Alba: Celtic Scotland in the Middle Ages*. East Linton.

Cowan, EJ 2000 'The Invention of Celtic Scotland', *in* Cowan and McDonald (eds), *Alba*, 1–23.

Davies, RR (1990) *Domination and Conquest: The experience of Ireland, Scotland and Wales, 1100–1300*. Cambridge.

Dixon, P 2002 *Puir Labourers and Busy Husbandmen. The Countryside of Lowland Scotland in the Middle Ages*. Edinburgh.

Dodgshon, R 1980 'Medieval Settlement and Colonisation', *in* Parry, ML and Slater, TR (eds), *The Making of the Scottish Countryside*, London and Montreal, 45–68

Dodghson, R 1981 *Land and Society in Early Scotland*. Oxford.

Dodgshon, R 2002 *The Age of the Clans: The Highlands from Somerled to the Clearances*. Edinburgh.

Donaldson, G 1974 *Scottish Historical Documents*. Glasgow.

Donaldson, G 1990 *A Northern Commonwealth: Scotland and Norway*. Edinburgh.

Dunbar, J 1981 'The Medieval Architecture of the Scottish Highlands', *in* MacLean, L (ed), *The Middle Ages in the Highlands*, 38–70.

Duncan, AAM (ed) 1988 *Regesta Regum Scottorum V: The Acts of Robert I King of Scots, 1306–29*. Edinburgh.

Duncan, AAM (ed) 1997 *John Barbour's The Bruce*. Edinburgh.

Frame, R 1990 *The Political Development of the British Isles, 1100–1400*. Oxford.

Ganshof, FL 1964 *Feudalism*. Revised edn. New York.

Grant, A 1984 *Independence and Nationhood: Scotland, 1306–1469*. London.

*Grant, A 1988 'Scotland's 'Celtic Fringe' in the Late Middle Ages: The MacDonald Lords of the Isles and the Kingdom of Scotland', *in* Davies, RR (ed), *The British Isles, 1100–1500. Comparisons, Contrasts and Connections*, Edinburgh,118–141.

Grant, IF and Cheape, H 1987 *Periods in Highland History*. London.

Gregory, D 1975 *The History of the Western Highlands and Isles of Scotland from AD 1493 to AD 1625. With a brief introductory sketch from AD 80 to AD 1493*. First published 1836. Second edn 1881. Repr. Edinburgh, 1975.

Haldane, ARB 1952 *The Drove Roads of Scotland*. Edinburgh.

Houston, RA and Knox, WWJ (eds) 2001 *The New Penguin History of Scotland From the Earliest Times to the Present Day*. London.

Jackson, KH 1951 *Common Gaelic: The Evolution of the Goidelic Languages*. London.

Lamont, WD 1960 'The Islay Charter of 1408', *Proceedings of the Royal Irish Academy* 60/4, 163–87.

Lamont, WD 1981 'Alexander of Islay, son of Angus Mór', *Scottish Historical Review*, 60, 160–9.

Lydon, J 1992 'The Scottish Soldier in Medieval Ireland: The Bruce Invasion and the Gallowglass', *in* Simpson, GG (ed), *The Scottish Soldier Abroad, 1247–1967*, Edinburgh, 1-15.

Lynch, M (ed) 2001 *The Oxford Companion to Scottish History*. Oxford.

Macdougall, N 2000 'Achilles' Heel? The Earldom of Ross, the Lordship of the Isles, and the Stewart Kings, 1449–1507', *in* Cowan and McDonald (eds), *Alba*, 248–77.

MacInnes, J 1972-74 'West Highland Sea-Power in the Middle Ages', *Transactions of the Gaelic Society of Inverness* ,48, 518–56.

Macinnes, J 1981 'Gaelic Poetry and Historical Tradition', *in* MacLean, L (ed), *The Middle Ages in the Highlands*, 142–63.

MacKenzie, WC 1949 *Highlands and Islands of Scotland: A Historical Survey*. Revised edn Edinburgh and London.

*MacLean, L (ed) 1981 *The Middle Ages in the Highlands*. Inverness.

McDonald, RA 1995 'Images of Hebridean lordship in the twelfth and early thirteenth century: The seal of Raonall MacSorley', *Scottish Historical Review*, 74, 129–43.

*McDonald, RA 1997 *The Kingdom of the Isles: Scotland's Western Seaboard c. 1100– c.1336*. East Linton.

McDonald, RA 1999 'Coming in from the margins: the descendants of Somerled and cultural accommodation in the Hebrides, 1164–1317', *in* Smith, B (ed), *Britain and Ireland, 900– 1300: Insular Responses to Medieval European Change*, Cambridge, 179–198.

McDonald, RA 2003a *Outlaws of Medieval Scotland: Challenges to the Canmore Kings, 1058–1266*. East Linton.

McDonald, RA 2003b 'Old and new in the far north: Ferchar Maccintsacairt and the early earls of Ross c. 1200–74', *in* Boardman, S and Ross, A (eds), *The Exercise of Power in Medieval Scotland c. 1200–1500*, Dublin, 23–45.

McKerral, A 1951 'West Highland Mercenaries in Ireland', *Scottish Historical Review*, 30, 1– 14.

McLeod, W 2004 *Divided Gaels. Gaelic Cultural Identities in Scotland and Ireland c.1200– c.1650*. Oxford.

McPhail, JRN (ed) 1914-34 *Highland Papers*. 4 volumes. Edinburgh.

Moll, R 2002 'Of quhat nacioun art thow?' National Identity in Blind Harry's *Wallace*', *in* McDonald, RA (ed), *History Literature and Music in Scotland, 700–1560*, Toronto, 120– 143.

Moncreiffe, I 1967 *Highland Clans*. London.

Munro, J 1981 'The Lordship of the Isles' *in* MacLean, L (ed), *The Middle Ages in the Highlands*, 23–37.

Munro, J and RW (eds) 1986 *Acts of the Lords of the Isles, 1336–1493*. Edinburgh.

Munro, RW (ed) 1961 *Monro's Western Isles of Scotland and Genealogies of the Clans 1549*. Edinburgh and London.

Munro, RW 1981 'The Clan System – Fact or Fiction?' *in* MacLean, L (ed), *The Middle Ages in the Highlands*, 117–129.

Newton, M 2000 *A Handbook of the Scottish Gaelic World*. Dublin.

Nicholson, R 1974 *Scotland: The Later Middle Ages*. Edinburgh.

Pálsson, H and Edwards, P (eds/trans) 1978 *Orkneyinga Saga. The History of the Earls of Orkney*. London.

Reid, WS 1960 'Sea-Power in the Anglo-Scottish War, 1296–1328', *Mariner's Mirror* 46/1, 7–23.

Reynolds, S 1994 *Fiefs and Vassals. The Medieval Evidence Reinterpreted*. Oxford.

Rixson, D 1998 *The West Highland Galley*. Edinburgh.

Robertson, EW 1862 *Scotland Under Her Early Kings: A History of the Kingdom to the Close of the Thirteenth Century*. 2 vols. Edinburgh.

Sellar, WDH 1971 'Family Origins in Cowal and Knapdale', *Scottish Studies*, 15, 21–37.

Sellar, WDH 1973 'The earliest Campbells – Norman, Briton or Gael?', *Scottish Studies*, 17.

Skene, WF 1837 *The Highlanders of Scotland: Their Origin, History and Antiquities; with a Sketch of their Manners and Customs, and an account of the clans into which they were divided, and of the state of society which existed among them*. 2 vols. London.

Skene, WF (ed) 1872 *Johannis de Fordun Chronica Gentis Scotorum*, trans. FJH. Skene. Edinburgh.

Skene, WF 1876-80 *Celtic Scotland: A History of Ancient Alban*. 3 vols. Edinburgh.

Smout, TC 1969 *A History of the Scottish People 1560-1830*. London.

Stokes, W (ed.) 1898 'Tigernach's Continuator', *Revue Celtique* 18, 9–59, 150–97, 267–303, 374–91.

Steer, KA and Bannerman, JWM 1977 *Late Medieval Monumental Sculpture in the West Highlands*. Edinburgh.

Thomson, D 1968 'Gaelic Learned Orders and Literati in Medieval Scotland', *Scottish Studies*, 12, 57–78.

Thomson, T and Innes, C (eds) 1814–75 *Acts of the Parliaments of Scotland*. 11 vols. Edinburgh.

Wainwright, FT (ed) 1962 *The Northern Isles*. London and Edinburgh.

Watson, WJ (ed) 1937 *Scottish Verse from the Book of the Dean of Lismore*. Edinburgh.

Watt, DER (gen. ed.) 1987–98 *Scotichronicon by Walter Bower, in Latin and English*. 9 vols. Aberdeen.

Watt, DER 1981 'Education in the Highlands in the Middle Ages', *in* MacLean, L (ed), *The Middle Ages in the Highlands*, 79–90.

Webster, B 1997 *Medieval Scotland: The Making of an Identity*. Basingstoke and London: Macmillan.

Young, A 1997 *Robert the Bruce's Rivals: The Comyns, 1212–1314*. East Linton.

www.mallaigheritage.org.uk/aileach/aileach1.htm (on the reconstructed 16th century West Highland galley *Aileach*)

CHAPTER SIX

The Medieval Church
Janet Foggie

The medieval church in Scotland was an organic structure that had grown out of the first seeds of Christianity spread on her shores, in part by famous saints such as Columba, but more frequently by word of mouth, marriage of Christian to pagan households, and the strength of religious ties in political alliances. The church was not planned and imposed by its hierarchy, the priests, bishops and archbishops, but rather the hierarchy grew to serve the spreading Christian church.

By 1100, the church had a long history and if changes were to be made to the structures of the church they took time and had a huge impact on the Scots themselves. No institution stands still. The introduction of monasteries, the coming of the friars, the founding of the universities and the developing consciousness of a Scottish national church, including the appointment of Scotland's first archbishop, are all considered below. The church shaped Scotland's rural landscape, her towns, and the hearts and minds of her people.

THE ECCLESIASTICAL MAP

In 1100 the map of Scotland's church was very different from the one that existed 400 years later. The basic unit of ecclesiastical organisation is the diocese. Each bishop controlled a diocese, which was known as their see – a term coming from the Latin word for a seat. The bishops were, usually, under the authority of an archbishop, and ultimately of the Pope in Rome. For Scotland this was not so straightforward. The relationship between the kings of Scots and the kings of England was frequently one of antagonism; the southern border of the realm was disputed and fought over in this period and the claims of the kings of Scots concerning their territories were not always reflected in reality. The Scottish bishops had to contend with claims of jurisdiction from the archbishop of York, who controlled Galloway and claimed to act as metropolitan of the dioceses of Scotland. The dioceses of Orkney and the Isles (Sodor) were ruled by the Norwegian crown and therefore ecclesiastically under the control of Trondheim, in Norway. The remaining dioceses (Aberdeen, Caithness, Dunblane, Dunkeld, Glasgow, Moray, Ross, St Andrews) were brought directly under papal control in 1189 in what is known as 'special daughter' status, because the pope referred to Scotland as his 'special daughter' in the bull freeing the Scots from the claims of York (McNeill and Nicholson 1975, 35–7, 136). In 1274, this bull was confirmed, including the practice – dating from as early as 1222 – of holding provincial councils in Scotland free of any metropolitan, or of any representative sent from the papal court with papal authority (Watt 2000, 44).

The reign of David I (1124–35) was significant in pushing forward in Scotland the development of a national church that was responsible for its own internal organisation, a process mirrored in other European states at the time. The pattern that had grown up since the establishment of Christianity was of irregular areas within dioceses run by priests living together and serving large areas of territory. Slowly these were replaced by a division of each diocese into parishes. This was a piecemeal change; slowly landowners would build a church for themselves and their townships, each one being staffed by a priest. The imposition by David I of the teind – a tax commonly collected in other European countries, which was paid to the church for the upkeep of the church and comprised a tenth levied on agricultural produce – formalised many of the parish boundaries. New landowners given land by the king as a reward for their loyalty would also set up a parish church. The teinds for that church would be collected from the area within the new landholding, and so the parish boundaries came into being. This tax was used to fund the church, paying for priests, buildings, books, art, vestments, chalices, patens – everything the church required. The teind was useful as a means of funding the parish priest and his vicar (taking the place of the priest who was termed the rector) although it was, from its introduction, intended to be used for other purposes. Just as the parish became more organised, so too did the formal structure of diocesan staff. A cathedral was either staffed by prebends (priests) under the supervision of the dean, or by a regular chapter, such as the Augustinian Canons at St Andrews. The cathedrals were funded by teinds from appropriated parishes. Under this system, the income from certain specified parishes was allocated to the cathedral and a small amount given back to the parish to pay for a vicar. Even when a parish was not appropriated it was unlikely that the entirety of its income would rest locally with the rectors, or the main parish priests. These priests were often absentees – living away from the parish – or pluralists – holding more than one benefice (church income) – and who employed a vicar in the parish in just the same way as the system of appropriation did (McNeill and Nicholson 1975, 37–8, 136–9).

The parish system was often a source of comfort and sustenance to the people of Scotland. Poor relief and healthcare began at parish level, as did education for many Scots, orally in the stories of the faith, and visually in the pictures, windows and statues that decorated their churches. From 1100 to around 1350, the church maintained literacy as a skill for those within its ranks, but later, certainly by 1400 and after, more and more wealthy lay people had access to reading and writing skills. Although it began as a unit of ecclesiastical taxation, the parish became the basis for personal local identities through the exercise of piety centred on the church, as discussed below.

RELIGIOUS ORDERS

The subject of Religious Orders is far from simple. Whatever the order, the purpose of the monastic life was the same from Egypt to Arbroath. Monks withdrew from the world in order to pray to God. They followed a threefold discipline of poverty, chastity, and obedience. In early Christian Scotland monastic foundations had been concentrated on the west coast. Known as the Culdees, the monks followed a life of discipline and devotion pioneered by St Columba and his disciples. The most famous Celtic monastery was at Iona, but there were others, such as Applecross and Lismore. On the east coast, the Culdees were to be found at St Andrews, which was to replace Iona as Scotland's foremost religious site, and at many sites of more minor significance such as Abernethy or Muthil. These foundations, like the Columban monks themselves, had come from the sweeping evangelism of the Celtic Church through Ireland and into Gaelic Scotland.

The desire to regulate and reform monasticism, and other aspects of ecclesiastical life and thought, was common throughout much of Europe and is sometimes known as the *Twelfth Century Renaissance*. This movement was initiated in the eleventh century by the reforms of Pope Gregory the Great (1073–1085). His reforming zeal began to be felt in the secular church and was followed by reforms of the Benedictine Rule made by several different groups. Most prominent amongst these in Scotland was the Cistercian order, following the ideals of Benedict as understood by St Bernard of Clairvaux (1090–1153) and following the mother house at Citeaux in France. The introduction of French monastic reform can be linked to the introduction of Anglo-French feudal landholders under David I. Two factors should be borne in mind in this respect. Firstly, the orders settled from mother-houses based in England were French, and had come very recently from Normandy itself. For example, the Augustinian canons established at Scone (1120) had come from Nostell in Yorkshire, which was itself established only six years previously. Secondly, the spread of reformed monastic houses was typical in the majority of Christian European countries and that broader context should be kept in mind.

The Cistercians – white monks – were particularly austere in the first years of their institution. They refused rents and steady incomes, depending instead on the labour of the monks and their lay brothers, the *conversi*, to work the land given to them by lay donors. This was ideally to be wilderness, untamed and remote, where the monks could live close to God and far from the temptations of human society. In the first hundred years, from the mid-twelfth century onwards, the labour of the Cistercians in places like Glenluce, Sweetheart and Melrose brought them a comfortable income and, as the houses became established, the farming of sheep and consolidation of the monastic incomes brought them great wealth.

The monastic foundations were important to Scotland for their wealth of learning. They were the great libraries of their day, and also acted as educational centres, educating oblates (young boys who were to become monks) in Latin, art, calligraphy, theology and all the skills required by monastic life. Monks were historians and chroniclers, they recorded the financial records and property holdings of their houses and there is often much detail of local interest in their charters. The monastic foundations were also very important to Scotland's nobility, as rivals for the country's wealth, but also providing careers for their sons. The aristocratic names of Scotland frequently appear in the lists of heads of religious houses and the links between the abbeys and the nobility clearly predated the introduction of commendators. That having been said, the humble monk was more likely to come from the middling rank of society as Dilworth expressed it, 'mostly teachable youngsters of average social standing, with a sprinkling of older literate men' (Dilworth 1995, 52).

Scottish monasteries were wealthy, and some were very wealthy indeed by 1500. The easiest reckoning of monastic wealth is the financial calculations done at the Reformation as the newly formed Reformed Church tried to assert its rights over the very wealth they had condemned. The three wealthiest houses in 1560 were St Andrews (annual income £12,500 Scots), Arbroath (£11,000) and Dunfermline (£9,630) (Cowan and Easson 1976, 55, 66, 89). The majority of houses, however, had an income of less than £5,000 per annum. The overheads of the monastic houses were high – fees paid to Rome and the expenses of keeping a commendator (a lay administrator of a monastic house) were often extortionate. The monks and canons themselves lived on a portion, or annual sum, which varied between 20 merks (£13 6s 8d) and £20 and was often collected from a particular source, a tenement of land or an appropriated parish.

THE COMING OF THE FRIARS

In 1215 another great reforming pope, Innocent III accepted the orders of Franciscans and Dominicans into the church. St Francis had, by then, a wide fame in Christian Europe as a holy man, an imitator of Christ and one who lived a poor, apostolic life. St Dominic had been in the forefront of fighting heresy in Spain and members of his order were renowned for their preaching, teaching and learning. One borrowed from the other, the Franciscans becoming more bookish as time progressed and the Dominicans quite self-consciously adopting the austerity of lifestyle of the heretics whom they sought to defeat. Both orders arrived in Scotland within a year of each other – the Dominicans in 1230, the Franciscans in 1231. Clement, the first Dominican bishop in Scotland, was consecrated in 1233. The advent of the friars was an urban phenomenon. They settled in the towns, or on the edges of them, and preached to the urban population first and foremost. Both orders were also able to preach in the rural areas by sending out pairs of friars to carry their message into the countryside.

With the friars came new interpretations of scripture, of theology, and of church practice. The doctrine of purgatory was emphasised and the need to pray for the dead to ease their passage through purgatory to heaven was filled by the holding of anniversary services in the friars' churches as well as in the churches of the parish clergy. For the truly wealthy, there was the opportunity to build a personal collegiate church to keep alive the prayers for the family. This became increasingly popular amongst Scotland's nobility. The fashion was to reach its height towards the end of the period with sixteen collegiate churches being founded in the fifteenth century (Cowan and Easson 1976, 173–86). It was not confined to the nobility, however, as the collegiate church of St Giles was the parish church of the burgh of Edinburgh and it was the provost, baillies and community of the burgh who petitioned the pope for the collegiate foundation, granted in 1469.

The benefactors of the collegiate churches were the aristocratic members of society, the tight-knit circle directly around the crown. The friars, however, enjoyed the patronage of the wealthy urban elite, the merchants and burgesses, from whose ranks they were mainly drawn (Foggie 1993, 80). The parish churches were often supported by the craft guilds of the towns and each guild would have some religious artefacts, statues, palls for coffins at guild funerals and so forth.

WOMEN IN THE CHURCH

The obvious route for a pious woman who wanted to devote her life to the church was to become a nun. This was not always what happened. A woman in medieval Scotland was not free to choose her path in life, this being decided for her by the men in her family – primarily her father. Marriage was a matter of some political importance for the women of wealthy families, and if a match could be made that was advantageous to the family, so much the better. There were some, however, for whom no match could be found or whose natural inclination to the religious life was so obvious from an early age that no other choice could be made. Widows were also able to enter convent life and a few of them did so. Scotland did not, however, have a particularly significant representation of female religious. There were no houses in Scotland bigger than a priory and no Scottish abbesses.

By 1300, there were eleven nunneries in Scotland and seven of these had been founded in the previous century. They were represented by three orders – Benedictines, Cistercians and Augustinians. Added to this were several other institutions, such as the Franciscan nuns at Aberdour, Dundee and Haddington, and the Dominican sisters of Sciennes. Scotland's comparative paucity of nunneries cannot easily be explained. It is possible that the relative independence of Scottish women, compared to their English counterparts, their ability to hold property and to be businesswomen (usually as wives or widows), meant that there was less need for nunneries. But then the noblewomen who comprised most nuns would never have had business concerns – that was the place of the alewife or fishwife of the burgh, not for the daughter of a lord. Perhaps it was that the burden on the economy of religious houses for monks was already fairly heavy before the real expansion of nunneries in the twelfth century. Whatever the answer, Scottish nuns wielded little power, lived simple lives of prayer, work and obedience and were, as far as can be ascertained, faithful to their calling.

This is not the last word that may be said on religion and women in medieval Scotland. Some of Scotland's most powerful noblewomen were patrons of the church. As a widow, a Scottish woman could have quite a degree of independence. As the widow of a king, she had real power. Ermengarde was the widow of William the Lion and, as such, she founded the monastery of Balmerino in Fife around the year 1227 with her son, Alexander II. Devorgilla (John Balliol's widow, and mother of King John) founded Sweetheart Abbey – a house of Cistercians – in the 1270s.

THE CHURCH IN THE HIGHLANDS

The three most important sources for the medieval church in the Highlands are the records of the Vatican Archives, the material contained within Gaelic scholarly manuscripts and the archaeological evidence, particularly of gravestones and other religious sculpture. The information contained within the Vatican Archives relating to Scotland has been being slowly pieced together over the past forty years. It is difficult to present any general picture from this information as it lacks sustained and serious study. As much material from Argyll as from any other area of Scotland has been found in the records of the Penitentiary and in the Register of Supplications, two of the largest bodies of records in the Vatican corpus. Latin provided an easy language of communication across Europe and clearly this was the case for Gaels as well as Scots speakers (MacGregor 1998, 8). The records in Rome relate to the daily requirements of the church: dispensations for illegitimacy, in order that someone born out of wedlock could be ordained priest, or dispensations for marriages within the forbidden degrees, to a cousin, second cousin, or other relative – a common practice when property rights and marriage were closely tied. All Scots had the right to apply to Rome in this way; that the Gaels and Scots shared this use of the Vatican courts demonstrates the unity of practice in Scotland.

The poetry of Gaelic Scotland was undergoing something of a revival in late fifteenth-century Scotland, as demonstrated by the work recorded in the *Book of the Dean of Lismore*. Although it was a cleric who recorded these compositions for posterity it has been argued by MacGregor that they contain quite harsh criticism of the clergy, and that the existence of disharmony between the clergy and the secular poets of Gaelic society may be inferred. This ambivalence in attitude to the clergy by the poets in Scottish Gaelic culture is compared by MacGregor to Ireland, where the relationship was characterised as being hostile owing to the greater power held in Irish society by the poets (MacGregor 1998, 12–17).

The sculptural evidence for medieval Christianity in the Highlands is quite strong. The church of the MacLeods in Rodel, Harris has one of the finest wall-tombs in Scotland, equal to the quality of sculpture anywhere in early sixteenth-century northern Europe. Yet it was not the MacLeods who were the biggest sponsors of late-medieval Celtic art. Most of the fine crosses and churches built in the Highlands in the period were due – directly or indirectly – to the sponsorship of the Lordship of the Isles, and the extremely powerful MacDonald family. Indeed, the end of this flourishing of sculptural art can be dated to the three years most closely marking the decline and final demise of the MacDonalds' fortunes – 1475, 1493 and 1545 – rather than to 1560 – the supposedly pivotal date of the Scottish Reformation (MacGregor 1998, 15).

THE SCOTTISH UNIVERSITIES

By 1300 there were between 15 and 20 universities in Europe. Collegiate in structure, they were built out of a meeting of academic minds, gathered into one place to train the clergy of the next generation more effectively. They extended their teaching to law and sometimes a little medicine, but primarily they were concerned with the business of staffing the church. Usually the students were between fourteen and eighteen years of age, though it was possible to study for much longer periods, especially if a student became a Franciscan or Dominican or was training to become an academic himself. They stayed in pedagogies or college accommodation, living together with their teachers. The teaching was by lectures on set texts, examinations being oral, by disputation. The appeal of this more organised gathering of intellectual activity was powerful. By 1500 there were 70 universities in Europe and the figure was to keep on growing. Scotland accounted for three of these, a remarkable number considering the population base and wealth of the country.

All three Scottish institutions were founded by bishops. St Andrews began informally at first with a group of masters meeting to teach and discuss learning from around 1410, but it was Henry Wardlaw, Bishop of St Andrews (c.1402–1440) who applied to the Pope for confirmation of his charter of incorporation and privileges. He was rewarded in part for Scotland's loyalty to the antipope, Benedict XIII who gave the *imprimatur* in 1413. The countries of Europe had become divided in their allegiance to pope and antipope from 1378–1417, a period known as the Great Schism. The significance of this event for Scotland lay in the fact that it was one of the last countries to abandon loyalty to the antipope, in the main because England had followed the opposite path. The councils that deposed the antipopes and in the end solved the schisms did much to strengthen the power of the national churches. Over 60 Scottish churchmen took part in the Council of Basle, though not all at once – it was a protracted business. Some were more prominent than others, most notably Thomas Livingstone, Abbot of Dundrennan. The conciliarists were to bring back to Scotland with them new ideas, and also a vision of a church run by agreement as well as decree. This rise in nationalism was also identifiable in the religious orders. The Franciscans and Dominicans, who had come to Scotland in the 1230s, were contained within the English Province of their orders, but they broke free in the later fifteenth century: the Observant Franciscans in 1467, the Dominicans in 1481, and the Franciscan Conventuals in 1483.

In St Andrews, the Augustinian canons of the cathedral priory became very closely linked with the university, as did the Dominicans, a little later in the century. Next came Glasgow – again an episcopal project – as William Turnbull, a graduate of St Andrews and dean of the faculty of arts there, made it one of his first priorities upon being appointed to the see of Glasgow (in late 1447 or early 1448) to found his own university. The first general chapter of the university was held in the Dominican convent in Glasgow in 1451, and the links between the two institutions remained so close that the Dominican bell regulated the hours for the students and staff. Just as Turnbull had been a student of St Andrews so a student of canon law at Glasgow – William Elphinstone – went on to become the bishop of Aberdeen (1488–1514) and there he founded the third university in the realm in 1495.

Elphinstone was doing more than simply founding an institution of higher learning. He had a broader picture in mind for the religious life and wellbeing of his diocese and beyond. He travelled in person to Rome in 1494–5 to have the foundation of his university confirmed by Pope Alexander VI. Aberdeen was to have a single college coterminous with the faculty so that the frictions and disputes between colleges and between college and faculty that had so crippled St Andrews and Glasgow could be avoided. Indeed, it was so successful that Glasgow later adopted a similar system. The funding for Aberdeen was also tightly drawn up so that the new institution could find its feet. The university was tied in Elphinstone's plans to the general revival in interest in Scottish identity.

The Great Schism, it has been argued, was one of several factors to weaken the authority of the papacy, just as the national identities of the European states were strengthening. As the national identity of Scots began to rise they asserted themselves in poetry, history and song. The *Book of the Dean of Lismore* is thought by Donald Meek to contain fifteenth-century compositions, perhaps signalling a revival in the arts of Gaelic poetry at that time. So too, in Scots, the works of Robert Henryson (c.1450–c.1505) would fit into this period and meets these ideals. Elphinstone actively encouraged the link between the national and the international, the local and the elite. In this spirit he commissioned researchers to collect information about Scottish saints and finally to produce a breviary including the usual European saints but also over 70 Scottish saints, presented with historical biographies and feast days. The wider, European context should again not be forgotten; to Elphinstone the Scottish saints were not qualitatively different from their continental counterparts nor were they 'new' to the late fifteenth-century scholars who recorded them. Although Boece wrote that the Scottish saints had been sadly neglected during the fourteenth century, they were not completely forgotten. This was a conscious rediscovering of what it meant to have a Scottish Christian faith set firmly in the context of a Christian Europe.

THE FIRST ARCHBISHOP

The government of the Scottish church (excepting Galloway) lay for most of this period with the provincial council. Although the statutes of this council are now lost there is enough evidence to suggest that this was a fairly successful method of managing the ten dioceses of Scotland. The relationship with Rome was not particularly close. There was no need to have the council's acts ratified in Rome nor any particularly regular or close scrutiny of the Scottish prelates from Rome. The Church was given sufficient independence to run itself as a national body.

The territories held by the Scottish crown were altered by the winning of Orkney and Shetland from Norway: by 1468–9, the diocese of Trondheim thus being no longer their metropolitan they became part of the Scottish province of the church. No doubt this caused some jostling as the bishops absorbed the new system, but there was no particular reason to see change on the horizon. The pressures on the crown to change the church were not political, but financial.

While bringing prestige, setting the Scottish church within its European context and maintaining its place on the world stage was expensive. The steady flow of Scots bullion to Rome for barratry (the buying of benefices) was beginning to have an adverse effect on the Scots exchequer, causing a steady devaluation of the Scots coinage. This was a problem that had been addressed by the Scottish crown several times since 1424. Leslie MacFarlane (1969) has argued that given that the crown did not want 'the possibility of an awkward or intransigent primate bent on enforcing dubious papal policies', it must have been Sixtus IV who initiated the creation of an archiepiscopal see at St Andrews in 1472. Donald Watt (1984), on the other hand, argued that the Archbishop must have had some measure of royal support, or at least the crown must have known of the Archbishop's intentions. Roland Tanner (2001) subsequently demonstrated that the relationship between Patrick Graham and the king had been tense, if not hostile, for some time. This is unsurprising in one sense because Graham was related to the Kennedy family, favourites under James II, and had been given rapid promotion through the ranks of the church due to his family connections, finding himself bishop of St Andrews in 1465, at the age of only 30.

MacFarlane (1969) has also argued, furthermore, that the rest of the hierarchy was not best pleased by the rapid promotion of one so young over the heads of more senior, more capable and more experienced churchmen. It does seem that Graham was the sort of man who fought for his benefices with tenacity, not caring whose pride he may have been injuring. Thus, a good solution to the problems of the Scottish church, keeping bullion at home by awarding most benefices within Scotland, uniting the territory of the dioceses with the geography of the realm, and providing a strong unified structure for the national church, was rejected by its king and bishops. It is difficult to see how Sixtus IV would have thought this a good solution, except in its neatness of execution, but for the king it should have been ideal. It is also easy to see that none of the rest of the hierarchy would have liked this plan, whoever was its sponsor. The truth appears to be that it was Graham's plan. It was unfortunate for him that he planned himself to be its main beneficiary. He ran up significant debts in Rome securing his archbishopric, and also the commendatorship of the abbey of Arbroath – a not inconsiderable benefice – perhaps granted to Graham by Sixtus IV with a view to having the outstanding debts to the curia repaid. The Scottish bishops – already apoplectic – and the king – feeling that Graham had gone too far – united in their opposition to him. By August 1473, Graham was forfeit of his lands and revenues in Scotland. In 1476, he had suffered some form of mental breakdown. This was the saving of the situation as James III was able to appoint his own favourite, physician and courtier, William Scheves as coadjutor. The curia had to accept that it would not see its money, and the position of the crown in relation to the papacy seemed stronger than ever before. The hierarchy of the Scottish church were not quite so contented: Scheves was resented in his own way, being a layman and a royal favourite, but it seems unlikely that the bishops would ever have accepted a Primate, whoever it might have been, without complaint. It is not surprising that this episode has been dubbed, 'one of the more intractable problems of Scottish History' (McRoberts 1968, 12). It was probably obvious to most of the bishops that the appointment of Scheves to the archbishopric, not long after Graham's deprivation, on 11 February 1478, was something of a foregone conclusion.

If the story had ended there, all might have been well for the new Scottish national church, united behind one archbishop and able to work more closely together, and in less frequent conflict with the crown. It is easy to wonder how closely the papacy followed the impact of its decisions upon the Scottish church, for in 1488 Robert Blackadder, Bishop of Glasgow was granted exemption from the primatial authority of Scheves, and then, in January 1492, Innocent VIII erected Glasgow into an archbishopric. Two archbishops, each with tiny areas to govern, each in competition with the other, was an enormous burden to bear for such a small national church. Slowly, St Andrews reasserted its supremacy with two royal successors to Scheves. The first was James IV's brother, James, Duke of Ross (who died in early 1504). He was followed by the king's illegitimate son, Alexander Stewart a gifted, if young, appointment who died at Flodden alongside his father. It was not lost on the hierarchy of the church that such royal appointments did two things – firstly, they brought ecclesiastical revenue into the hands of the king and secondly, they freed royal lands to be retained in royal hands, which would otherwise been granted to these family members.

The struggle for the primacy, the reaction against Graham and the consequent power of the crown over church appointments was to weaken the ability of the Scottish church to conduct reform and to serve the people of Scotland. The problems of the Scottish church in relation to the crown were not unique, and many national churches found that increased independence from Rome could also lead to increased dependence on secular government. It is to be remembered that throughout this period noble birth, a close relationship to the royal line, or abilities prized at court, such as Scheves's medicinal training, were as important to churchmen as to those seeking secular power. It is difficult but worthwhile to endeavour to understand these men by the standards of their day.

THE CHRISTIAN YEAR

Though high politics and the destinies of national churches and nation states form the skeleton of history, the people, their lives and stories, give it flesh. People's experience of Christian worship varied widely through time, and region by region. Some areas had a particular connection with a saint, like St Columba in Iona, St Kentigern in Glasgow, or St Triduana in Restalrig, near Edinburgh. Pilgrimage was a journey undertaken as a penance and a devotion which could take the pilgrim a couple of miles down the road to the local shrine or as far as the Holy Land, as a simple pilgrim, or as a crusader. The collection of funds for crusades was a constant theme in this period and the dream of going on crusade a romantic notion shared by many. Money flowed from Scotland out to the crusades but the local church collected its fair share of pilgrims' wealth – shrines such as that of St Andrew in St Andrews being specially designed with the needs of pilgrims in mind.

In the late fifteenth century, there was revived interest in Scottish saints, as was argued above for the Aberdeen Breviary. St Triduana was the recipient of a new six-sided chapel at Restalrig, provided for her relics by the king, James III. Right at the end of the fifteenth century Archbishop Robert Blackadder of Glasgow improved the shrine of St Kentigern in his cathedral, and also had a chapel placed at the site considered to be his birthplace, in Culross. This was matched by a corresponding increase in pilgrimage to such sites, by the ordinary Scots but also by their kings.

Not only did the saints have places – they also had days. The lives of saints were read upon their day in monasteries at mealtimes and people celebrated when the day of the saint after whom they were named came round. The year itself was predicated on Christian values, not only being calculated from the supposed birth of Christ, but also beginning on Lady Day (25 March). This was nine months before Christmas, thus calculated to be the day of the annunciation. The year was also divided into two by Whitsun and Martinmass, the days, traditionally, of fairs. On these days, new farm hands were hired for work, rent was collected, people moved house, were married, or conducted other transactions. Holy days were holidays. The Scots celebrated Yule, or Christmas, with feasting, plays and other enjoyments. Plays were also held at other times of the year, for example in Haddington on midsummer day. Processions were also popular, the Corpus Christi being one of the most lavish, indeed too expensive to keep running in some areas. However there is good evidence for it in Edinburgh, Aberdeen and several other burghs. In this procession the craft guilds were represented, walking in pairs through the town with the sacred host, the body of Christ, being carried by the priests in an ornamental pyx, so that the whole town might share in veneration of the sacrament.

PEOPLE AND PIETY

The people of Scotland have left us a record of what they did, rather than what they thought. In the absence of sources such as diaries which exist for later periods, it is not easy to assess what a religion – with its outward observance of prayers, sermons, feasts and processions – meant to people as individuals. There is no method of discovery of the true devotion of hearts and minds. One obvious feature of piety for the Scots was the marking of the rites of passage of life. Baptism of newborn infants was a high priority, welcoming them into the community of the church as quickly as possible, in case they died young. Another rite that was observed until quite recently in Scotland, although not a sacrament, was the 'kirking' of a mother after childbirth. This was the return of the mother, safely delivered, into the church and back into her public role in the community.

The sacrament of marriage was usually celebrated at the door of the church. For the better-off, formal betrothals preceded marriage, and property and titles could pass from one family to another this way. It was also used as a means of bridging divides and stopping feud, using relationships to salve the ill-feeling from hurts and wrongs. There were very strict and complicated rules of consanguinity (blood relationship) and affinity (relationships brought about by marriage, i.e. brother-in-law) that governed marriage, and these would have prevented many medieval marriages if it were not for the twin forces of ignorance of the law on the part of many priests, and the system of dispensations for the conscientious. If a man discovered that his future wife was his mother's second cousin then he could pay for a petition to be taken to the *curia* where a dispensation would be issued for the degrees of consanguinity between the pair, and they were then free to marry. Once this process had been completed, however, there was no possibility for divorce on the same grounds (a fact that was to displease Henry VIII of England!).

Death must be acknowledged by all societies. In medieval Scotland the rites surrounding death, grief and bereavement were complex. The funeral, known as *placebo* and *dirge*, was preceded by a bell being rung through the town by a bell-man, calling people to pray for the souls of the deceased. Belief in purgatory grew steadily in the period 1100–1500 and the faithful hoped that the prayers of those left alive would speed the progress through purgatory to heaven for the departed. The body would be placed in the church on a *mort claith* and the services would be said before the burial, either in the church or in the church grounds. Often at funerals of relatively wealthy people there was a dole to the poor, especially when buried in the churches of the friars. Charity was beneficial to the deceased in the same way that prayers were; foundations often included clauses to pray for all the faithful dead, sharing their prayers with others not fortunate enough to pay for the church to maintain their memory.

CONCLUSIONS

From 1100–1500 the church in Scotland was not a static monolith. This was a false impression of the medieval church that was later formed by post-reformation historiography. In fact, during this period the church slowly evolved a working system of parish areas that could be served by priests, taxed efficiently and bound into larger areas called dioceses. The dioceses themselves, each ruled by a bishop, were able to work together through the provincial councils of the Scottish church until 1472 when a metropolitan see was created and the archbishop of St Andrews became the primate of all Scotland, unifying at the same time the church with the geographical realm of Scotland. Yet this hierarchical picture is not all, as the intricate network of monastic institutions spread across the south and east, each bound to its mother house, each functioning as a nexus of trade and power in its local community. The older Celtic monasteries fell into disuse or were modernised to meet the new Norman ideals. No sooner had this system settled into place than a new movement of Dominican and Franciscan friars settled in Scotland bringing with them their ideals of poverty, teaching and preaching. Ideas changed too as the legal and structural reforms of the twelfth-century renaissance gave way to the new theology of Aquinas in the thirteenth century, spread powerfully by the friars, and then onto the conciliarism and humanism of the fifteenth century.

People, by their very nature, have ambiguous relationships with their institutions, and can combine criticism and loyalty in the same breath. It was no different for the medieval Scot. The observance of the rites of human passage gave structure and meaning to their lives, yet their intellectual assent cannot be guaranteed. What they thought and felt must remain theirs alone. Without intruding into the private space of piety and devotion the historian can say much about the practises of religion in medieval Scotland, celebrating its richness in education, art, social welfare, health-care and community living. Within the poetry and popular literature of the day there is a mixture of criticism and praise for the institutions of the church. The works of Sir David Lindsay written in the period 1530–50 drew upon a long tradition of Scottish verse that held in balance the faults and achievements of the church in the minds of the poets of the day. Whatever the final verdict, changing patterns of church structure and personal religion were fundamental to the experiences of the people of medieval Scotland.

REFERENCES TO BOOKS AND ARTICLES MENTIONED IN THE TEXT

Cowan, I and Easson, D 1976 *Medieval Religious Houses in Scotland*. London.
*Dilworth, M 1995 *Scottish Monasteries in the Late Middle Ages*. Edinburgh.
Foggie, JP 2003 *Renaissance Religion in Urban Scotland: the Dominican Order, 1450–1560*. Leiden.
McNeill, PGB and Nicholson, R 1975, *An Historical Atlas of Scotland, c400–1600*. St Andrews.
*McRoberts, D 1968 'The Scottish Church and Nationalism in the Fifteenth Century', *Innes Review*, 19, 3–14.
*Macfarlane, L 1969 'The Primacy of the Scottish Church, 1472–1521', *Innes Review*, 20, 111–29.
Macgregor, M 1998 'The Church in the Highlands', *in* Kirk, J, *The Church in the Highlands*, Edinburgh, 1–36.
Tanner, R 2001 *The Late Medieval Scottish Parliament: Politics and the Three Estates, 1424–1488*. East Linton.
Watt, DER 1984 'The Papacy and Scotland in the Fifteenth century', *in* Dobson, B (ed), *The Church, Politics and Patronage in the Fifteenth Century*, Stroud, 115–29.
Watt, DER 2000 *Medieval Church Councils in Scotland*. Edinburgh.

FURTHER READING

The references marked * in the above list are recommended further reading, along with the following:

Grant, A 1994 *Independence and Nationhood: Scotland, 1306–1469*. Edinburgh.
McNeill, PGB and MacQueen, HL 1996 *Atlas of Scottish History to 1707*. Edinburgh.
MacDonald, AA, Cowan, IB and Lynch, M (eds) 1994 *The Renaissance in Scotland: Studies in Literature, Religion, History and Culture*. Leiden

CHAPTER SEVEN

Scotland and Europe

David Ditchburn

In 1320 the Scottish nobility sealed a letter that was then dispatched to Pope John XXII. The letter, now known as the Declaration of Arbroath, is widely acknowledged as a masterpiece of political rhetoric. In one of its most evocative passages, the pope was invited 'to admonish and exhort the king of England to leave in peace us Scots who live in this poor little Scotland beyond which there is no dwelling place at all'. The unknown author was cleverly playing on commonly held views about the isolation and impoverishment of his homeland. On the famous thirteenth-century world map, now in Hereford Cathedral, Scotland was placed close to the circumference of the known world and for continental authors this was a suitable habitat for cannibals – and even the Devil. If isolation offered an almost credible setting for uncivilised inhabitants, for others the periphery was equated with poverty. The twelfth-century Moroccan writer Abu Abdallah Muhammad al-Sharif al-Idrisi offered an especially bleak assessment, noting that Scotland was 'uninhabited and has neither town nor village'. This was, of course, untrue, but even foreigners more familiar with the Scottish landscape, such as the French knights who visited Scotland in 1385, regarded the terrain of their allies as inhospitable (Ditchburn 2001a, 266–75).

Impressions can be misleading. Scotland was regarded as distant from a world traditionally centred on Jerusalem, but it was nonetheless within the known world – and the Declaration of Arbroath is also a clear and clever reflection of the kingdom's European identity. Pope John and his predecessors, Clement V and Boniface VIII, had taken a keen interest in the Anglo-Scottish wars, initially encouraging the Scots, but latterly censuring them. The eloquent Declaration indicated that papal goodwill mattered to them (Simpson 1977, 11–33). Yet the extent to which it mattered – and to whom – is debateable. The Declaration was a manifesto of the elite. Its author was probably a leading clergyman, its signatories were secular aristocrats and its instigator was probably the king, Robert I. Medieval society was hierarchical and hierarchy was regarded as natural and God-given. At the same time, however, society was divided by function, into those who prayed, those who fought and those who worked. These responsibilities cut across hierarchy, but they were important in establishing contrasting visions of Europe among the medieval Scottish population.

THE FIRST ESTATE

Medieval Christendom was an intensely religious society. Religious belief was not a matter of personal choice but rather a state of mind. In such a society the clergy played a particularly significant role, for it was their job to pray for the living and the dead. There were perhaps between three and four thousand clergymen in medieval Scotland (Grant 1985, 89). Together with their counterparts throughout the Western Christendom they all owed earthly obedience to the bishop of Rome – or pope. The pope's pre-eminence derived from his association with St Peter, Christ's foremost apostle and the first bishop of Rome. This conferred upon the papacy unrivalled prestige, which was enhanced by a widespread acknowledgement that the pope was the final arbiter of religious doctrine and law. Doctrinal issues were normally discussed by leading clergymen in general councils, which were summoned periodically by the pope. From 1163 (when Bishop Gregory of Dunkeld attended a general council at Tours) most were attended by at least some of Scotland's leading clergymen. Decisions made by these general councils required papal ratification and the assertion made at the council of Constance in 1415 – that the powers of a general council were derived directly from Christ and were therefore superior to those of a pope – met with a frosty papal response. In 1460 this opinion was declared heretical.

Aside from approving doctrine, the pope also possessed legal powers. His written rulings – or decretals – were binding on the whole church and formed the basis of church – or canon – law. This was systematized from the twelfth century and papal representatives (especially the papal legates who visited Scotland frequently in the twelfth and thirteenth centuries) were probably instrumental in disseminating awareness of it (Ferguson 1997; Watt 2000). Manuscript copies of canon laws also circulated and in 1436 Aberdeen Cathedral possessed commentaries by leading jurists, as well as collections of canon law (Ditchburn 2001a, 92). These laws were applied in church courts, the most authoritative of which were located at the papacy, though others were established in each diocese of Christendom. Church courts held exclusive jurisdiction over the clergy; but because the remit of canon law was extensive – covering marital and testamentary issues, matters of morality and belief (such as illegitimacy, blasphemy and heresy) and even commercial matters (such as usury) – laymen and women also appeared at their sittings. In addition, both clerical and lay supplicants used the offices of the Chancery, Datary and Penitentiary located at the papacy, which were empowered to absolve sinners from sin as well as to dispense individuals from canon law stipulations. Scottish clerics were regular customers – proportionately more numerous than those from other 'peripheral' areas such as Scandinavia. At the Penitentiary most petitioned regarding illegitimacy, although in 1487 David Barbour, from the diocese of St Andrews, was one of a few who sought dispensation for corporal defects, in his case poor vision (McDonald, 2005, 99). Without dispensation neither bastards nor the disabled could become priests.

While canon law was one means by which papal authority was asserted, the provinces of Christendom were also bound to the papacy by financial strings. Clerical income tax was instituted in order to pay for crusading ventures. It was levied on several occasions in Scotland during the thirteenth century, but then largely abandoned in favour of taxing individual clerics who had been appointed to their position by the pope. This provided an incentive for the papacy to increase its powers of clerical appointment. Before the fourteenth century these had been negligible but by the end of the fourteenth century the pope was making roughly thirteen appointments to clerical office in Scotland annually. It was not necessary for clerics to visit the pope personally in order to secure an appointment; some did so by correspondence and through the offices of an agent (or 'procurator') present at the papal court. Nevertheless, clerical visits to the papacy were far from unusual.

Papal authority was thus exerted through a variety of mechanisms. Although lay society was not immune from these developments, clergymen and women were its most direct targets. In Scotland, as in all other parts of Christendom, clerics came in two guises: regulars (who followed a rule and who usually lived together in distinctive cloistered communities) and seculars (who ministered directly to the laity in churches). Before 1100 regular life followed patterns of monasticism found throughout the Celtic world. Thereafter monastic communities increasingly resembled those in continental Christendom. Benedictine monks – who followed the rule of St Benedict – were established at the ancient royal centres of Dunfermline and Iona, and also at Coldingham (in Berwickshire), the Isle of May and Urquhart (in Moray). In Iona they superseded a well-established community of monks adhering to Irish norms, while Dunfermline's recruits came initially from Canterbury, those at Coldingham from Durham, and those at May from Reading. Variants of the Benedictine rule were also introduced into Scotland. They included Cluniacs (who took their name from the abbey of Cluny, near Mâcon, in Burgundy), Tironensians (modelled on Tiron, near Chartres, in France) and Cistercians (named after the abbey of Cîteaux, near Dijon, in Burgundy). The first Scottish Cistercians, recruited from the Yorkshire house of Rievaulx, settled at Melrose and others followed at Balmerino, Coupar Angus, Culross, Deer, Dundrennan, Glenluce, Kinloss, Newbattle, Saddell and Sweetheart in Galloway. The monastic mix was completed with three Valliscaulian houses (based on the rule followed at Val des Choux, near Langres, in France) and the belated arrival of Carthusians at Perth in 1429, who took their lead from Grande Chartreuse, near Grenoble, in France. There were also a few nunneries – though opportunities for religious women were considerably more limited than those for men.

Other regular communities of both men and women followed the rule ascribed to St Augustine of Hippo, or variants of it, such as those followed at Arrouaise and Premontré in France. Again many of these Scottish communities recruited initially from abroad. Both Scone (the first Augustinian foundation, dating from c.1120) and Holyrood drew their initial recruits from Merton in Surrey while Cumbuskenneth (in Stirlingshire) was populated from Arrouaise. Aside from monks and canons regular two other types of religious order also appeared on the Scottish landscape. The crusading movement had spawned the creation of military orders – communities of armed knights who followed monastic rules – and two of these (the Templars and the Hospitallers) received extensive endowments in Scotland. More popular still were the mendicants (or 'friars'), who originated in the thirteenth century with the dual purpose of spearheading the church's fight against heresy and ministering to the growing number of urban poor. By comparison with many continental countries, Scotland proved infertile ground for heresy and its towns remained small. Nevertheless, the leading mendicant orders of Franciscans (named after St Francis of Assisi), Dominicans (named after St Dominic Guzman) and Carmelites (named after Mount Carmel in Sinai) made a significant impact in Scotland. Friaries were established in twenty-four Scottish towns, by comparison with 116 locations in England and 155 in France.

Regular communities were thus radically transformed during the twelfth and thirteenth centuries. Irish influences waned significantly, and even those communities that maintained Irish links (such as Saddell in Argyll, a daughter house of Mellifont in Ireland) did so within a continental framework. Nevertheless, there is a danger in exaggerating the cosmopolitan nature of these new institutions. Most soon lost contact with their foreign mothers, although the Cistercians, the Hospitallers and the mendicants retained their international contacts longer. In part this was a consequence of their more rigid managerial structures. All Cistercian abbots were summoned to an annual general meeting ('chapter general') held at Cîteaux every September, the costs of which were met from a levy on all Cistercian houses. These tax obligations brought the Scottish Cistercians into contact with continental financial markets, but because of the distance they had to travel Scottish abbots were required to attend the chapter general only every four years. These meetings constituted a policing mechanism. Specifically Scottish concerns were occasionally debated, during the thirteenth century at least, most notably in 1234 when the English abbots of Rievaulx, Roche and Sawley were instructed to 'correct, reform and punish' misdeeds at Dundrennan and Glenluce – perhaps signifying an attempt to suppress lingering Celtic eccentricities that also affected Cistercian houses in Ireland (Canivez 1933–41, ii, 136; Miller 2003, ch. 6). The watchful Cistercian eye was supplemented by tours of inspection, which each mother house was obliged to undertake of its daughters. Thus Rievaulx inspected Melrose, as well as Dundrennan, Wardon (Lincolnshire), Revesby (Lincolnshire) and Rufford (Yorkshire); and Melrose, in turn, inspected Newbattle, Kinloss, Coupar Angus, Balmerino and Holm Cultram in Cumbria. These inspections occurred regularly in the twelfth and thirteenth centuries but were subsequently disrupted by warfare involving Scotland, England and France and by the papal schism lasting from 1378 to 1418 – during which England recognised a pope based in Rome while Scotland and France were obedient to his rival in Avignon.

The hierarchical structures of the monastic world had their parallels in the secular arm of the church. The Latin West was divided into archiepiscopal units, presided over by an archbishop. Each archdiocese was in turn subdivided into diocesan units under the oversight of a bishop; and each diocese might be further subdivided in archdeaconries. A clear chain of command was thus established from the pope at its apex, through archbishops, bishops and others, extending down to the priests who administered the sacraments at parish level and the chaplains who might assist them. Most of these units were established in Scotland by the twelfth century, with one key exception. There was no Scottish archbishop. The Isles and Orkney came under the jurisdiction of the Norwegian archbishop of Trondheim, while the archbishops of

York and Canterbury vied for charge of the mainland bishops, their claims opposed by Scottish kings and bishops. The papacy was unwilling to settle the matter by appointing a Scottish archbishop, but in 1189 or 1192 (the date is uncertain) it sought compromise by declaring the mainland bishops a 'special daughter' of the papacy itself (Barrell 1995, 116–38). Galloway remained under York's jurisdiction, but both it and the Isles were integrated into the Scottish mainstream once the papal schism impeded the maintenance of cross-border ecclesiastical structures. The papacy's arrangements for Scotland continued until the bishop of St Andrews was elevated to archiepiscopal status in 1472, followed by Glasgow in 1492 (Watt 1984, 123–26; Macfarlane 1992, 99–118).

It was not just the bonds of papal bureaucracy that linked Scottish churchmen to their continental counterparts. Many of those who aspired to senior clerical office began their careers at universities, which were quasi-ecclesiastical institutions. For most of this period university study was undertaken abroad. St Andrews, the first Scottish university, was only founded in 1413, and although two further Scottish universities were established (at Glasgow in 1451 and at Aberdeen in 1495), this did not stem the student exodus. The Scottish universities remained under-resourced and unable to offer the range of subjects or (by and large) the famous teachers associated with the most renowned continental schools. As late as 1560 the bishop of Orkney advised his nephew to study abroad since 'he can leyr na guid at hame' (Napier 1834, 67). In the thirteenth century many, including John Duns Scotus (the most significant Scottish intellectual of the middle ages), headed for Oxford and Cambridge. Some continued to study there in later centuries, though both became less appealing in times of Anglo-Scottish conflict. As a result, many Scots looked elsewhere. Bologna in Italy was famed for its legal teaching while Paris (where Duns Scotus also studied) acquired a reputation for both its basic arts courses and for doctoral study in theology. Both attracted sizeable numbers of Scots by the thirteenth century, though by the fifteenth century many others were to be found at the newer universities of Orléans, Cologne and Leuven in particular.

Some university graduates stayed in academia following acquisition of their first degrees, proceeding to study for higher degrees in canon law, civil law, medicine or theology and then, perhaps, to a teaching career. For most graduates, however, an ecclesiastical career beckoned. The papacy's increasing control of clerical appointment encouraged approaches from ambitious graduates in their quest for employment. In many parts of Christendom this led to foreigners being appointed to lucrative ecclesiastical positions. Some Scots benefited from this papal largesse: William Lauder, an Angers student, held clerical positions in the French bishoprics of St Malo and Rennes before his appointment as bishop of Glasgow in 1408, while the Parisian graduate John Kirkmichael held posts in France as well as Scotland before becoming bishop of Orléans in 1426 (Watt 1977, 311–12; 331–33).

In many countries this process stirred xenophobic resentments, prompting secular authorities to seek control of church appointments within their jurisdiction. In Scotland there was little sign of such trouble, partly because relatively few foreigners sought provision to the comparatively poor Scottish benefices, but also because the papacy normally acquiesced to royal wishes in the appointment of senior clergymen. An enormously bitter dispute between King William the Lion and the papacy over the appointment of a bishop of St Andrews – which lasted from 1179 to 1188 – was something of an exception, and it was not until 1487 that the crown and the papacy felt a need to formalise the crown's rights in the appointment of senior clergymen. From then, Pope Innocent VIII agreed to an eight-month delay in making appointments to cathedral churches and wealthier monasteries, allowing the king to indicate in the interim his preferred candidates for these posts (Thompson 1968, 23–31).

However and wherever appointed, clergymen in all parts of Christendom were expected to undertake their duties in similar fashion. The Christian message was theoretically universal and respective of no political frontiers. Churches were built to a roughly similar Romanesque and then Gothic design (even in Gaelic Ireland and Scotland) (O'Keefe 2004, 28–32) and the wealthier of them were adorned with familiar religious iconography. Little of the latter has survived – thanks to the iconoclastic efficiency of later Protestant reformers – but archaeological and documentary evidence provides some indication of its content. Statues and images of Christ and internationally popular saints such as Mary were common, while Glasgow Cathedral housed relics associated with Saints Bartholomew, Blaise, Catherine, Eugene, Mathew, Thomas Becket, as well the remnants of the Virgin Mary's girdle, hair and breast milk. Throughout Europe, in a setting that was colourful and perhaps instructional, priests wore distinctive garb and (except in parts of Croatia) conducted church services in Latin, which few members of the congregation understood. Communal prayer and the Eucharist – collectively known as the liturgy – were the most prominent element of church services. In Scotland these followed a model originally fashioned in France and Italy, which by at least the thirteenth century had come to supersede older Celtic rites. Before printing was invented in the mid-fifteenth century the standardisation of liturgical texts was, however, difficult and several variants of the Romano-Gallican model developed. Most Scottish churches (including the cathedrals of Aberdeen, Dunkeld, Glasgow, Moray and Ross) followed a liturgy originally devised at Salisbury in England and supplemented by prayers to specifically Scottish saints. Its observance survived the Wars of Independence and attempts mounted by the ecclesiastical hierarchy towards the end of the fifteenth century to revise the Salisbury model radically into a distinctively Scottish Use or to abandon it in favour of the Roman Use met with only limited success.

THE SECOND ESTATE

Although prayer was primarily the business of priests, other sections of society were also deeply imbued with a Christian mentality. Lay society attended church regularly and was theoretically bound by the stipulations of canon law. Marriage within four degrees of consanguinity was prohibited, unless ecclesiastical dispensation was obtained, and during the fifteenth century the Penitentiary received an average of ten petitions each year from Scots seeking such authorisation (Furneaux

2004, 60). The devout also petitioned the papacy for relief from ecclesiastical strictures on diet and for permission to possess portable altars. Piety could be exemplified in other ways too. The wealthy patronised monasteries and churches and all sections of society participated in pilgrimage, even although this was not a compulsory element of devotional practice. Pilgrimages were undertaken for different reasons, but all pilgrimage shrines possessed saintly relics in which, it was believed, the spiritual powers of the saint remained. Prayer at such locations brought pilgrims – or their representatives – into contact with saints and their miraculous powers: Alexander Sutherland of Dunbeath was not unique in dispatching his son to Rome on his behalf in c.1456 (Bannatyne Club 1855, 96).

In the eleventh century at least one Scottish king – Macbeth – had apparently undertaken a pilgrimage to Rome, which remained a popular pilgrimage destination. In Jubilee Years – which were declared periodically from 1300 – the pope offered a plenary indulgence to those from outside the city who spent fifteen days visiting prescribed sites. This amounted to a full remission on the penance imposed following the confession of sin and among those lured by this amnesty on penance were William, eighth Earl of Douglas, his son and several other knightly members of the Douglas affinity, as well as the Bishop of St Andrews, who all visited Rome in 1450.

Rome's popularity also stemmed from its enormous collection of saintly relics, especially those connected with St Peter. It was, however, a distant location for Scots, as were the other two great pilgrimage destinations, the Holy Land and Santiago de Compostella, in north-western Spain. Those who undertook such journeys were proud of their accomplishment and some, such as Sir Thomas Maule of Panmure, boasted of their achievement by incorporating the internationally recognised symbol of Compostella – the conch – on their coats of arms (Laing 1850, nos 571; 676). For those with more limited time and/or assets, there were closer alternatives. Aside from Scottish shrines, England offered Canterbury (with shrines dedicated to St Thomas Becket) and Walsingham (a Marian shrine), as well as Durham (with the relics of St Cuthbert). The MacMalcolm dynasty displayed particular reverence for Cuthbert and many Scots, including some from the Hebrides, visited Durham in the twelfth and thirteenth centuries (Barrow 2004, 109–16). Anglo-Scottish hostilities did not extinguish the popularity of English shrines, though the continent was more hospitable territory. In 1383 miracles brought pilgrims from all over Europe to the German shrine of Wilsnack. In France, Amiens in particular attracted Scots – its assemblage of saintly wares included the head of John the Baptist. Or so it was claimed as two other locations also claimed this particular relic.

Religion was influential in shaping lay mentalities, but it was not the essence of the secular aristocracy. Instead, the primary function of aristocrats was theoretically military combat. On occasions it was possible to harness this altogether more deadly pursuit with a religious imperative, notably through involvement in crusades. In 1095 Pope Urban II had summoned Christians to wrest the Holy Land from Islamic control. His call met with unexpected success. The German chronicler Ekkehard of

Aura reckoned that one hundred thousand men were assembled from 'Aquitaine and Normandy, England, Scotland, Ireland, Brittany, Galicia, Gascony, France, Flanders, Lorraine and from other Christian peoples' and their obedience was rewarded with a plenary indulgence (www.fordham.edu/halsall/source/ekkehard-cde.html#opening). The integrity of the crusading ideal was, however, somewhat tarnished by the attack launched by crusaders on the Orthodox Christian city of Constantinople during the Fourth Crusade in 1204. Latin interventions in the Holy Land itself ended following the loss of Acre (the last Latin Christian outpost in the Holy Land), which fell to the Turks in 1291. Crusading opportunities remained, however, notably in North Africa, Iberia (where the objective was to recover territory captured by Muslims in the eighth century) and in the Baltic (where the Prussian-based Teutonic Order campaigned against the pagan Lithuanians).

Scottish aristocrats participated in many of these campaigns, most famously when Sir James Douglas accompanied King Robert I's heart on an expedition mounted against the Moorish citadel of Teba de Hardeles in 1330 (Cameron 2000, 108–17). This was a fitting tribute to the late king, whose father and grandfather had both undertaken crusades and whose son, David II, was also to demonstrate a keen interest in crusading ventures. Yet, despite the spiritual benefits to be gained, crusading remained an essentially individual or familial, rather than national, experience. There are several reasons for this. Other than the Bruce kings Robert I and David II, crusading enthusiasm was more circumspect among Scottish kings than among their European counterparts, many of whom personally participated in the crusades of the twelfth and thirteenth centuries. Subsequently, the spectre of Anglo-Scottish warfare distracted potential Scottish crusaders, including Robert I. The Declaration of Arbroath clearly indicates that crusading was a secondary priority to victory over England – though the regret expressed for this attitude probably reflects the genuine sentiments of the king at least.

Scottish crusading activity was generally limited to times of truce in Anglo-Scottish conflict. Similarly, in moments of peace aristocratic foes became colleagues who collaborated on the tournament field. Tournaments had developed in the eleventh century and involved both teams of warriors fighting in a *mêlée* and jousting contests, which pitted two participants fighting on horseback with lances against each other. These contests were originally fought under war conditions and thus constituted an authentic setting for the practice of skills required on the battlefield. Increasingly, however, tournaments served other purposes too. Often set to a storyline, enacted upon lavish sets and fought with blunted weapons, tournaments became entertainment. They were often staged to mark royal marriages or as vehicles for political propaganda. In 1358 Edward III of England staged a tournament at Windsor with the express intention of celebrating recent English victories against the French and the Scots. On this occasion English champions pitted their skills against Scottish knights, and Anglo-Scottish tournaments were not unusual. London Bridge was the spectacular setting for an encounter between Sir David Lindsay of Glenesk and Lord Wells in May 1390, their clash followed in the same month by another between teams led by the Earls of Moray and Nottingham.

Aside from these and similar contests, both Scots and Englishmen participated in tournaments held abroad such as that staged at Compiègne in 1278. Stars of the international tournament circuit visited Scotland too. In 1449 a Burgundian team, led by Jacques de Lalaing, fought a contingent of Douglas knights in the presence of James II – and Lalaing, who had arrived from a similar engagement in Spain soon departed for another performance at Chalons-sur-Saône in France.

For aristocrats, fighting was not just a function but a culture. Even amid the carnage of a tournament staged at Berwick in 1342 there were discernible chivalric elements. Contemporaries applauded the attributes of courage, honour and largesse, even in an adversary and those who supervised the Berwick tournament awarded prizes for the best performances. The Scots chose an English knight who had run his lance through William Ramsay's head; and the English, significantly, selected a Scotsman, Patrick Graham. Graham had killed one English knight in the tournament and would have killed a second, had he not worn protective armour beyond that agreed by the two teams. This was cheating and the English deplored it as much as the Scots. Culture, it is worth remembering, was a matter of death, as well as life (Ditchburn 2001a, 96–105).

Crusades and tournaments offered the aristocracy an arena in which to display military prowess. They also constituted an important element in an aristocratic culture that bridged nationality. National animosities were, however, not always absent from such events and the murderous brawl that crusaders played out at Königsberg in 1391 is a potent reminder that most Scottish aristocrats displayed their military prowess in the name of their king rather than their God. By comparison with their English, French and Iberian counterparts, Scottish kings and aristocrats had remarkably few external enemies. Geographical remoteness had its advantages. Between 1100 and 1500 the Scottish political community faced only two potential threats against which its military prowess might be tested. One was located to the west and north, the other to the south. The western and northern seaboard constituted an international frontier beyond which, in the Hebrides, Orkney and Shetland, lay Norwegian territory. Despite a Norwegian attack on Aberdeen in 1151, the Scandinavian presence posed little threat to the Scottish kingdom during the period under consideration, though its limited control over native Islesmen was a potential source of friction. By contrast, during the mid-thirteenth century Scottish kings and aristocrats (most notably of the Stewart family) mounted an ambitious and aggressive effort to wrest control of the western isles from a weakened Norwegian monarchy. This provocation prompted the Norwegian king Hakon IV to lead his army into battle against the Scots at Largs in 1263. The outcome remains contentious, but it was insufficient to prevent a Scottish takeover of the Hebrides (including the Isle of Man), which was formally recognised by the Treaty of Perth in 1266 (Cowan 1990, 103–31). Both Orkney and Shetland still remained Norwegian possessions, though by the fifteenth century covetous royal eyes were beginning to focus on further gain at Norwegian expense. In the event, military manoeuvres proved unnecessary. In 1468 Orkney, and in the following year Shetland too, came into James III's possession, following his astute marriage to

Margaret, daughter of King Christian IV of Denmark and Norway. The Scandinavian king was unable to deliver his daughter's dowry and therefore substituted the Northern Isles.

Political threats from the south were both more powerful and less easily overcome. The twelfth century began with the Scots on the offensive. Taking advantage of civil war in England, David I (1124–53) had secured control of Cumberland, Westmorland and Northumberland by the 1140s. Keith Stringer has argued that his objective was even more ambitious and entailed the incorporation of Durham, Yorkshire and Lancashire too, thus establishing a domain coterminous with the archbishopric of York (Stringer 1993, 36). Through conquest, David perhaps hoped to acquire what the pope had declined to grant: an archbishop of his own. Political and religious aspirations were, however, more than matched by economic benefits. Cumbria included rich deposits of silver, which financed an enormous expansion in the Scottish economy, symbolically manifested in the issue of the first Scottish coinage (Blanchard 1996, 23–45).

Whatever his motives, David's expanded domains crumbled quickly after his death. A claim to the northern counties was all that remained, though this was sufficient to fuel the imagination of David's grandson, King William the Lion (1165–1214). William faced sterner and more formidable opposition than his grandfather, for the northern counties were now more firmly incorporated within the domain of the new Angevin king of England, Henry II. William's ill-considered military campaigns ended in the humiliation of capture and his forced acceptance of Henry II's overlordship, formalised by the Treaty of Falaise (1174). Although William was subsequently able to purchase his kingdom's release from this imposition – by the Quitclaim of Canterbury (1189) – Anglo-Scottish relations remained at times tense. They were only pacified when, in the Treaty of York (1237), King Alexander II (1214–49) and King Henry III agreed on a border between their two kingdoms.

Anglo-Scottish hostilities of the twelfth and thirteenth centuries were conducted largely in an insular 'British' context. William's reign was, however, marked by one significant diplomatic initiative: an attempt to harness French and Flemish aid for campaigns across the Anglo-Scottish frontier. Some was forthcoming, though not enough to prevent military failure in 1174. Nevertheless, it was ostensibly to France again that the Scottish political community turned when Anglo-Scottish relations deteriorated at the end of the thirteenth century. This time it was emboldened by a formal treaty of alliance, agreed in 1295 and renewed periodically thereafter. In reality direct French assistance was normally limited to small numbers of men, arms and/or money; and Scottish armies which crossed the Anglo-Scottish border in support of French initiatives often encountered disaster – for instance at Neville's Cross (1346) and Flodden (1513). Only in 1385 did a substantial French force set foot in Scotland. The ensuing Franco-Scottish invasion of England achieved little, however, partly because (as in 1174) a French attack on southern England did not materialise, but also because of acrimony between the visiting French and their Scottish hosts.

The French alliance became a hallmark of Scottish diplomacy from 1295 until

1560. Arguably it promised more than it delivered. Such a judgement fails, however, to take account of domestic French problems. Anglo-French conflicts peppered the thirteenth and early fourteenth centuries and became more consistent with the onset of the Hundred Years War (1337–1453). Some Scots, such as Sir William Douglas and two hundred companions who fought at Poitiers in 1346, extended *ad hoc* aid to the beleaguered French crown, although in only one period did substantial Scottish forces travel to France (Watt 1987–98, vii, 299). Between 1419 and 1424 thousands of Scottish soldiers, led by leading aristocrats such as Sir John Stewart of Darnley and the Earls of Buchan, Douglas and Wigtown, fought on behalf of the beleaguered Dauphin, the future King Charles VII, who had been effectively disinherited by his father, Charles VI (Ditcham 1978, ch. 2). This, and the consequential prospect of a single, united Anglo-French realm, was deeply threatening to Scottish interests. If implemented, Scotland might remain the only Anglophobic power in Christendom. Although hardly altruistic, Scottish intervention was critical. Before defeats at Cravant (1423) and even more catastrophically at Verneuil (1424), where the dead included both Buchan and Douglas, a Franco-Scottish victory at Baugé (1421) blocked the English advance from Normandy into central France. It was not, however, responsible for turning the tide – an accolade arguably belonging more to Joan of Arc.

English ambitions in both France and Scotland were responsible for the Franco-Scottish alliance. There was, however, a complicated fourth element in the equation. The Netherlands was a politically fragmented but commercially precocious region in which all three kingdoms held a significant interest. The southern Netherlands, including most of Flanders, were technically part of the French kingdom, but the Netherlandish textile industry relied on copious supplies of wool from the estates of English and Scottish landowners. These external loyalties were a source of friction within Netherlandish society and added to domestic tensions between Netherlandish rulers and their powerful towns. Scottish interests were best served when political antagonisms (both between France and Flanders and within Flanders) were mute. Often they were not. In such circumstances the Scottish government faced a conflict between its commercial and political interests. It was to avert such possibilities that several marital alliances were arranged between the Scottish royal house and Netherlandish rulers. In 1282 Alexander III's elder son married Margaret, daughter of the Count of Flanders; and in 1444 James I's daughter Mary married the Lord of Veere in Zeeland, a familiar haunt of Scottish merchants. Even more strikingly, in 1449 James II married Mary of Guelders, a niece of Philip the Good, Duke of Burgundy, whose domains included most of the Low Countries – the marriage constituting the symbolic embodiment of a full military alliance agreed by the Treaty of Brussels (Ditchburn 1996, 59-75). Despite these precautions, historians remain divided as to the significance of the dilemma facing Scottish government. Some, such as Norman Macdougall, effectively discount economic considerations in the formulation of foreign policy. For them the primacy of the French alliance remained uncontested (Macdougall 2001; Bonner 1999, 5–30). By contrast, Alexander Stevenson has argued that economic imperatives were central to diplomatic considerations and that the Scots only agreed a French alliance in 1295 because French influence was then paramount in Flanders. It was, in other words, primarily with Flanders not France that the Scots sought alliance (Stevenson 1996, 28-42; Ditchburn 2001b, 33–55).

THE THIRD ESTATE

While the clergy prayed and the aristocracy fought, the remainder of the population worked. Their lives were shaped by the same religious concerns and obligations as other sections in society and by similar social and economic realities to those pertaining elsewhere in Christendom. Rich and poor alike were, for instance, expected to confess their sins and take communion annually, as decreed by the Fourth Lateran Council in 1215; and poverty did not prevent the poor from undertaking pilgrimage in search of a miracle. Despite the similarities of life, there were also sharp differences. The leading clergyman, Walter Bower, Abbot of Inchcolm, compared peasants with dogs, whatever their nationality (Watt 1987–98 vii, 395); and, no matter in which country they lived, the harvest (rather than the battlefield) was the most critical moment in the peasant year.

The numerically largest section of society was not, however, heterogeneous. It included wealthy urban merchants as well as impoverished and landless peasants – and its direct experience of foreign contact was, not surprisingly, diverse. Foreign influences were at their most intense in the towns. Trade was the fundamental *raison d'être* of the town, its importance reflected physically (in the focus of the market-place), institutionally (in the political and social dominance exercised by merchant guilds) and legally (in the protection afforded to traders). Although most trading activities involved interaction between towns and their landward hinterlands, towns also offered a point of commercial contact with other countries. By at least the thirteenth century the vast monastic (and probably aristocratic) estates of the Scottish countryside had been overrun by sheep, which were producing quantities of wool beyond that required for Scottish cloth production. The excess was exported. Wool and cloth were not the only commodities which Scots sold to foreign merchants. Leather was another significant by-product of a significantly pastoral economy; and fish, including both fresh- and salt-water species, were abundant. Unlike wool, cloth and leather, fish were, however, perishable. Salting was one means by which they might be preserved and supplies of relatively poor quality salt – and also coal – were particularly abundant in the Forth estuary. Scotland thus produced a surplus of agricultural and raw materials (Ditchburn 2001a, 142–9; 163–6; 176–80; 183–9).

There was demand for all of these goods abroad. An extensive textile industry had developed in Flanders and Artois, the most densely urbanised region north of the Alps, and then in Brabant and Holland too. Netherlandish looms were supplied with wool from England and Scotland, as well as the Low Countries. In the thirteenth and early fourteenth centuries Netherlandish demand for Scottish wool was buoyant, its sale financing a significant increase in the circulation of coinage in Scotland

(Mayhew 1990, 53–73). From the later fourteenth century, however, Scottish wool exports declined significantly. There are several explanations for this, chief among them a decline in Netherlandish demand. In response to new and growing competition from English cloth manufactures, many Netherlandish towns, including Brussels, Leiden, Maastricht and Ypres, focused production on cloth of the highest quality. Scottish wool was inadequate for this purpose and its use was prohibited. It was still perfectly adequate for producing poorer quality cloths (both in Scotland and in the Netherlands), but in the Netherlands it faced increasing competition from Spanish wools and, periodically too, from those of the Rhineland, Pomerania and Silesia. Although there was some expansion in domestic Scottish production, demand for cheap Scottish cloths remained comparatively stagnant. Unlike England, Scotland failed to transform itself from a major wool exporter into a major exporter of woollen cloth (Ditchburn 2001a, 172–81).

Religious concerns ensured that demand for fish was more constant. Adam's sins in the Garden of Eden had prompted a divine judgement cursing the ground. As penance the church decreed that on Wednesdays, Fridays, Saturdays and additional periods of particular religious contemplation – such as Lent and Advent – Christians should avoid consumption of foodstuffs derived from the land. For roughly half of the year all but the poor and sick were expected to abstain from the consumption of meat and dairy products, providing an enormous stimulus to the fish trade. In northern Europe much of this demand was met from the herring sold in Skania, on the southern tip of Scandinavia, and from cod caught off the Norwegian coast. The fish trade in these areas was dominated by merchants from the Hanseatic towns of northern Germany, who were also active in Shetland both before and after its incorporation into the Scottish kingdom in 1469 (Friedland 1983, 86-95). Elsewhere, Netherlandish fishermen caught fish in Scottish waters from the thirteenth century, though without the intercession of Scottish fishermen or merchants and thus with little or no profit to the Scottish economy. Nevertheless, Scots were able to profit from their own fish sales in France and England.

Profits made from sale of exports enabled merchants to purchase commodities not grown or manufactured in Scotland. Since the aristocracy (together with the urban elite) was by far the wealthiest section of the population, merchants tended to cater for their demands, rather than those of the poor. Aristocratic tastes had originally been fashioned in France, by the ancestors of those Anglo-French nobles who settled in Scotland from the twelfth century. The elite dined on meat, fish and wheaten bread, supplemented by wine. Scottish production of meat and fish was adequate to satisfy their palate but, while some wheat was grown in Scotland, it seems unlikely that production met demand, for wheat often figured among imported commodities. Since Scotland was to the north of viticultural limits, so did wine. Spices, several of originally Asian origin, were also familiar to aristocrat households. The most expensive included saffron, mace and galingale, though cinnamon, cumin, ginger, nutmeg and pepper were also used to flavour, rather than preserve, foodstuffs.

Other imports included manufactured goods and raw materials, including timber and timber-based products, such as tar and ash. Manufactures, meanwhile, included expensive items of clothing, notably silk-based materials, such as velvet, satin, damask and taffeta, as well as woollen cloths of superior quality to those produced in Scotland. The elite expected to dress, as well as to eat, in conformity with continental fashions – and their homes were further adorned with continental furniture, art, manuscripts and (after the invention of the printing press in the mid fifteenth century) books. In addition, many metal-based artefacts were purchased abroad. In an ambiguous passage often interpreted as an indication of Scotland's poverty, the chronicler Froissart specifically mentioned 'iron to shoe horses', though other more mundane accoutrements, such as frying and dripping pans and kettles, were also imported. So too were weapons, including by the mid-fifteenth century cannons and bombards such as the famous 'Mons Meg' (now displayed in Edinburgh Castle), which was presented to James II by Philip the Good, Duke of Burgundy.

Supply and demand for goods, rather than geographical proximity, dictated the patterns of commerce. This explains the relatively limited extent of trade with Scandinavia (Ditchburn 1990, 73–89). By contrast, England and Ireland were a source of both grain and goods such as wine, re-exported from elsewhere, though these links were periodically disrupted by Anglo-Scottish warfare. By the fifteenth century grain and timber products came from Prussia and Poland (mainly through the ports of Stralsund and Danzig/Gdansk), while wine was shipped directly from Bordeaux, which the French captured from the English in 1453. Throughout the period, Scotland's chief commercial links were, however, with the Netherlands. Scottish wool and leather were legally directed to a 'staple' located in the Nether-lands and it was here too that Scottish merchants purchased an array of merchandise either produced in the Low Countries or brought there by merchants from other countries. In return for their business, Scottish merchants were awarded commercial privileges, agreed by treaty and protected by a 'conservator', who normally resided in the staple town. This was usually located at the great commercial emporium of Bruges, though it was occasionally transferred to Middelburg and from 1507 to Veere. Not surprisingly vibrant migrant communities of Scots emerged in several Netherlandish towns (Stevenson 2000, 93–107).

If towns and, to differing degrees their complex populations, formed part of a commercial network which transcended political boundaries, the horizons of the rural poor were more restricted. Before the fourteenth century military service provided one of the few experiences available of foreign terrain, as able-bodied men joined campaigns across the Tweed. Peasant livelihoods were, however, also in the frontline of invasions. On their northward incursions English armies frequently ravaged the countryside, while Scots reciprocated with scorched-earth tactics. Aliens were a threat and in 1297 peasants near Annan derided an English force as 'tailed dogs', a popular term of Anglophobic abuse throughout Christendom (Rothwell 1957, 307; Ditchburn 2001a, 276). Froissart noted that contempt for French allies was no less reserved and fully reciprocated.

These limited and unfriendly experiences of the foreigner were transformed in the later fourteenth and fifteenth centuries, as the social and economic consequences of the Black Death became apparent. Plague was later medieval Scotland's most significant import, killing an estimated one third of the population. Yet, for many of those who survived the plague, life improved. The shortage of labour ensured that serfdom – by which peasants had been tied to the land, obliged to work for their landlords and sometimes traded like chattels – disappeared. Its last recorded appearance was in 1370 when David II formally freed William son of John, from the royal thanage of Tannadice in Angus (Thomson 1984, no. 345). No longer tied legally to the land, some peasants took advantage of the buoyant demand for labour to find more lucrative remuneration. Military service continued to provide one such opportunity, though the ordinary soldier's horizons were no longer confined to the Anglo-Scottish frontier. Between 1419 and 1424 some 15,000 Scots struggled to thwart resurgent English ambitions in France. This amounted to perhaps one per cent of the entire Scottish population, and its number included men who tradition-ally worked the land as well as the aristocrats who led the campaigns. Thereafter, opportunities in France declined, though several hundred Scots continued to serve the French crown, each engaged on average for about twelve years, with between thirty and forty new recruits arriving annually (Contamine 1992, 19–20). Others – especially in the Highlands and Isles – found service as galloglass, in mercenary forces recruited by the Gaelic lords of Ireland. One (probably exaggerated) estimate suggested that in 1474 ten thousand and more Scots were in Ulster, allegedly planning 'to subdue al thys land to the obeysaunce of the Kyng of Scottes' (Bryan 1933, 18–19).

Soldiering was an intermittent occupation and its rewards were at least as likely to result in death as in fortune. A safer, if less rewarding, option entailed labouring in return for wages. Despite unresolved Anglo-Scottish political tensions and the harsh penalties imposed on migrant labourers in England, many Scots crossed the border in search of work from the fourteenth century. By the 1440s several thousand migrant Scots laboured in Cumberland, Westmorland, Northumberland, Durham and Yorkshire. We know very little about these migrants – from where most came, why they went, how long they stayed, how much they earned – but many were women and several sought naturalisation in England. For most, however, the experience was probably temporary – English employment offering a quicker means to the acquisition of wealth before marriage than was possible in Scotland. England was not, however, the only migrant destination. Others ventured to the Netherlands, France and Scandinavia, though, England aside, most probably headed for eastern Europe. Complaints about Scottish peddlers in Prussia and Poland became frequent from the last quarter of the fifteenth century, and often focused on their attempts to sell cheap merchandise to the rural poor, thereby flouting trading conventions and undermining the interests of established merchants. On other occasions they were accused, as in England, of vagrancy – which suggests a transient labour force seeking short-term employment, as and when it became available.

Migrants clearly believed that better returns for their labour were available abroad. This, in turn, suggests domestic impoverishment, with little economic expansion. Support for this hypothesis is derived from the data relating to overseas trading activities. Imports were, in the main, expensive. They could be paid for either through the sale of exports, or with credit. By the thirteenth century booming wool and leather exports meant that the country enjoyed a balance of payments surplus. But the decline in wool and leather exports from the later fourteenth century, coupled with a deteriorating Anglo-Scottish exchange rate, has led many historians to argue that this trend was subsequently reversed (Grant 1985, 79–82). Not all agree with this assessment. Fish exports were probably more valuable than has previously been thought and to some extent compensated for declining wool sales (Ditchburn 2001a, 192–96). But even if commerce brought wealth to merchants, it did not translate into wider economic development; and many of the poor voted with their feet and walked away.

CONCLUSION

Medieval Scotland's connections with Europe defy simple generalisation, for they varied according to status, gender, location and period. In the twelfth century Scotland was situated on the frontier between Celtic and continental influences. Irish influences did not disappear, but by the fifteenth century they had diminished significantly, even in the north and west. The context in which religious, political and economic life was conducted became increasingly influenced by continental norms and concerns. This transformation is obvious from the reign of David I, who spent most of his youth and middle age at an English court, immersed in French culture. David encouraged like-minded aristocrats and townsmen to settle in Scotland and, though small in number, their cultural, religious and economic expectations soon became fashionable, or at least influential, on all sections of society. Cosmopolitanism was superimposed on an existing society, but did not displace it. Medieval Scots inhabited a world that was simultaneously local, national and international; and although tensions sometimes materialised between these contrasting loyalties, they were neither irreconcilable nor inherently and mutually exclusive.

The principal threats to this tripartite paradigm emerged in the form of David's royal successors and Anglo-Scottish warfare. When Englishmen denied the very existence of the Scottish king's kingdom, it was above all in the latter's interest to ensure that national allegiances transcended all others. The royal interest was coincidentally advanced by the decline in cross-border landholdings and marriage, which had brought Scottish aristocrats into contact with the still largely French-influenced cultural instincts of their English counterparts. Occasional pilgrimages and/or military service abroad were no substitute. French literature did not circulate in later medieval Scotland as freely as it had done in the high middle ages and aristocratic familiarity with the French language diminished. Nevertheless, English ambitions were not thwarted in isolation. Economic and diplomatic connections with the continent were not only maintained but intensified; religious impulses remained fundamentally conditioned by supra-national concerns; and through the stimulus of death and poverty the horizons of the humblest sections of society expanded. The title of this chapter and its rationale is therefore fundamentally misleading. Europe is not a concept to be attached to medieval Scotland. Medieval Scotland was instead both an integral and distinctive component of Christendom.

REFERENCES TO BOOKS AND ARTICLES MENTIONED IN THE TEXT

Barrell, ADM 1995 'The Background to *Cum universi*: Scoto-Papal Relations, 1159–1192', *Innes Review*, 46, 116–38.

Barrow, GWS 2004 'Scots in the Durham *Liber Vitae*', *in* Rollason, D *et al* (eds), *The Durham Liber Viate and its Context*, Woodbridge, 109–16.

Bannatyne Club, 1855 *The Bannatyne Miscellany. Volume III.* Edinburgh.

Blanchard, I 1996 'Lothian and Beyond; the Economy of the 'English empire' of David I', *in* Britnell, R and Hatcher, J (eds), *Progress and Problems in Medieval England: Essays in Honour of Edward Miller*, Cambridge, 23–45.

Bonnar, E 1999 'Scotland's 'Auld Alliance' with France, 1295–1560', *History*, 84, 5–30.

Cameron, S 2000 'Sir James Douglas, Spain and the Holy Land', *in* Brotherstone, T and Ditchburn, D (eds), *Freedom and Authority: Scotland, c.1050–1650*, East Linton, 108–117.

Bryan, D 1933 *Gerald Fitzgerald: The Great Earl of Kildare, 1456–1513.* Dublin and Cork.

Canivez, J-M (ed) 1933–41 *Statuta Captulorum Generalium Ordinis Cisterciensis ab anno 1116 ad annum 1786.* Louvain.

Contamine, P 1992 'Scottish soldiers in France in the second half of the fifteenth century', *in* Simpson, GG (ed), *The Scottish Soldier Abroad, 1247–1967*, Edinburgh, 16–30.

Cowan, EJ 1990 'Norwegian Sunset – Scottish Dawn: Hakon IV and Alexander III', *in* Reid, N (ed), *Scotland in the Reign of Alexander III, 1249–1286*, Edinburgh, 103–31.

Ditcham, BGH 1978 'The Employment of Foreign Mercenary Troops in the French Royal Armies, 1415–1470'. University of Edinburgh: unpublished PhD thesis.

Ditchburn, D 1990 'A note on Scandinavian trade with Scotland in the later middle ages', *in* Simpson, GG (ed), *Scotland and Scandinavia, 800–1800*, Edinburgh, 73–89.

Ditchburn, D 1996 'The place of Guelders in Scottish foreign policy, c.1449–c.1542', *in* Simpson, GG (ed) *Scotland and the Low Countries, 1124–1994*, East Linton, 59–75.

*Ditchburn, D 2001a *Scotland and Europe: The Medieval Kingdom and its Contacts with Christendom, c.1215–1545. Volume I: Religion, Culture and Commerce.* East Linton.

Ditchburn, D 2001b 'Scotland and the Netherlands in the Later Middle Ages: the Other 'Auld Alliance', *Handelingen van de Koninklijke Kring voor Oudenheidkunde, Letteren en Kunst van Mechelen*, 105, 33–55.

Ferguson, PC 1977 *Medieval Papal Representatives in Scotland: Legates, Nuncios and Judges-delegate, 1125–1286.* Edinburgh.

Friedland, K 1983 'Hanseatic Merchants and their Trade with Shetland', *in* DJ Withrington (ed), *Shetland and the Outside World, 1469–1969*, Oxford, 86–95.

Furneaux, I 2004 'Pre-Reformation Scottish Marriage Cases in the Archives of the Papal Penitentiary', *in* Jaritz G, Jørgensen, T and Salonen, K (eds), *The Long Arm of Papal Authority: Late Medieval Christian Peripheries and their Communication with the Holy See* Bergen, Budapest and Krems,60–69

Grant, A 1985 *Independence and Nationhood: Scotland, 1306–1469.* Edinburgh.

Laing, H 1850 *Descriptive Catalogue of Impressions from Ancient Scottish Seals* Edinburgh.

*Macdougall, N 2001 *An Antidote to the English: The Auld Alliance, 1295–1560.* East Linton.

Macfarlane, LJ 1992 'The Elevation of the Diocese of Glasgow into an Archbishopric in 1492', *Innes Review*, 43, 99–118.

McDonald, J 2005 'The Penitentiary and Ecclesiastical Careers: The Scottish Clergy and their Requests to the *Sacra Apostolica Penitenzieria*'. University of Aberdeen: unpublished PhD thesis

Mayhew, N 1990 'Alexander III – A Silver Age? An Essay in Scottish Medieval Economic History' *in* Reid, N (ed), *Scotland in the Reign of Alexander III, 1249–1286*, Edinburgh, 53–73.

Miller, KE 2003 'Ecclesiastical Structural Reform in Ireland and Scotland in the Eleventh and Twelfth Centuries'. University of Aberdeen: unpublished PhD thesis.

Napier, M (ed) 1834 *Memoir of John Napier of Merchiston*. Edinburgh.

O'Keefe T 2004 *The Gaelic Peoples and their Archaeological Identities, A.D. 1000–1650*. Cambridge.

Rothwell, H (ed) 1957 *The Chronicle of Walter of Guisborough*. London.

*Simpson, GG 1977 'The Declaration of Arbroath revitalised', *Scottish Historical Review*, 56, 11–33

Stringer, KJ 1993 *The Reign of Stephen: Kingship, Warfare and Government in Twelfth-Century England*. London.

*Stevenson, A 1996 'The Flemish Dimension of the Auld Alliance', *in* Simpson, GG (ed), *Scotland and the Low Countries*, 28–42.

Stevenson, A 2000 'Medieval Scottish Associations with Bruges', *in* Brotherstone, T and Ditchburn, D (eds), *Freedom and Authority*, 93–107.

Thomson, JM (ed) 1984 *Registrum Magni Sigilli Regum Scotorum. The Register of the Great Seal of Scotland, 1306–1424*. Edinburgh.

Thomson, JAF 1968 'Innocent VIII and the Scottish church', *Innes Review*, 19, 23–31.

Watt, DER 1977 *Biographical Dictionary of Scottish Graduates to A.D. 1410*. Oxford.

Watt, DER 1984 'The Papacy and Scotland in the Fifteenth Century', *in* Dobson, RB (ed), *The Church, Politics and Patronage in the Fifteenth Century*, Stroud 115–29.

Watt, DER (gen. ed) 1987–98 *Scotichronicon by Walter Bower, in Latin and English*. Nine volumes. Aberdeen.

Watt, DER 2000 *Medieval Church Councils in Scotland*. Edinburgh.

FURTHER READING

The items above marked * are recommended for further reading, along with the following:

Brotherstone, T and Ditchburn, D 2000 '1320 and a' that: the Declaration of Arbroath and the Remaking of Scottish History', *in* Brotherstone, T and Ditchburn, D (eds), *Freedom and Authority*, 10–31.

Cowan, EJ 2003 *For Freedom Alone. The Declaration of Arbroath, 1320*. (Chs 3 and 4 especially.) East Linton.

Ditchburn, D 1988 'Trade with Northern Europe, 1297–1540' *in* Lynch, M, Spearman, M and Stell, G (eds), *The Scottish Medieval Town*, Edinburgh, 161–79.

Stevenson, A 1988 'Trade with the South, 1070–1513' *in* Lynch, M, Spearman, M and Stell, G (eds.), *The Scottish Medieval Town*, 180–206.

CHAPTER EIGHT

Townlife and Trade

— *Elizabeth Ewan*

Modern Scotland is a highly-urbanised country, with most of its people living in towns and cities, but in the middle ages the vast majority of the population lived in the countryside. Although there are no population statistics to tell us exactly what proportion of the population lived in rural areas, historians estimate that the medieval urban population was never more than 10 per cent. However, the impact of the towns on the medieval realm was out of proportion to their share of the population.

What would a traveller have seen on approaching a medieval Scottish town? The first building visible would probably have been a castle and/or a cathedral or monastery, the residence of the town overlord. Unlike many urban communities in medieval Europe, the town was unlikely to have been marked off by a town wall. Few medieval Scottish towns had walls, Perth and Berwick being early exceptions. Some towns such as Edinburgh built walls in the fifteenth century, but most relied on natural defences or on relatively flimsy gates at the end of individual properties. As a result, the sharp physical distinction between town and countryside found in many European countries was not as marked in medieval Scotland.

On entering the town itself, perhaps by crossing a bridge across a river, or embarking from a ship in the harbour, the visitor would have been confronted with a long main street. This often widened out in the middle to accommodate a market place. Here were sited the most prestigious structures in the town – the homes and shops of merchants and wealthy craftsmen, the parish kirk, the tolbooth (the townhouse, the seat of municipal government and the place where market tolls were collected), the tron (the public weighbeam) and, presiding over all, the market cross, the symbol of the king's peace. The marketplace was the heart of the medieval town, trade its very reason for existence.

Houses were usually crowded together along the street, each with its own long narrow plot, known as a burgage, so that as many households as possible could take advantage of the commercial opportunities offered by frontage on the market place. Between them ran narrow wynds and closes, giving access to the extensive backlands of these properties and leading to secondary streets. Here the majority of the urban population lived, less visible in the records but just as crucial as the merchant and craft elite for the successful functioning of the town. Together these inhabitants made up a town, a place where 'a significant proportion (but not necessarily a majority) of its population lives off trade, industry, administration, and [a variety of] other non-agricultural occupations' (Lynch, Spearman and Stell 1988, 1).

HISTORIANS AND THE MEDIEVAL TOWN

While there has long been interest in the history of individual Scottish towns, the study of urban history in general is a more recent development. The seeds were sown in the nineteenth and early twentieth centuries with the work of historical publishing clubs which published extracts from the surviving local records of towns such as Aberdeen, Edinburgh, Peebles, and Inverness. These works inspired some historians to publish records from other towns such as Dunfermline, Stirling and Lanark. Some local historians and town archivists produced histories based on the manuscript records (Kennedy 1818; Maxwell 1891; Adams 1929). The few studies of Scottish towns in general tended to focus on such issues as origins and local government (Murray 1924–32; MacKenzie 1949).

Urban history in Europe and England began to flourish as a discipline in the 1960s, partly as an offshoot of the new interest in social history, although in Scotland it did not really begin until the late 1970s. The Scottish Burgh Survey, established at the University of Glasgow, and later continued by the Centre for Scottish Urban History, surveyed the surviving historical and archaeological evidence for Scotland's towns, pointing the way to future research (Dennison 1999). Studies of individual towns appeared from the 1980s (Torrie 1994; Booton 1988a; Torrie 1990). A 1988 essay collection demonstrated a variety of ways to approach the subject, examining trade, architecture, industry, guilds, parish churches, townscape and law (Lynch, Spearman and Stell 1988). More general studies of medieval towns also began to appear (Lynch 1988; Ewan 1990). Recently, urban historians have turned to such subjects as women's work, urban families, and popular piety (Mayhew 1999; Ewan 2000; Dennison 2002). Work on Scotland is beginning to be integrated into studies of urban life in the British Isles as a whole (Swanson 1999; Palliser 2000), although for some recent medieval European historians, urban life still appears to have come to a halt at the Tweed (Nicholas 1997).

What types of sources exist? The earliest records for most towns are the royal charters that granted them the special legal and commercial privileges associated with burghal status. Such documents are often all that survive for the twelfth and thirteenth centuries. From the late fourteenth century, the records of local government, especially those of the local council and burgh court, begin to appear – the earliest, those of Aberdeen, start in 1398 (with a fragment from 1317). In the fifteenth century, records of guild merchants, which regulated many of the trading activities of the town, also appear for towns such as Perth and Dunfermline. In these sources can be found the statutes that local officials passed to regulate the life of the community, the admissions of individuals as burgesses, the records of wrong-doing by those who broke local laws, the complex webs of debt and credit among the inhabitants, responses to crises such as plague, warfare, and shortages of food. There are records of celebration and civic pride, the erection and improvement of civic buildings and local churches, religious processions and mystery plays, festive occasions and saints' days. Registers of religious houses and parish churches can tell historians much about the spiritual life of the town and its inhabitants.

From the later fifteenth century much information can be found in the protocol books of urban notaries who recorded the many transactions involving urban property. Land was the main form of wealth in the middle ages – it also conferred prestige and legal status. To be a burgess one had to hold property in the burgh. Detailed descriptions of the property boundaries sometimes allow the reconstruction of the layout of medieval tenements, while inheritance cases throw light on family and social networks.

Central government records also reveal much about medieval towns. The Exchequer Rolls, beginning in the early fourteenth century, record exports of goods that were subject to customs duties. At first, these consisted of wool, woolfells (fleeces) and hides, but later other commodities were added. These records thus provide a picture of Scotland's overseas trade, which was centred in the burghs. The Treasurers' Accounts from the later fifteenth century illustrate the activities of Scottish merchants who supplied the royal household, as well as the monarch's interactions with local people. Other royal records show grants by the kings to the towns and individual inhabitants. English and European records also provide glimpses into the activities of Scottish merchants (Flett and Cripps 1988).

As well as these traditional documentary sources, there are many others; one of the hallmarks of recent urban history has been historians' increased willingness to use non-traditional sources (Dennison 2000). Literary sources often shed light on contemporary urban settings (Bawcutt 1992, 45–7, 150–3; Fradenburg 1991, ch. 1– 4). A poem by William Dunbar, addressed to the merchants of Edinburgh, paints a particularly vivid picture of the bustling and smelly marketplace of Scotland's most important town at the end of the fifteenth century. Accounts by foreign travellers from the late thirteenth century onwards often include comments on Scottish towns (Hume Brown 1891).

Unfortunately few visual sources survive. The earliest representation of a town, in a mid fifteenth-century manuscript of Walter Bower's *Scotichronicon*, shows Stirling as background to a depiction of the Battle of Bannockburn. The earliest map is one of St Andrews from the mid-sixteenth century. However, because of the tendency of plot boundaries, streets, and major institutions such as townhouses and churches to remain static for centuries, later maps can be used to reconstruct medieval towns and their expansion and growth over the medieval period (Dennison 2000, 279–80).

Medieval parish churches (often much altered by later building work) still exist in many towns, although few secular buildings remain. Provand's Lordship in Glasgow was the townhouse of a cathedral priest. However, medieval remains have been identified in a number of urban buildings (Dennison 2000, 282), and possibly more will be found, adding to our knowledge. A house in Advocate's Close, Edinburgh may date from the fifteenth century, as may parts of other High Street houses such as Gladstone's Land.

Since the 1970s, archaeological evidence has become the most important new source for those studying Scotland's medieval towns. Excavations in Perth's High Street in the mid 1970s revealed a hitherto unsuspected wealth of evidence lying under the streets and houses of the modern town. Since then, there have been other excavations in several towns such as St Andrews, Canongate (the Scottish Parliament site) and Linlithgow, although it is the work in Aberdeen and Perth that has been most extensive to date (Murray 1982; Holdsworth 1988). Archaeological evidence is especially valuable for what it can tell us about those features of urban life which do not appear in the records – types of housing, diet, craft activities (Dennison 2000, 277–8; Yeoman 1995, ch. 4, 5).

ORIGINS AND GROWTH

The origin of Scotland's towns has been much debated, partly because historians have defined towns in different ways. If a strictly legal definition is used – a town must have a charter creating it as a burgh with defined jurisdictional privileges – it can be argued that the first towns were created in the reign of David I (1124–53). However, if a more organic view of the town is used, evidence suggests that many burghs existed as urban settlements before the twelfth century. Probably the earliest 'urban' settlements were the later iron-age hillforts, places such as Traprain Law in East Lothian. In later centuries, the populations shifted to adjacent sites more suited for their needs, closer to water transportation routes, and arable land. Other towns such as Glasgow and St Andrews grew up around pilgrimage sites and shrines associated with the work of early saints, with a small trading community beside the shrine providing for the needs of visitors. David I and his successors' grants of legal and commercial privileges to many of these settlements helped bring them into the network of European medieval towns which had been developing from c.1000 (Lynch, Spearman and Stell 1988, 1–3; Hall 2002, 10–11).

The Scottish kings' main motive for establishing burghs was to promote trade, especially overseas trade, although other concerns such as defence were involved in some foundations – for example, several of the Moray burghs were probably established to create a strong royal presence in a previously turbulent area (McNeill 1996, 197). Inducements were offered to encourage settlement, both by Scots and by people from outside the realm. Surname evidence suggests that many of the early settlers came from Flanders or England. Settlers were offered certain legal privileges – the right to hold land in return for a money rent instead of labour service, the right to alienate property, and the freedom to buy and sell free of toll. In some burghs, the first inhabitants were offered *kirset*, a period of time in which they could hold their property rent-free. After this, they owed a yearly rent for their land to the burgh overlord. Unusually for European medieval towns, many burghs were also granted 'liberties', an area in their hinterland where burgesses enjoyed a monopoly on the trade in wool, woolfells and hides. All such goods had to be brought to the burgh for sale. These liberties could be very extensive – Aberdeen's included all of Aberdeenshire (McNeill 1996, 234–5). Foreign merchants were also restricted to purchasing goods from the burgesses – there were no officially sanctioned rural markets in Scotland (although occasional glimpses are caught of unofficial ones when burghs complained about them to the king).

Most early burghs were established by the king or by ecclesiastical lords. The great numbers of market towns chartered by local lords in other parts of Europe were not typical of Scotland's early urban development. However, in the fifteenth century the foundation of burghs of barony dramatically increased. This was very late by European standards; elsewhere such towns were numerous by the thirteenth century. Proportionately, many more of the baronial burghs failed than the royal or ecclesiastical burghs. In contrast to royal burghs, the new foundations had much more limited trading rights and privileges, and most functioned mainly as centres of local trade (McNeill 1996, 213).

Because of the centrality of trade to town life, urban fortunes were closely tied to economic developments in the kingdom as a whole. Some early towns became the sites of mints as kings began to produce a Scottish coinage. The majority of burghs were established in the east of the kingdom, facing Scotland's main trading partners on the Continent and the east coast ports of England. Scotland was primarily an exporter of raw materials and an importer of manufactured goods. The twelfth and thirteenth centuries were a period of increasing international trade. The growing cloth towns of the Low Countries were hungry for wool, and Scotland was well-positioned to supply them. Scottish merchants were numerous enough in Bruges to have their own quarter in the town in the later thirteenth century. As a major entrepot for trade between Northern Europe and the Mediterranean, Bruges provided the manufactured and luxury goods that Scottish merchants could take back to customers at home (Stevenson 1988). On the west coast, there was a more limited trade with Ireland and some western English ports. There must also have been fairly extensive inland trade, although this has left less trace in the records and, as a result, is harder to quantify.

This heyday of trade and prosperity came to an end with the outbreak of the Wars of Independence. English embargoes ended Anglo-Scottish trade while English ships disrupted Scottish trade with the Continent (although illegal trade and piracy flourished). Relations with the Low Countries remained generally amicable, although periodically affected by English attacks and the changing political allegiances which resulted from the Hundred Years War between England and France (1337–1453). Indeed Flemish trade may have increased from the 1350s. Increasing expansion in the production of cheaper wool cloth meant a renewed demand for Scottish wool, which was of inferior quality and cheaper than English wool, and wool exports boomed in the 1370s. The effects of the Black Death of 1347–50 and war, however, affected all European trade, and Scotland's wool trade declined drastically in the later fourteenth century. Although there were short-term recoveries during the fifteenth century, it never again reached the heights it had enjoyed during the 1370s.

The vacuum created by the loss of Berwick to England in the fourteenth century was filled by the rise of Edinburgh. Indeed the story of Scotland's trade and towns in the later middle ages is dominated by the increasing power of Edinburgh, economically, administratively, and culturally. By the late fifteenth century, the town controlled 70 per cent of Scotland's total wool exports. To meet the challenge of changing trade patterns, some towns diversified. Perth expanded its manufacturing base, while Dundee sought out new markets for exports of woollen cloth. Stirling concentrated more on hide exports, northern burghs increasingly on salmon, west coast towns on hides and then herring (McNeill 1996, 244–7).

There has been some debate about the extent of Scotland's economic decline in the later middle ages. The export records show a sharp decrease in overseas trade, but how representative are they of Scotland's overseas trade as a whole? In the fourteenth century, only wool, woolfells and hides were subject to customs duties and therefore recorded. Scots also exported other goods, including fish, animal skins and salt. In the fifteenth century, although duties were imposed on more exports, the records still only provide a partial picture. Wool in the form of cheap cloth may have made up for some of the decline in wool exports, as well as encouraging domestic industry. Falling exchange rates may also have encouraged domestic production by making imports more expensive. The shortage of silver, which has been seen as evidence for a growing trade deficit, was a condition affecting most European countries at this period. It has even been argued that the price inflation that affected Scotland in the fifteenth century could be indicative of rising demand, implying that some people had money to spend (Gemmill 1995, 371–81). The building projects taken on in several towns in the late middle ages suggest that at least some of these were townspeople. Moreover, there are almost no records of the trade within the kingdom that would have made an important contribution to the economy of the towns. (Booton 1988b).

How did those townspeople who were not overseas merchants make their living? The focus of existing records on exports means that it is harder for historians to uncover evidence for crafts than for trade. However, archaeological evidence has helped reveal something of the variety of activities.

Basic needs of nourishment were supplied by food producers, the most important being bakers of bread and brewers of ale. The activities of baxters (bakers) and brewsters (brewers) were regulated from the twelfth or thirteenth century, and it became common practice in Scottish towns to regulate the price of both commodities to ensure a reasonably-priced supply for the townspeople. Brewing was dominated by women throughout the middle ages; baking was more commonly practised by men, although in some towns, especially smaller ones, female bakers were also common. Baking was both a domestic and commercial activity – professional baxters probably used larger ovens, some of which have been uncovered in excavation. In larger towns such as Aberdeen, female cake-bakers provided competition to the bakers of wheat bread, providing the cheaper oatcakes that were the staple food of the poor. These could be baked over a hearth fire while the cakebakers were carrying out other domestic tasks, and thus fitted the patterns of women's lives better than full-time baking (Ewan 2000). For the wealthier inhabitants of the town, meat was also available – there is some evidence that the consumption of meat increased in the later middle ages in Scotland, although it was to fall back again in the sixteenth century. Other foodstuffs came from the sea and the countryside. Townspeople also earned a living by selling such goods, either buying them directly from rural producers, or purchasing supplies in the market and reselling them in smaller quantities to those who could not afford to buy wholesale.

Most crafts used the raw materials that came into the town from the countryside. Wool provided materials for small-scale local cloth industry; the presence of dyers and fullers in many early towns suggests that not all wool was exported. The decline in the wool trade in the later fourteenth century may have led to a revival of the domestic cloth industry – dyers, weavers, fullers and tailors all appear in the town records of the fifteenth century. Other workers included combers, carders and spinners who turned the wool into yarn, the majority of them probably women.

The export trade in hides helped provide leather and other products from cattle for local craftspeople. This was supplemented by the livestock kept by many townspeople, who grazed them on the common lands of the town and kept them in byres and pens in the backlands behind their houses. Leather provided raw materials for tanners, saddlers, shoemakers, cobblers, belt-makers, armourers and others; excavated shoes show some townspeople keeping up with the latest fashions in medieval footwear. Cattle and goats also provided the raw material for horn and bone workers – in Perth horn-working appears to have been a major industry. Antler working was also practised in many towns.

Wood provided shelter and fuel – most urban dwellings were built of wood. Wood was crucial for boats and ferries to make water transport feasible, and for bridges. There was a boat-building industry at Inverness in the late thirteenth century. Coopers provided barrels, woodworkers produced bowls, plates, spoons and cups. There is some evidence of a shortage of good wood in the later middle ages and imports from the Baltic and Scandinavia became more common.

Another craft revealed by archaeology is the pottery industry. The pottery evidence, however, illustrates the care with which archaeological evidence must be used. Because pottery survives better than most other artefacts, there is a danger in overestimating its importance. Moreover, it is not clear that the pottery industry was an urban one – a kiln has yet to be found in an urban excavation. There is more substantial evidence for working of metals such as bronze, silver and iron, although the iron was probably smelted outside the town. Lead was used for roofing, windows and pipes. In some of the larger towns, with sufficient wealthy inhabitants to support them, luxury trades such as goldsmithing also existed (Spearman 1988).

Trade was tightly controlled, with numerous regulations intended to deter cheating and sharp practice, and ensure fair treatment of the customer. Some of the earliest laws dealt with weights and measures; each burgess was allowed to have a measure for corn, an ellwand for measuring cloth, and a stone and pound weight to weigh other goods – each of these measures was to be marked with the burgh seal in order to indicate that it conformed to standards set by the town. For historians, these local statutes, as well as court cases involving those who broke them, provide a vivid picture of the medieval marketplace.

Responsibility for regulating local trade and industry lay largely with the burgesses themselves. From the thirteenth century, it becomes possible to trace the growth of urban government. Burghs were originally under the control of the overlord's officials. The official chose local men, known as *prepositi*, to assist him. During the thirteenth and fourteenth centuries, many towns took on increasing responsibility for their own affairs. In some, it became practice to choose each year one *prepositus* (provost) who would be aided by three or four *ballivi* (baillies). In many towns, the work of the provost and baillies was aided by a council, chosen annually. The size of the council could vary considerably; late thirteenth-century Berwick had a council of 24 members, although this was unusually large, reflecting its position as Scotland's pre-eminent town at that time. As the economy and occupational structure of towns grew more complex, additional offices were established, including sergeands to carry out the administration of justice and sentences ordered by the burgh court, ale and wine tasters to supervise the quality and price of ale and wine, flesh prisers to do the same for meat, liners to safeguard boundaries between burgage plots, a treasurer to look after the burgh revenues and a town clerk to keep a record of government decisions and burgh court proceedings.

Many early burghs also had guild merchants, associations of the leading members of society. The laws of the Berwick guild survive from the thirteenth century. Seventeen burghs had such guilds by 1500. They were often involved in the organisation of the town and admitting burgesses. With the same individuals being both members of the guild and part of the town government, the functions between the two bodies often overlapped, although the guild tended to focus largely on issues relating to trade, especially overseas trade. Weavers, fleshers, dyers and fullers were supposed to be excluded, but when the guild records of Dunfermline and Perth begin in the fifteenth century, these crafts are found among the members. In some larger towns such as Edinburgh, the formation of craft guilds in the fifteenth century may have led to increasing social differentiation between the members of the merchant and craft guilds, but in smaller towns the guild merchant remained an organisation for both merchants and craftsmen (McNeill 1996, 215).

One development which may have helped strengthen the progress of burghs towards self-government was the granting of feu-ferme charters. Originally each burgess owed an annual payment for his property to the king. Market tolls and the fines of justice were also paid to the king, being collected by royal officers. By the mid-thirteenth century, some towns may already have been paying the king a lump sum in place of the individual rents, but Berwick was the first town to benefit from a formal feu-ferme charter, which replaced the individual revenues owed to the king with one fixed annual payment in perpetuity. Robert I granted a feu-ferme charter to Aberdeen in 1319 while Edinburgh received one in 1329. At least 22 burghs had them by the early fifteenth century (McNeill 1996, 212). The burgesses were now responsible for the collection of the annual payment, but they also benefited from the use of any surplus, known in most towns as 'the common good'. Where there was money to spend, an administration would usually develop to spend it.

The burgh court was the central administrative organ in most towns – here statutes were decided by the town officials, burgh accounts were presented, new burgesses and guild brethren were admitted, court cases involving the townspeople were heard, debts, agreements and property transactions were registered, and fines were collected. If a town had its own tolbooth, this was usually the site of the court. Such buildings became increasingly elaborate in the later middle ages, and symbolised the power and status of the town. In smaller towns, burgh courts might be held in church buildings or even in the open air.

The head courts of the burgh were held three times a year. All burgesses had a duty to attend these courts; those who did not were fined. At the head courts, acts and statutes affecting the whole community were proclaimed and actions were taken concerning urban property. At the Michaelmas headcourt (held shortly after 29 September) the year's burgh officials were elected. Disputes would also be heard at other courts which met more frequently. Burghs had the right to 'repledge' (claim jurisdiction over) their burgesses from other courts, and could hear most civil cases, although their competence over criminal cases was more limited. However, beginning with Perth in 1394, several towns began to be granted increased criminal jurisdiction when they received royal grants giving them the legal powers of sheriffdoms.

There is evidence that town government in Scotland, in common with that of most medieval countries, became less representative and more oligarchic in the fifteenth century. Where evidence exists for early elections, councils seem to have been chosen by all the burgesses of the town. However, an act of parliament of 1469 stipulated that in future the new council would be chosen by the old council, thus ensuring a perpetuation of office holding among a small elite. Although the act may not have been observed in every town, 11 families dominated the office-holding of Aberdeen from 1450 to 1530 (Booton 1988a). Other fifteenth-century parliamentary legislation included statutes establishing deacons for the crafts to supervise their work. This could be seen as broadening participation in local government responsibilities, but because the deacons were answerable to the council, it was more likely that it was intended to give the merchant-dominated council more control over the crafts (Swanson, 1988). In the later fifteenth century there is evidence of some agitation by the crafts for more representation on the town council – the issue would dog many town governments in the sixteenth century, although recent work has suggested that the traditional picture of merchant-crafts conflict was more complex than it first appears (Lynch, 1984).

Burghs also played a role in national politics – the earliest recorded burghal participation in national assemblies occurred in 1296 when six royal burghs added their seals to the Franco-Scottish treaty. Their first participation in parliament was probably in 1326. More active participation began when money was needed to raise David II's ransom from 1357 – because the main revenues would come from wool exports, the merchants' agreement was required. The representatives of royal burghs (and later a selected number of non-royal burghs such as St Andrews), who made up the third estate of parliament, appear to have regularly attended parliament from the later years of David's reign. David's grant of privileges to 'our burghs' in 1364 helped set royal burghs apart from others in their trading privileges, and parliamentary representation and responsibility for paying parliamentary-imposed taxation came to symbolise another difference in status.

The burgh commissioners gradually became less representative of the community as a whole. The 1469 act of parliament which brought in the practice of the old council choosing the new meant that the burgh commissioners, chosen by the council, were representative only of the elite. The influence of the burgess members of parliament may have been felt mainly in legislation on trade, taxation, and urban privileges, although burgesses sat on the judicial committees of parliament in the fifteenth century. However, the extent of burgh participation in parliament in the later fifteenth century was not great – the majority of burghs entitled to send representatives from 1490 to the mid-sixteenth century did not do so (MacDonald 2005).

The burghs also had their own national forum, unique in Europe. The court of the Four Burghs met from at least the late thirteenth century. It heard cases from local burgh courts and deliberated on matters affecting urban communities as a whole. It became the practice for burgh representatives to meet before sittings of parliaments or general councils, in order to prepare proposed legislation. In the later fifteenth century, the court developed into the Convention of Royal Burghs, which was officially established by parliament in 1487, although the act may not have taken effect immediately (MacDonald 2005).

The propensity among the royal burghs for collective action may have been strengthened by another feature uncommon in medieval Europe. Scotland had its own collection of burgh laws, the earliest ones dating from the twelfth and thirteenth centuries. There is some debate about the extent to which towns felt bound to follow these laws exactly, but local governments make reference to the burgh laws in stating decisions, and the general practices laid down in them seem to have been carried out in most burgh courts. The Court of the Four Burghs heard cases arising from the burgh laws, and provided a forum for the burghs to decide amongst themselves how they should be interpreted.

LIFE IN THE TOWN

Scottish towns were small in comparison to many of their English and European counterparts. Most had less than 1000 people. Even the largest towns probably had under 5000 inhabitants for most of the middle ages. The earliest surviving tax list for a Scottish town was compiled in Aberdeen in 1408 and has 350 names on it – this may suggest a population of about 3000 (Ewan 1990, 5). Only Edinburgh, which far outstripped all other Scottish towns in its dominance of trade and politics, was an exception, possibly reaching 12,000 by the mid-sixteenth century.

There is little documentary evidence about the dwellings in which most of these people lived; although some descriptions can be found in the notaries' protocol books, most evidence for early housing comes from archaeology. Early dwellings were mainly of wood. The commonest type of house was a one-storey, wattle-and-daub structure. This consisted of wooden upright stakes, between which were woven wattles or flexible twigs, with a cladding of clay (or occasionally dung) to provide insulation. The roof was of thatch, the floors of clay or gravel, covered with straw. Warmth, light and cooking facilities were provided by a central hearth. Water came from a nearby well or from rainwater collected in barrels. In some early houses, as in the countryside, a byre was attached, the body heat of the livestock providing additional warmth for the inhabitants. It has been estimated that the typical life-span of one of these dwellings was about twenty-five years. (HK Murray 1982).

Over time, changes in construction techniques extended the life of domestic buildings. Larger houses were probably timber-framed with wattle-and-daub infill. By the fourteenth century, the first stone houses are mentioned, although they did not become common until towards the end of the middle ages. In some constricted urban sites, physical limits to expansion outwards, led to expansion upwards, and buildings began to grow in height. The most extreme example of this was Edinburgh, where by the sixteenth century, many of the houses along the steep ridge extending down from the castle reached a height of five or six storeys. In most towns, however, two storeys with perhaps a cellar, was the maximum height for most domestic buildings.

Frontage buildings often combined a workshop/shop with living quarters for the family, either above or behind the business premises. The stone commercial booths can still be seen today at the front of John Knox's House in Edinburgh. Sometimes the workshop was situated further back in the property, with the booth on the frontage used for selling the products of the workshop. The backlands had gardens for growing vegetables to supplement the family diet, stockades for livestock, living quarters for servants and other employees, and middens for waste disposal. As towns grew in size, the backlands often became subdivided and filled in with housing for other families.

Urban households were economic as well as social units. Workshops and businesses generally involved the whole family with the male head of the household (or the female head if the male head had died) in charge of business decisions, the wife and children as workers and sometimes retailers of the products, and servants and apprentices also working there. As was common across Europe, the husband was legal head of the household. Any property belonging to the wife came under his administration for the duration of the marriage. Women could inherit property if there were no male heirs; it was common also to provide for daughters at the time of their marriage. As a result, marriages often resulted in considerable transfers of ownership of property. The protocol books show considerable amounts of female property-holding. One common practice was for a spouse to resign his or her property and have it regranted to both spouses as a conjunct fee, which ensured that the surviving spouse continued to hold the property after the other spouse's death. Although a widow was legally entitled to a third of her husband's property for the rest of her life, it could be difficult to enforce this – the conjunct fee seems to have developed to provide a more secure holding for widows. The need to provide for widows was widespread as they headed between 10 and 20 per cent of urban households.

Women's responsibilities included the care and provisioning of the household. As well as producing food and drink in the home, and sometimes selling the surplus for profit, in urban families they and their servants carried out most of the marketing. The marketplaces of medieval towns were thronged with women; men might dominate in the more formal public arenas of the court, the church and the tolbooth, but women were a ubiquitous and vocal presence on the streets.

There were schools in several towns by the late middle ages, although probably only a minority of burgh children received formal education. A few may have attended the universities founded in St Andrews, Glasgow and Aberdeen in the fifteenth century. Boys were often apprenticed to a craft. Girls were occasionally apprenticed, but were more likely to spend their adolescence in a period of domestic service, learning the skills required for running their own household. Servants, like children, came under the authority of the head of the household. While lands generally went to the eldest son, moveable goods were divided between all the children – boys and girls – although the eldest son as heir was entitled to certain heirship goods.

Because much family life took place in the private sphere it is difficult for historians to penetrate the walls of medieval households and to eavesdrop on the relationships between family members, although there has been an increasing interest in such topics in urban history. Glimpses of interpersonal relations can be had through the occasional recording of family disputes, when aggrieved parties wished to have their complaints formally recorded by a notary. Inheritance disputes sometimes surfaced to disrupt peaceful family relations, some of them originating at the deathbed itself.

Death came to every family, but disease and war could hasten it. Increasing numbers of hospitals were established in towns in the fifteenth century (McNeill 1996, 344–5), although many were intended for the poor rather than the sick. The infirmaries of religious houses might also offer health care. Most medical care was carried out at home, although from the fourteenth century apothecaries, physicians (leeches) and surgeons (barbours) began to be numbered among the inhabitants of several towns.

The disease which cast most fear into people's hearts from the fourteenth century onwards was the plague, usually referred to as 'the pest'. The Black Death of 1348–50 is estimated to have killed up to a quarter of the population, but there were frequent outbreaks for the rest of the middle ages. Towns, with their crowded living conditions and poor sanitation, may have been particularly badly hit. Local authorities made stringent efforts to try to ward off an approaching plague or to control its spread once it had hit. All strangers coming from an area known to be infected were forbidden to enter the town, and any infected townsfolk were either quarantined in their house until they had died or recovered, or were sent to isolated areas outside the town. The penalties for disobeying such laws included banishment and even death.

As well as outbreaks of plague, the inhabitants of towns suffered from other diseases. Skeletal remains from over 2,000 individuals have been excavated in recent decades and have begun to provide evidence for some of the other diseases which townspeople suffered, including tuberculosis, malnutrition, and arthritis (Yeoman 1995, 84–5). One of the most endemic diseases in the medieval town was leprosy, although other disfiguring diseases were sometimes lumped together with it. A person diagnosed with leprosy was removed from the town, usually to the leper hospitals, which were established just beyond the borders of the town. Lepers were isolated in order to prevent infection of others, although the infection feared may have been as much moral as physical, as leprosy was associated in the popular imagination with sexual sin.

Another disease that hit medieval towns at the close of the fifteenth century, more securely linked with sexual behaviour, was syphilis. One of the first towns hit was Aberdeen in 1497. On April 24, the authorities put into place measures to prevent the spread of the disease. The focus was on 'light women' (prostitutes) whom the council attempted to force into other trades; their customers faced no such restrictions. However, when the disease reached Edinburgh in September, all persons, men and women, suffering from it were banished to the island of Inchkeith in the Forth until they recovered (Dennison 2002, 75–6).

The sick people described above were banished temporarily from the town, but was there a place for everyone within the urban community? To what extent was there a sense of community in the medieval town? Some historians have suggested that a medieval sense of community was increasingly lost with the population growth, increasing poverty and religious changes of the sixteenth century (Lynch 1984). Others have questioned whether such a sense of community embracing the whole population of the town ever existed at all (Dennison 1998). Looking beyond the burgess elite at those groups (the poor, non-burgesses, women) who were not enfranchised members of the burgh, historians have questioned to what extent they were considered part of the community.

Although there is not room here to discuss all groups, something can be said about the poor. The early burgh laws recognised that some inhabitants might fall into poverty and made provisions to help them, for example by making it possible for them to alienate land away from their heirs if necessary. Guild laws made provision for brethren who fell into poverty. Hospitals were also founded for the poor. The poor were originally regarded as suitable recipients of Christian charity, but by the fifteenth century there is evidence of hardening attitudes to at least some of the poor, perhaps as worsening economic conditions and population growth made them more visible to the authorities. Parliament legislated against beggars as early as 1425, trying to force them to find work. Towns also began to pass laws regulating beggars; licensed beggars, generally those who had been born in the town or had lived there for a long time, were given tokens permitting them to beg, while unlicensed beggars were ordered expelled from the town. Increasingly distinctions were being made between those who were considered part of the town and those who were not.

On the other hand, there were also forces that acted to unify the community, especially those connected with religion. It has been estimated that in Aberdeen around 1500 about one in every 20 adult males was a priest, chaplain, monk or friar. As well as churches and chapels, and the abbeys or cathedrals of overlords in ecclesiastical burghs, the towns, as centres of population, were the favoured sites for the orders of friars which began to come to Scotland from the thirteenth century. Some of the larger burghs had three or four houses of friars by the late middle ages (Dennison 2002, 289).

One feature that distinguished Scottish towns from those elsewhere was the fact that the inhabitants all belonged to the same parish. This meant that the inhabitants worshipped as a community, a *corpus christianum* (a Christian body) and that the parish church acted as a symbol of the town, its 'architectural and ritual focus' (Fawcett 1997, 13). In the mid-fourteenth century, individual townspeople gave to St Nicholas' kirk in Aberdeen new images of many saints, priests' vestments and two great bells named Lawrence and Mary (Cooper 1892, 12–17). In towns where craft guilds developed, individual crafts, such as the websters of Edinburgh in 1475, maintained altars which became the visible symbol of their piety and wealth (not necessarily in that order) and acted as a focus of their identity. Many merchant guilds established an altar of the Holy Blood, reflecting the popular religious cult which had become widespread in the Low Countries in the fifteenth century, and was probably brought back by merchants trading overseas (Ditchburn 2001, 52–3). Wealthy individuals also established altars, where masses were said for their soul to ensure the safety of their soul after death, and where the very visible signs of their wealth and piety ensured that the reputation of their families would live on in the collective memory of the town's inhabitants. St Nicholas, Aberdeen had at least 30 altars by the late middle ages, while St Giles, Edinburgh had over 40. Some towns campaigned to have their parish church erected into a collegiate church incorporating all the priests into one college, emulating cathedrals. The first of these was Dunbar. Of the larger towns, only Edinburgh was successful before 1500 after a campaign which lasted several decades, although several more towns were able to establish collegiate churches in the early sixteenth century (McNeill 1996, 346; Fawcett 1997).

From the later fourteenth century, a number of towns rebuilt and extended their parish churches such as St John's in Perth and Holy Rude in Stirling. While some of the rebuilding was a response to earlier destruction, much of the late medieval work on parish churches arose from other motives – pride in the town's identity and the building which represented the heart of the Christian community. Often these projects involved the town taking on new responsibilities. In many burgh churches, part of the building belonged to a religious house, but in the fifteenth century many towns made agreements with these houses to take over the maintenance of the entire church. The masons engaged were often the best available, men who had worked on royal palaces and other prestigious projects and were familiar with the latest architectural fashions from the Continent (Fawcett 1997). The interesting thing about these building programmes is that they seem to have developed just as the overseas trade which provided the revenues was decreasing. Some historians have argued that this shows the importance of religion to the town, as an increasing proportion of decreasing revenues was devoted to such purposes; others have suggested that perhaps the decline in prosperity was less than has been thought.

Religion permeated every aspect of medieval life; this was especially true of those occasions on which local authorities tried to bring the townspeople together. Guilds united their members in the upkeep of services at their chosen altar, and emphasized their solidarity by requiring all brethren to be present at the funeral of any member. The resources of the guild were also used in acts of Christian charity, paying for the funeral of impoverished members and providing maintenance for poor widows and orphans. Holy days provided other opportunities to bring the entire community of the town together. Annual Corpus Christi processions, as well as processions on the day of the town's patron saint, involved all the different crafts of the town in putting on pageants and processing through the town. In many towns, one or two men were chosen annually as the 'abbot of unreason' and his prior (or later Robin Hood and Little John) to look after such plays and festivities (Mill 1969).

However, as historians have pointed out, such activities could create a sense of exclusion as well as one of inclusion (Dennison 1998). Even among those groups who were included, there was a definite sense of hierarchy which might not be conducive to feelings of harmony – every craft had its place and disputes sometimes broke out over who should enjoy the most prestigious positions within the procession. Nor did every craftsman wish to participate. Some town councils had to threaten penalties against those who did not appear. Moreover, the disorder which sometimes accompanied the festivities presided over by the Abbot of Unreason led to periodic clampdowns on the office by the authorities both local and national (Mill 1969).

What did community mean for the individual townsperson? Did most inhabitants feel that they belonged to the urban community? It can be argued that the authorities wished to think so and they believed that they controlled access to it. This can best be seen in the way in which towns dealt with serious discord between their inhabitants. Rather than simply fining or punishing the guilty party, there was often an elaborate ceremony, based on religious penance rituals, which was used to restore peace to the fractured community and to bring the offender back within it. Whether this was really effective for the individual concerned remains open to question.

The Scottish medieval town was a vibrant living community. Historians, archaeologists and other scholars continue to shed new light on the towns, although more studies of individual towns are needed, as well as more studies of the different social groups within the town. Many questions are still being debated. Was there a sense of community? How did towns react to the changing fortunes of the late middle ages? To what extent were towns separate from the countryside? Such questions can take us beyond the realm of urban history and shed new light on medieval Scottish society as a whole.

REFERENCES TO BOOKS AND ARTICLES MENTIONED IN THE TEXT

Adams, I et al 1929 Edinburgh, 1329–1929. Edinburgh.

Bawcutt, P 1992 Dunbar the Makar. Oxford.

Booton, H 1988a 'Burgesses and Landed Men in North-East Scotland in the Later Middle Ages; A Study in Social Interaction', University of Aberdeen: unpublished PhD thesis.

Booton, H 1988b 'Inland Trade: A Study of Aberdeen in the Later Middle Ages', in Lynch, M, Spearman, M and Stell, G (eds) The Scottish Medieval Town, Edinburgh, 148–60.

Cooper, J 1892 *Cartularium Ecclesiae Sancti Nicholai Aberdonensis.* Aberdeen.

*Dennison, EP (ed), *Conservation and Change in Historic Towns.* York.

Dennison, EP 1999 'The Scottish Burgh Survey and the Centre for Scottish Urban History', *in* Dennison, EP (ed), *Conservation and Change in Historic Towns,* York, 77–89.

Dennison, EP 2000 'Recreating the Urban Past', *in* Brotherstone, T and Ditchburn, D (eds), *Freedom and Authority. Scotland, c.1050–c.1650,* East Linton, 275–84.

Ewan, E 1990 *Townlife in Fourteenth-Century Scotland.* Edinburgh.

Ewan, E 2000 'Mons Meg and Merchant Meg: Women in Later Medieval Edinburgh', *in* Brotherstone, T and Ditchburn, D (eds), *Freedom and Authority,* 131–42.

Fawcett, R 1997 'The Churches of the Greater Medieval Cities', *in* Mays, D (ed), *The Architecture of Scottish Cities,* East Linton, 13–25.

Flett, I and Cripps, J 1988 'Documentary Evidence', *in* Lynch, M, Spearman, M and Stell, G (eds) *The Scottish Medieval Town,* Edinburgh, 18–43.

Fradenburg, LO 1991 *City, Marriage, Tournament. Arts of Rule in Late Medieval Scotland.* Madison.

*Gemmill, E and Mayhew, N 1995 *Changing Values in Medieval Scotland.* Cambridge.

Holdsworth, P (ed) 1988 *Excavations in the Medieval Burgh of Perth 1979–81.* Edinburgh.

Hume Brown, P (ed) 1891 *Early Travellers in Scotland.* Edinburgh.

Kennedy, W 1818 *Annals of Aberdeen.* 2 vols, London.

Lynch, M 1984 'Whatever Happened to the Medieval Burgh?', *Scottish Economic and Social History,* 4, 5–20.

Lynch, M 1988 'Towns and townspeople in fifteenth-century Scotland', *in* Thomson, JAF (ed), *Towns and Townspeople in the Fifteenth Century,* Stroud, 173–89.

MacDonald, AR 2005 'The Burghs and Parliament, c.1300–1707' *in* Brown, KM and MacDonald, AR (eds), *The Scottish Parliament: A Thematic History,* Edinburgh.

MacKenzie, WM 1949 *The Scottish Burghs.* Edinburgh.

Maxwell, A 1891 *Old Dundee, Ecclesiastical, Burghal and Social Prior to the Reformation.* Edinburgh.

Mayhew, N 1999 'Women in Aberdeen at the end of the Middle Ages' *in* Brotherstone, T *et al* (eds) *Gendering Scottish History,* Glasgow, 142–55.

*McNeill, PGB and MacQueen, HL 1996 *Atlas of Scottish History to 1707.* Edinburgh.

Mill, AJ 1969 *Medieval Plays in Scotland.* New York.

Murray, D 1924–32 *Early Burgh Organization in Scotland.* Glasgow.

Murray, HK 1982 'The Excavated Secular Buildings' *in* Murray (ed), *Excavations in the Medieval Burgh of Aberdeen,* 224–8. Edinburgh.

Murray, JC (ed) 1982 *Excavations in the Medieval Burgh of Aberdeen, 1973–81.* Edinburgh.

Nicholas, D 1997 *The Later Medieval City, 1300–1500.* London.

Spearman, RM 1988 'Workshops, Materials and Debris – Evidence of Early Industries', *in* Lynch, M, Spearman, M and Stell, G (eds) *The Scottish Medieval Town,* 134–47.

Stevenson, A 1988 'Trade with the South, 1070–1513', *in* Lynch, M, Spearman, M and Stell, G (eds) *The Scottish Medieval Town,* 180–206.

Swanson, H 1988 'The Illusion of Economic Structure: Craft Guilds in Late Medieval English Towns', *Past and Present,* 121, 29–48.

*Swanson, H 1999 *Medieval British Towns.* Houndmills.

Torrie, EPD 1984 'The Gild of Dunfermine in the Fifteenth Century', University of Edinburgh: unpublished PhD thesis.

Yeoman, P 1995 *Medieval Scotland.* London.

FURTHER READING

Items above marked * are recommended for further reading, along with the following:

Dennison, EP 1998 'Power to the People? The myth of the medieval burgh community', *in* Foster, S *et al* (eds), *Scottish Power Centres*. Glasgow.

Dennison, EP *et al* (eds) 2002 *Aberdeen Before 1800. A New History*. East Linton.

Ditchburn, D 2001 *Scotland and Europe. The Medieval Kingdom and Its Contacts with Christendom, 1214–1560*. East Linton.

Hall, D 2002 *Burgess, Merchant and Priest. Burgh Life in the Scottish Medieval Town*. Edinburgh.

Lynch, M, Spearman, M and Stell, G (eds) 1988 *The Scottish Medieval Town*. Edinburgh.

Palliser, D (ed) 2000 *The Cambridge Urban History of Britain volume 1, 600–1540* Cambridge.

Torrie, EPD 1990 *Medieval Dundee. A Town and Its People*. Dundee.

CHAPTER NINE

Medieval Archaeology
—— *Derek W Hall and Catherine Smith*

Urban archaeology in Scotland came to the fore in the 1970s when the first major excavations were carried out in advance of urban regeneration in Elgin, Aberdeen, Perth and St Andrews. Current conservation and planning policies now ensure that major building projects are unlikely to take place in the cores of historic burghs, although there are still some exceptions. The recent excavations at the new site of the Scottish Parliament in Edinburgh probably represent the largest urban excavation ever undertaken in Scotland (Moloney *et al* forthcoming). Whilst this offers the opportunity to reconstruct an accurate picture of lifestyle and living conditions of the medieval period, it comes at a very high financial cost. All the excavations mentioned in this chapter are 'rescue' excavations, having been undertaken as a result of modern development projects.

Urban archaeology can provide the most information and the most plentiful finds of any sort of excavation, since many medieval towns are situated on sites where continuous occupation has resulted in deep archaeological deposits of up to three or four metres. The burghs of Perth, North Berwick and parts of the Old Town of Edinburgh probably represent the best Scottish examples of such survival. These deep deposits are often waterlogged and under anaerobic (without oxygen) conditions, with the result that the process of decay of organic materials like leather, wood and bone is either very slow or does not occur at all.

Medieval deposits survive better in some of Scotland's burghs than in others. Important centres such as Elgin, Forres and Dunfermline often prove to have no archaeology surviving on their street frontages. All three of these burghs are built on ridges, their high streets running along the tops. Thus every phase of urban renewal scrapes the archaeology off, down to the natural subsoil. Downhill from the ridge, archaeological deposits do survive, often to some depth, but the important link to the buildings on the frontage has gone. The modern urban archaeologist therefore has to attempt to predict where the deposits will survive and to react to development pressures accordingly.

Environmental analysis of waterlogged archaeological deposits has shown that among the remains of plants found at the Perth High Street excavation (hereafter PHSE) were cereal grains, seeds and achenes (fruit seeds), leaf fragments, wood, moss ropes and hazel nut shells (Fraser and Smith forthcoming). Animal remains included the bones of domestic and wild mammals, birds and fish, fragments of ox horn, cattle, goat and horse hair and sheep's wool, leather, shells of marine and freshwater mollusca, eggshell fragments and even feathers (Bogdan *et al* forthcoming).

PROBLEMS OF DATING THE DEPOSITS

The dating of medieval archaeology is based on a combination of information provided by pottery and other excavated finds. Some types of pottery can be dated by relating them to finds elsewhere, but there are often problems when the only pottery recovered is of local production for which there is still not a usable chronology. Work is currently ongoing to try to determine the sources of clay and the kiln sites themselves (Chenery *et al*, forthcoming). Radiocarbon (C^{14}) dating may be less useful for archaeology of the medieval period because the margin for error can often span several centuries. Perhaps the most useful dating technique is dendrochronology (tree ring dating). However, to employ this dating technique it is necessary to recover substantial pieces of timber, a rare occurrence. As with much of the information for medieval Scotland, it is the burghs of Perth and Aberdeen which provide such samples (Crone forthcoming).

BEFORE THE BURGHS

It is very likely that when many of burghs were given their foundation status, some sort of settlement already existed on the sites. Such pre-burghal evidence from archaeological excavation is still quite limited, but a tantalising glimpse from Perth was the discovery of a ditch lined with wattle (woven tree branches), radiocarbon dated to AD 990-1040. This feature may be part of an enclosure around an earlier version of St John's church and seems to indicate settlement at Perth at least 100 years earlier than its foundation as a burgh in the twelfth century (Moloney and Coleman 1997). Ongoing research into a type of pottery found at PHSE, known as Shellyware, also indicates dates 100 years older than the date of the foundation of Perth as a burgh (Hall 2005, 8–9).

Another Scottish burgh with evidence of pre-burghal origins is St Andrews in Fife. St Andrews originated as an early religious centre, located on the headland at Kirkhill. Excavations in 1980 located part of a substantial cemetery, which included bodies buried in stone boxes known as long cists, dating to the sixth to eighth centuries AD (Wordsworth and Clark 1997). There would almost certainly have been a settlement associated with this early religious centre, although this has yet to be located. It seems likely that many early religious settlements may have formed the nucleus of what were later to be consolidated by charters as burghs.

DAILY LIFE IN THE BURGHS

Most surviving Scottish medieval documents concern the Crown and religious matters, rather than the mundane facts of everyday life. Thus archaeological excavation is the most practical way of discovering what it was like to live and work in medieval Scotland. Well- preserved deposits in Perth, Elgin, St Andrews and Aberdeen present the opportunity to reconstruct medieval life right through from the buildings and streetscape to clothing and foodstuffs.

The most productive elements of a medieval burgh from the archaeologist's point of view are the town middens. It is somewhat surprising to learn that some efforts (however futile) were made to keep the streets clean. In fifteenth-century Aberdeen, a burgh 'scaffyngir' was appointed to remove rubbish (a job still done by the 'scaffies' of the north-east) (Wyness 1966, 71, 140). Nevertheless, the scaffyngir was no match for the inhabitants of medieval Aberdeen and great midden deposits were allowed to accumulate as revealed by the excavations at Queen Street (Murray 1982). In Perth, the job of street cleaning or 'gait dychting' seems to have fallen within the province of the 'pynnouris', the shore-porters at the harbour. They were also responsible for 'sowping and dychting of the mercattis' (Stavert 1993, 237). 'Sowping' seems to have implied slopping out of the market area with water. The rubbish itself was probably thrown into the Tay; the pynnours were charged with the obligation to 'dicht all the mercattis of the toune and carry the muk thairof to the wattirside, and clengis the gaittis and mercattis thairof with couppis and sleddis . . . and als cleng and dycht the mydding at lyis besid the peir beneath the trone and all possible haist betwix this (11 November 1511) and Youll' (*ibid*, 458).

Archaeological evidence shows that domestic rubbish was disposed of by being spread out in the backlands of the burgage plots or even out into the street. In Perth, a build-up of rubbish was starting to cause problems by the fifteenth century, particularly where it was building up along the access road at the foot of the town defences: the burgh eventually passed a law to prevent this from happening. The deep middens of Perth contain preserved wool textiles, silk, leather and wood, evidence of the clothing and footwear being worn. The most commonly found textile is a very coarse hand-woven woollen fabric, which was presumably very good at keeping out the cold. Finer types of clothing are best represented by an ornate silk hairnet from Perth High Street (Bogdan and Wordsworth 1978, 29). Other fragments of silk with woven bird designs were recovered from the Kirk Close excavation in Perth: the best parallel for this textile comes from royal graves in Spain dated to the thirteenth century (Muthesius 1987, 169).

Some of the inhabitants of Perth made an effort towards a degree of comfort in their domestic sanitary arrangements; at Kirk Close, a covered latrine or earth closet was constructed with an oaken seat, on which one user had incised a graffito of decorative lines (Ford 1987, 145). The user may have utilised a sphagnum moss or lint toilet 'paper', the latter type having been used at Elgin (Robinson 1987). The shed containing the earth closet was found attached to the back of a medieval building fronting the High Street at Kirk Close, so by implication such facilities may have been common in the medieval burgh.

In its medieval heyday Perth appears to have become a very crowded place, and pressure on the available High Street frontage seems to have been intense; this is best illustrated by the results of excavations at the House of Fraser site in the early 1980s, where a vennel (or alley) between two properties on the street frontage was turned into a very small booth by roofing over the gap between the two buildings. The enterprising occupant may have been in the business of selling hot food, as there is a small hearth with an associated wattle-built animal pen, perhaps for chickens (Clark and Blanchard 1995, 932). In contrast, there is evidence from excavations in Perth that in some periods, possibly as early as the mid-thirteenth century, some of the street frontages became derelict and were occupied only by pits either for rubbish or the quarrying of sand; later examples of such bad times for the burgh economy may reflect the effect of the Wars of Independence.

The most distinctive feature of the plans of Scotland's medieval burghs are the backlands. These reflect the way in which land was divided when the burghs were founded – an extent on the street frontage where the first buildings were erected, and a long strip of land stretching back to the next boundary, often the limit of the burgh. In Perth, St Andrews and Aberdeen the boundaries of many of these plots of land have remained unchanged throughout the centuries, although now disappearing as a result of modern development. The owners of the properties would often conduct their trade here, and it is from these backlands that much of the archaeological evidence for the different industries of the burgh is recovered. From the surviving documentary evidence in the Rental Books of the King James VI Hospital in Perth we can see that these backlands are often further subdivided into 'forelands' and 'innerlands' (Milne 1891).

SOCIAL ORDER

The most striking social change that took place following the foundation of the burghs was the creation of a sense of community amongst their inhabitants. This consensus was vital to ensure that trade and industry would prosper. To qualify for burgess-ship and all the privileges that came with it, a serf had to be able to prove he had been resident in the relevant burgh for a year and a day. In the early days of the burgh most adult males would have become burgesses – women and children enjoyed privileges through their husbands and fathers but were not involved in the political life of the burgh. As the new burghs became the focus for immigrants from the surrounding countryside, the number of non-burgesses increased. Most of these incomers lacked the necessary finance to purchase the plots of land required for burgess-ship and would have found employment as servants or labourers for the established inhabitants. The results of excavations in Aberdeen have led the excavator to suggest that these non-burgesses may have been housed in the buildings, excavated in the burgh backlands, which are generally of a poorer quality than those on the frontages (Murray 1982, 247). Interestingly, however, excavations on Mill Street in Perth have located backland buildings dating to the fourteenth and fifteenth centuries with tiled roof ridges, surely a sign of wealth (Hall 1995, 970).

BUILDINGS AND TOWNSCAPE

Excavations in Perth and Aberdeen allow us to suggest what the standard domestic dwellings of the medieval burgh must have looked like. Until at least the fifteenth or sixteenth centuries, all the buildings were built of wood – the only stone-built structures were likely to have been churches and monastic establishments, although there is an intriguing reference to a stone house in fourteenth-century Perth. A standard medieval house would have had timber foundation-beams holding upright posts, which supported wattle walls daubed with clay tempered with dung. Occasionally, evidence is found for a slightly more sophisticated wall structure, such as upright planks fitted together with tongue and groove. Roofs seem to have been thatched with straw or heather, although it has been argued recently that wooden shingles may also have been used – there is a single excavated example of a shingle from the PHSE site in Perth. An account of the Perth flood of 1209 refers to some of the burgesses escaping from the rising waters by going upstairs into the 'solars' of their houses, implying that some of these houses must have had at least two storeys (Corner *et al* 1994, 257).

The buildings would have been concentrated on the street frontage and along the sides of any vennels or closes running back from these major thoroughfares. Vennels or wynds were a very common feature of the burghs, and some still exist to this day, for example Horner's Vennel and Cutlog Vennel in Perth, Couttie's Wynd in Dundee or the many closes of Edinburgh's Royal Mile. The name 'vennel' is French in origin and provides some evidence for Norman influence in the planning of the burghs. Evidence is growing that the high streets of the north east burghs were often much wider than at the present day, by up to as much as two or three metres on either side. It appears that these wide streets were the sites of the burgh markets; the market square, so common in England, is a rare phenomenon in Scotland. Access to a harbour was important to the success of a medieval burgh; Perth, Dundee and Dumbarton prospered as a result, whereas burghs like Elgin had to rely on a harbour some five miles away at Spynie. Although St Andrews did have a harbour, it could not accommodate very large ships and therefore did not attract much foreign trade.

Very few burghs were provided with formal defences against attack; Perth was one of the few that had a substantial stone wall surrounded by a deep water-filled ditch (the Town Lade). In most other burghs the rear of the long backlands (known as head riggs) would also have served as a boundary to the burgh. Most major Scottish burghs also possessed a royal castle, although few now survive; Perth's castle was washed away in the floods of 1209 and was never rebuilt. That the king subsequently stayed at the Blackfriars' monastery when visiting Perth implies that the main function of these castles was as royal lodgings and not as defensive strongholds. One of the few burgh castles excavated by archaeologists is that which stood on Ladyhill at the west end of the modern High Street in Elgin; evidence for at least two defensive ramparts surrounding a timber palisade was recovered when it was examined in 1973. The finds include a substantial number of bones of red deer, indicating that hunting played an important part in the life of the occupants of the castle (Smith 1998, 771). Excavations at the castles of Strachan in Aberdeenshire and Peebles in the Scottish Borders have suggested that these buildings often comprised a circular timber hall surrounded by a palisade standing on an artificial mound or motte (Yeoman 1984). Slezer's eighteenth-century view of Elgin seems to indicate a similar structure standing on Ladyhill.

TRADE AND INDUSTRY

Many of the burghs were hives of commercial activity and different parts of the town were used by different trades, as reflected in some of the surviving street and vennel names – Skinnergate and Horner's Vennel in Perth being good examples. Thirteenth-century documents give us an idea of the number and types of trades or professions that existed in Scotland's burghs. People's names included their trade: *Willelmus galeator* (helmet maker) and *Robertus faber* (smith). Such trade names were associated with a range of industrial process involving cloth or clothing, metalwork and leatherwork. It is out of this wide range of professions that the Guildry Incorporation developed. By 1400, at least thirteen burghs are on record as having guilds; unfortunately, no earlier records of these important organisations survive which makes it difficult to understand their function and composition. In Perth, the Guilds of Glovers and Hammermen (metalworkers) claim that their origins go back to the time of William the Lion (1165–1214). The presence of guilds in most of the burghs involved in overseas trade suggests that they had a monopoly over trade in certain goods such as cloth and hides.

Some industries, however, were not members of the Guildry, implying that they were not based within the burgh limits – the pottery industry for example. Kiln sites, where pottery was manufactured, do not seem to have been located within the burgh limits, although from the PHSE excavations in Perth alone there are c. 50,000 sherds of pottery. The kilns would, of course, have been an enormous fire hazard in a town built of timber. Until the post-medieval period, basic cooking equipment was made of ceramic material, although plates and bowls were exclusively made from wood. Whereas broken wooden implements could be disposed of by burning, pottery is virtually indestructible and so is a common find from excavations. In the case of Perth there are at least three possible sites for pottery kilns: at Claypots, Potterhill and Kinnoull. However, no evidence for anything relating to such an industry has been found at any of these sites. It is possible that the kilns may have been further afield, although the first piece of kiln furniture from medieval Perth was found during the excavations on the site of the new Council Headquarters at the former Pullar's works, just to the north of the medieval burgh. It seems likely that a whole series of small kiln sites situated in rural settlements may have been supplying the major burghs, since in many cases this is where the resources – clay, fuel and water supplies – were located.

Although very few kiln sites have been either located or indeed excavated, the products of a native pottery industry have been identified in Scotland (Hall 1998). From at least the twelfth century, Scottish White Gritty ware was being produced, possible production centres being located in the Borders, Lothian and Fife. There is a strong possibility that the technology for producing this well-fired pottery may have been brought to Scotland by some of the monastic orders, particularly those whose mother-houses were in Yorkshire, where good quality pottery was being produced at this period.

Until the thirteenth century, most pottery in the burghs had been imported from England and the Low Countries. From several sites in Perth, only imported pottery was found in the early layers. From the early thirteenth century, a type of pottery called Scottish Redware came into use, found in excavations from Stirling to Dornoch. A local Redware fabric has also been found on the west coast at sites in Dumfries and Galloway and in parts of Strathclyde. In thirteenth- and fourteenth-century Scotland, the very well-made products of the Yorkshire kilns became the dominant type and had an enormous effect on the style and technique of the local potters. The Yorkshire kilns produced distinctively lustrous green glazed vessels, often decorated with figures on horseback – for example the so-called 'knight jug', and tableware such as the aquamanile, which was designed to hold water for washing the hands. Excavations at the site of the new Scottish Parliament in the burgh of Canongate (now in Edinburgh) have recovered an important group of sixteenth- and seventeenth-century pottery, including sherds from high-quality vessels from northern Germany and France and olive jars from Seville in Spain (Hall forthcoming). The same assemblage also contains a piece of ceramic stove-tile, which possibly originated in the Baltic. Fragments of these stoves are very rare finds indeed and are evidence for a type of central heating popular in elite households in Britain in the sixteenth century. Recent excavations in the Skinnergate in Perth have also located a piece of tile from one of these stoves.

The nature and extent of trade in medieval Scotland is a matter of considerable debate. The lack of surviving medieval port books makes it very difficult to prove conclusively that pottery was being traded in its own right rather than as containers for other goods such as wine and honey. However, the use of cooking pots imported from the Low Countries or Scandinavia in the early centuries in the burgh of Perth suggests that these vessels were being bought for that very purpose.

The surviving customs records indicate the export of wool from Scotland to the Low Countries and Flanders, much of which may well have originated in the major monastic estates of the Borders, for example Jedburgh and Melrose. Following the end of the war between the Hanseatic League and the kingdoms of Denmark and Norway in 1370, the reopening of the Sound of Skagerrack to shipping provided direct contact between Scotland and the Baltic. It is difficult to work out just how extensive the use of this trade route was, although by 1497 the Sound Toll Register lists 21 Scots ships from Dundee, Leith, Aberdeen, St Andrews and one unknown port. Recent important work on the tree-ring dating of timbers from Stirling Castle seems to indicate that timber from the Baltic was certainly being imported into Scotland in the fifteenth and sixteenth centuries.

Animal skins, hides, cheap cloth, wool and salmon were all exported from Scotland. In fact, much of the export economy was based on materials derived from animals and other primary resources such as salt and coal. In the later middle ages there was a large-scale emigration of Scots to northern Europe; some of these were students heading for universities in Germany, France and the countries surrounding the Baltic, but many were merchants who settled in coastal ports such as Danzig. There may also have been even earlier contacts between the Baltic States and Scotland, for example a type of imported pottery found in early levels in Perth has been identified as possibly originating in Jutland.

Archaeological excavation has also recovered evidence for metalworking indus-tries in Perth, as evidenced by the smelting and working of iron for the manufacture of knives, horseshoes and barrel padlocks at Meal Vennel (Cox 1995). Important evidence for the source of the raw material for this industry has also been recovered, with the suggestion that 'bog iron' was probably the most commonly used and that this would have been available to both urban and rural smiths alike. Excavations at King Edward Street in Perth located a small workshop on the High Street frontage, which contained a small hearth and possible evidence for the working of either gold or silver (Clark 1995). Moulds for manufacturing rings and brooches have been recovered from sites on the High Street and in the Skinnergate. Leather-working was also an important industry in the Scottish medieval burgh, producing shoes, belts, scabbards and perhaps items of clothing. The area around the Skinnergate in Perth was probably the focus of this industry and many hundreds of pieces of leather have been recovered from excavations in the burgh, particularly PHSE (Thomas forth-coming).

In addition there is ample evidence from PHSE of skinning, horn working, commercial butchery, possible glue and neats' foot oil production, yarn spinning and textile manufacture. Backland activities included grain drying and malting at Canal Street III, Perth (Coleman 1996). Evidence from a watching brief at St John's Square, Perth has also provided evidence for small-scale antler and horn working: this is of great interest to the interpretation of craft industries in medieval Perth. Nowhere else in the burgh has such a concentration of antler offcuts been found, and it is apparent that a workshop, perhaps producing combs, was located there. These antler deposits are matched only in Scotland by an assemblage recovered from Linlithgow High Street, a town famed also for its leather work (Smith, forthcoming). Crafts for which we, as yet, have no direct evidence were also known to have been carried on in medieval burghs, for example, tallow rendering, candle making, flax retting and dyeing.

RELIGIOUS INSTITUTIONS

It seems fair to say that religion played a much greater part in people's lives in the medieval period than it does today, perhaps reflecting the uncertainty of people's existence. Religion therefore offered a common experience for everyone. For the various religious orders, a thriving medieval burgh offered a substantial source of revenue. These institutions were often founded by the king or a local abbey who had identified the need for such a monastic presence and the opportunity for the relevant order to become landowners.

At the core of most Scottish medieval burghs was the parish church, and many of the more important burghs also possessed at least one friary, usually built beyond the burgh limits where land was much cheaper. Like many thriving medieval burghs, Perth became a focal point for the foundation of religious houses. By the mid-fifteenth century Perth possessed four – all of them beyond the burgh limits. The earliest foundation was that of the Dominicans or Blackfriars in 1231. This friary lay on the north side of the burgh to the east of Kinnoull Street at its junction with Carpenter Street, confirmed by archaeological excavation. Following the destruction of the castle by the flood of 1209, the Dominican friary seems to have become the favoured lodging of Scottish kings when they were visiting the burgh. Indeed, it was in the Blackfriars monastery that James I was murdered in 1437.

The second foundation was that of the Carmelite friary of Tullilum in 1262, lying to the west of Perth on the southern side of the Longcauseway. Why it is located so far away from the burgh limits is still not understood – possibly a church already in existence on the site was granted to the Carmelites. The eastern end of the friary complex was excavated in advance of redevelopment in 1982, and some idea of the layout of the complex and the nature of the buildings was gained (Hall 1989). The friary seal matrix was recovered from the excavation at Whitefriars. This object would have been used to impress the insignia of the friary on official letters and documents. It is made of copper alloy and depicts the Virgin Mary nursing her son Jesus, above a friar kneeling in adoration. Around the outside of the seal is inscribed 'S' Prioris Fratrum Carmel de Pert' – the seal of the prior and brethren of the Carmelites of Perth. This seal is the first to be found from an excavation of a friary in Scotland. Although others exist, they are in private antiquarian collections and their precise findspots are unknown.

Perth's other two religious houses were the Franciscan and Carthusian friaries. The Franciscan or Greyfriars monastery was founded in 1460 and lay to the south-east of the burgh in the area now occupied by Greyfriars cemetery. The Carthusian friary was founded in 1429 and lay to the south west of the burgh close to the site of the King James VI hospital. Known as the 'Vale of Virtue', it was the only Carthusian house in Scotland, reflecting the importance of Perth at that time. James I and his consort, Joan of Beaufort, were both buried there. Both Franciscan and Carthusian friaries remain archaeologically unexplored at the time of writing. Two other Carmelite friaries at Linlithgow and Aberdeen and a Franciscan friary at Jedburgh have also been excavated. Both the Linlithgow and Jedburgh friary excavations produced important information about the layout of these monastic complexes (Lindsay 1989).

The Reformation of 1559/60 played a major part in the disappearance of many of these religious institutions, although the concept of wholesale mob destruction of the buildings may need to be revised. It seems much more likely that the roofs of the buildings were removed, the occupants ejected, and the stonework then gradually removed for re-use elsewhere.

CHURCH AND GRAVEYARD

Many medieval parish churches are still in use today and thus very few have been excavated. It is quite striking how the locations of many of the burgh graveyards have been forgotten, and it is only appreciated that some of the former inhabitants of the burgh are buried under present-day pavements when graveyards are exposed by modern development such as water and sewer-pipe renewal. The burgh graveyard of

Perth, for example, used to surround the church of St John before relocation to Greyfriars in 1580. A few medieval parish churches such as St Christopher's, Cupar, and St John's, Ayr, however, were not situated inside the burghs and may indicate important early religious foci that continued in use. Holy Trinity, the parish church of St Andrews, lay inside the precinct of the Augustinian abbey and cathedral until 1415 when it was moved to its modern site in South Street. Occasionally tantalising clues to the early origins of some of these sites are found. During nineteenth-century roadworks in Elgin, a Pictish cross-slab was found directly outside St Giles' Church. Possibly this stone, known as the Elgin pillar, indicates a much earlier ecclesiastical settlement in the area.

CLIMATE AND ENVIRONMENTAL CONDITIONS

Flooding in the centre of towns is not a modern phenomenon, as archaeology can demonstrate (Bowler 2004). As early as 1209, the royal castle of Perth was washed away and in 1621 'a fearful inundation of waters' swept away the bridge over the river. At very low water the timber pile foundations of this bridge can still be seen in the riverbed running across to Stanners Island.

Archaeological excavation may retrieve information that can be used to reconstruct the weather conditions and climate of medieval Scotland. We know from a combination of documentary sources and environmental evidence (tree-ring growth and lake sediments) that between AD 1000 and 1200 the climate was much warmer than it is today and therefore crop yields were much higher. But after c. AD 1300, conditions changed for the worse, with the onset of what is known as the 'Little Ice Age', which lasted for nearly five centuries. Marginal land that had previously been used for growing cereal crops was abandoned. During this period the annual temperature seems to have dropped by at least one degree centigrade, and the prevailing winds seemed to have shifted to a northerly or north-easterly direction (Lamb 1996). Several excavations on the east coast have indicated that wind-blown sand could pose problems. In North Berwick, Montrose and Arbroath, for example, archaeologists have recognised banded layers of sand between occupation deposits. A similar situation seems to have existed on the west coast, which is why the Sandgate in Ayr is so named.

THE BURGH HINTERLANDS – ENVIRONMENTAL EVIDENCE FROM PERTH AND ABERDEEN

Each medieval burgh was surrounded by a rural hinterland on which it depended for the production of agricultural raw materials, which generated the wealth of the medieval economy. In its turn, the hinterland was dependent on the burgh because its goods must be sold there. Agricultural and craftsmen's produce from the countryside was only allowed to be sold at legal fairs and markets within the burghs. The exact extent of each burgh's hinterland in the medieval period is not known precisely, although in the case of Perth, its borders probably corresponded with those of the sheriffdom of Perth, which probably first came into existence in the twelfth century.

Perth's main competitor over both the hinterland and over control of shipping in the Tay would have been Dundee, some 35 km by land to the east. However, the borders of the hinterland would not have remained static throughout the entire medieval period, but would have been in a state of fluctuation as territory was continually disputed and perhaps reallocated. There is still to the present day a rivalry between Perth and Dundee, which although people are no longer aware of it, began – over trade – some 800 years ago.

As well as the cultivated crops and domestic livestock raised in the burgh's hinterlands, a wide range of wild plants and animals were potentially available for exploitation. Of the cultivated crops, study of the botanical remains has shown that bere barley (*Hordeum vulgare tetrastichum*), white oat (*Avena sativa*), grey or bristle oat (*Avena strigosa*) and rye (*Secale cereale*) would all have been grown locally. Wheat (*Triticum aestivum*) was probably grown in small quantities on the more fertile land, as at Craigie, just outside Perth (Duncan 1975, 322), although some may have been imported from outwith Scotland. Peas and beans were probably also grown, although they may not have been extensively cultivated in Scotland. Certainly both peas and beans were imported in the thirteenth and fourteenth centuries (*ibid*, 324). Cultivated green vegetables were also scarce, but included *Brassica* species (kail or turnip). Fruit such as apples were also grown (Fraser and Smith, forthcoming).

The domestic livestock for which we have evidence were cattle, sheep, pigs, goats, and horses (Hodgson, Smith and Jones, forthcoming). All of these animals were of rather smaller stature than their modern day counterparts. In appearance, the cattle were probably of a short-horned type. Most of the cattle were either females, used for breeding or milk production, or castrated oxen kept for draught work pulling the plough. Very few bulls were found. Sheep were small spindly-legged creatures of a range of shades of grey, brown and black – very few of them would have been white – and were horned in both sexes. Some of the sheep had multiple horns, rather like the Jacob breed known today. They were kept chiefly for wool and woolfell production, although their milk was also valued in cheese-making. This cheese was economically important, as it often contributed to payments of rent in kind. Rentals of abbeys frequently specify payments of large quantities of cheese, for example 40 stones weight (Duncan 1975, 358), some of which would have been sold on at market.

A further important function of domestic stock was as walking producers of manure. Both cattle and sheep may have been *tathed* (folded) on the infield at certain times of the year in order to spread the dung where it was needed. Sheep may have been housed overnight in bughts or cots, not primarily in order to protect them from the elements, but in order to collect their dung, which was favoured over that of cattle (Shaw 1994, 112).

Goats do not seem to have played a role in this system of manuring and were less commonly kept than sheep. However, goat bones are more plentiful from sites in

Perth than elsewhere in medieval Scotland. This is possibly because those parts of the Perthshire highlands that may have been unsuitable for cereal production would have provided ample grazing for goats (which can eat almost any vegetation, however woody, because of the structure of their hard palate). Goat-keeping was part of the highland agricultural tradition from at least the medieval period until the mid-nineteenth century, but fell out of favour because of the goats' propensity to eat increasingly valuable woodland.

Pigs were not present in great numbers in animal bone assemblages from Perth and Aberdeen and it is quite likely that many were kept within the confines of the town itself rather than in the hinterland (Smith 2000). Unlike cattle and sheep, which produce milk, meat and wool or hides, pigs are less valuable in terms of their by-products. Their value was in turning the pannage from oak woodlands (particularly acorns) into meat. The privilege of allowing pigs to forage in this way was a jealously guarded right.

Woodlands provided far more than food for swine, however. Afforested land was probably managed in various ways in order to maintain a renewable source of raw materials. Oak woods were probably coppiced to produce a renewable source of bark, rich in tannins, for tanning leather. Other coppiced trees were hazel, from which wattling was made, ash for tool handles and sheep hurdles, alder for making turned bowls and birch for wattling, making besoms and for its bark, also used in tannery. A grant to Lindores Abbey, Fife, in the year 1250, of a hundred loads of hazel rods annually is evidence of the practice of coppicing (Duncan 1975, 363; Smout 1993, 44). The birch wattling found at PHSE may have been produced in this way. Because much of the woodland grew within the boundaries of Royal Forests or was granted to favourites of the King and to abbeys such as Coupar Angus by Free Forest Grant (Gilbert 1979, 183, 234), access by the common people to large trees may have been restricted. Thus at Kirk Close, Perth, much of the timber was thought to have been re-used, and was probably gleaned from stands of trees growing beside the Tay or from hedgerows (Crone and Barber 1987, 88).

Wood was also the main source of domestic fuel in the early medieval period, the use of coal being confined to those areas of small-scale mining such as Fife. Given that wood for building was at a premium, however, it is likely that any available scrub species were used for fuel. Wood charcoal was also of importance in smelting and metal working. It was probably produced on the site where wood was gathered, in earth-covered kilns. Woodland also provided a source of wild foods, gleaned for both human and animal consumption. Hazelnut shells are ubiquitous at medieval sites throughout Perth. Botanical evidence shows that fruits and berries were collected in season: strawberry, raspberry, bramble, rowan, rosehip, elderberry, gean, bullace and sloe have all been found in Perth (Fraser and Smith, forthcoming). These berries could have been eaten raw, providing a valuable source of Vitamin C, or fermented to make alcoholic drinks. Woodland was also a source of winter fodder for animals. Dried leaves or leafy branches harvested in late summer probably formed part of the winter feed for medieval cattle (Reynolds 1987, 56). That fodder of some kind was available is amply demonstrated by the large numbers of cattle that survived through at least four winter seasons.

Woodland was also exploited as a source of game animals. The larger species such as deer were a potential source of meat, while the smaller animals such as pine marten were hunted for their fur. Although there is as yet no evidence from Perth for exploitation of woodland bird species, evidence of feather remains from Pluscarden Priory shows that pheasant was present in fifteenth century Scotland (Cerón-Carrasco 1994, 414). Perhaps, as was the case with venison, the pleasures of hawking, by which woodland birds would have been taken, were also reserved mainly to the crown, nobility and clergy. The early sixteenth-century rental books of the Bishopric of Dunkeld, for example, show that a fowler (*aucupi*) was employed on 'each day when my Lord left hawking' (Hannay 1915, 65).

There is a wealth of evidence from Perth to show that moorland resources were imported into the town. Heather and moss fragments were probably the remains of roofing material or perhaps bedding for people and animals. Mosses were plaited into ropes, which might be used to hold thatch in place. Other moorland and bog plants such as bog myrtle, tormentil and bog cotton were all found in PHSE deposits, possibly having been deliberately collected. Bog myrtle has been used to make gale beer and also yields a yellow dye. Tormentil is rich in tannins and was used to tan leather, as at medieval Gallowgate, Aberdeen. Here a stone mortar found in connection with a series of tan-pits was encrusted with residues containing the pollen of tormentil, as well as oak and birch, all used as tanning agents (Evans 1987, 13; Moffat and Penny 2001, 297–99). Some moorland plants have medicinal uses, but it is not known whether they had been used in this way. However, in the absence of other medicines, the medieval townspeople would have had little option than to turn to locally available plant remedies and it is worth noting that some plant derived substances still have a place in the British Pharmacopoeia today. Thus mosses could have been used as a packing material for wounds: sphagnum is naturally antiseptic and highly absorbent. Eleventh-century chronicles relate how after battle, 'stricken Scots stuffed their wounds with moss' and this use continued until as recently as the Second World War (Mabey 1979, 102). Sphagnum was also useful as a 'toilet paper' (Robinson 1987, 200).

HUMAN HEALTH AND WELFARE

There is a strong possibility that the immediate environment of Perth, as in other burghs, was polluted to some extent by the craft industries that were indispensable to the creation of wealth in the burgh. Living conditions for the wealthiest merchants and the poorest labourers may have differed substantially, but it is probable that intestinal parasitic infestations were no respecters of social status. Whipworm (*Trichuris*) eggs were found in what may have been a cesspit deposit at PHSE and roundworm (*Ascaris*) eggs in a latrine deposit at Kirk Close (Robinson 1987, 201). Although we have no evidence for other intestinal parasites from Perth, it is quite likely that infestations of tapeworms were contracted via the dogs and pigs that roamed freely through the burgh. Cestode tapeworms (e.g. *Taenia solium*) and nematode roundworms (*Trichinella*) could be ingested through eating undercooked measly pork. This was perceived as a source of leprosy in the middle ages (Smith 1995). The fish tapeworm, *Diphyllobothrium latum*, could also have been troublesome if undercooked fish was eaten. Infestation by this parasite may lead eventually to Vitamin B12 deficiency.

The botanical contents of cesspits also reveal much about the diet of those who used them. As well as evidence of home grown cereals and wild berries found in medieval cesspits (Robinson 1987, 201-2), there are occasional remains of imported fruits such as figs and grapes, as at Aberdeen (Fraser 1981; Fraser and Dickson 1982, 240; Kenward and Hall, 2001, 29). Only the wealthy could have afforded these exotic fruits.

Meat from cattle and sheep was plentiful in the burghs, as a by-product of the hide and woolfell industries, but much more common in the diet of the rural labouring people were bannocks and porridge made from oats, rye and bere. However nutritious these must have been there was an ever-present danger of common weed seeds contaminating the processed grain. Corn cockle was a serious contaminant of the rye crop (Robinson 1987, 206) and has potentially serious poisonous effects on both people and their animals. (Cooper and Johnson 1984, 77–78). Another crop contaminant found at PHSE was stinking mayweed which, although not poisonous when ingested, was potentially troublesome during harvest time. Grigson (1975, 401) is of the opinion that 'in the days of hand husbandry no weed was more hated' because the entire plant has the power to raise blisters wherever it comes in contact with the skin, and often caused such pain that men were unable to work.

Ergot of rye, caused by the parasitic fungus *Claviceps purpurea*, was also a potential hazard in the medieval period, responsible for the disease known as St Anthony's Fire. Its spores have been found at a rural medieval site at Nethermills, Grampian (Boyd 1986). Ergot poisoning causes symptoms ranging from mild tingling in the arms and legs and burning sensations in the mouth to severe convulsions, mental confusion and gangrene (Cooper and Johnson 1984, 49). Mass episodes of poisoning have been recorded in the past, throughout Europe, from the sixth century AD onwards (Stuart 1987; Cooper and Johnson 1984, 49).

As well as the problems caused by accidental contamination or spoilage of food through damp or pilfering and polluting by mice, there was the very real risk of deliberate adulteration in order to make extra weight when sold. A curious practice that appears to have been indulged in by unscrupulous fleshers was to blow up joints of meat (presumably using straws) in order to make the meat appear plumper and more attractive. Documentary evidence for this trickery appears in the sixteenth-century burgh records of Dundee 'no flescher in brugh nor land bring blawin flesh to this merkit nor collipittit nor cuttit upon or under the skin . . . and na scheip be slitted down in the schulders' (Warden 1862, 12–13). 'Collipittit' implies cutting the meat in some way, perhaps in order to introduce air into it, or perhaps to remove identifying marks, such as ear marks, in the case of stolen animals. 'Blawin' of meat is commented on in *Ane satire of the thrie Estaitis* (Hamer 1931, 367). Meat was thus not to be tampered with in any way before reaching market. Part of the official duties of the appraisers of flesh (*appreciatores carnibus*) who came to be responsible for setting prices may have been to perform a carcass inspection.

Although perishable foodstuffs may have been contaminated either accidentally or deliberately, spoilage of meats and fish could be avoided by pickling, smoking and, particularly, salting. Salt was in great demand for this reason, and commercial salt-pans were in operation around the Fife coast by at least the late fifteenth century (Murdoch and Lewis 1999, 5; Whatley 1984). Home-produced salt was not considered to be as good in quality as that from the Mediterranean, however. Also important to the process of salting were the barrels in which the fish or meat was to be preserved. These had to be sound and leakproof, otherwise the brine would seep away and the contents putrefy. Richardson of Pitfour's eighteenth-century Tay salmon empire relied on skilled cooperage: his barrel staves were of the best oak, while the barrel hoops were of willow (Haldane 1981, 20–1). When the 'kitts' or barrels threw their hoops, the pickle was lost and the salmon spoiled. In the eighteenth century, this was a matter only of economic profit and loss. In the twelfth to fourteenth centuries the consequences may have been more far-reaching. We know that periods of crop failure and dearth occurred in the sixteenth century and there is every possibility that food shortages were common in earlier times; thus it was of prime importance to store food against time of famine.

Direct evidence of the value of the diet of the medieval people of Scotland may be seen in their skeletons. Two medieval graveyards in Perth – at the Carmelite and Dominican Friary sites – have been disturbed by modern developments and thus partly excavated (Bowler and Hall 1995, 939–52; Hall 1989, 99–110). There are further sources of evidence from both the Carmelite Friaries of Aberdeen and of Linlithgow (Stones 1989). From burials at these sites comes evidence of a condition called *cribra orbitalia*, characterised by pitting of the orbital area of the skull, which is thought to result from iron deficiency anaemia in childhood. Predisposing factors involved in this condition include parasitic infection, unhygienic living conditions (which, as we have seen, probably prevailed in medieval Perth) as well as prolonged lactation in women of child-bearing age and a diet deficient in iron (Cross and Bruce 1989, 135). Other deficiency diseases such as rickets, osteomalacia and osteoporosis, involving among other variables a lack of calcium in the skeleton, may have affected the medieval population; a skeleton of a child aged between six and ten years from St John's Kirkyard, Perth, for example, was thought to show signs of rickets (Roberts forthcoming). The high infant mortality rate amongst individuals found at the excavations at St John's Kirkyard may reflect the prevalence of infectious childhood diseases such as diphtheria, measles and whooping cough, against which there was little protection (*ibid*).

Our knowledge of the health and welfare of the occupants of the Scottish medieval burghs is, however, biased towards the information recovered from the excavations at several monastic houses, rather than from burgh graveyards. The average lifespan in medieval times has been estimated to be 35 years for males and 31 years for females. In the small sample from Perth Blackfriars, at least eight individuals approached or achieved this age. No individual showed evidence of age changes characteristic of what we would consider late middle or old age. Indeed, the oldest individual was considered to be no more than 40 years old. However, at monastic sites such as the Isle of May and the Carmelite Friaries at Aberdeen, Linlithgow and Perth (Cross and Bruce 1989) the average age at death was higher (Roberts forthcoming). This raises the question of how representative the Perth friary samples are of the general population of the medieval burgh. If the Blackfriars, for example, had a role in caring for the sick, it may be that this is the section of the population represented here. However, the absence of the very old and the very young may argue against this case. The relative absence of evidence of chronic illness may indicate that the role of the friary may have been related to the care of the acutely ill – possibly those suffering from infections. One skeleton excavated at Blackfriars may have come from a person who was accidentally buried alive – it was found lying face down, with elbows raised as if it trying to escape from the grave. Alternatively, the body may have been in deep rigor mortis when prepared for burial and was buried in the most practical pose.

Leprosy was widespread in Scotland from at least the twelfth century. It is generally assumed that the disease reached Britain via the Crusaders returning from the Levant. By the fifteenth century, all the major east-coast burghs possessed a leper hospital. Leprosy appears to have lasted in Scotland until the 1700s, when it gradually disappeared (the southern areas becoming free of it before the north). By the sixteenth century, every major Scottish burgh possessed a leper house and, although not all the inhabitants of these hospitals may have had the disease, these institutions performed an important function in everyday life in the medieval town. The Scottish leper hospital is still poorly understood and only one, just outside St Andrews, has been excavated in recent years (Hall 1995).

Smaller hospitals or hostels also existed in the middle ages specifically to aid pilgrims who were *en route* to a holy shrine. One such thirteenth-century foundation existed at Scotlandwell on the north side of Loch Leven. This establishment lay on the western pilgrim route to St Andrews and was administered by the Trinitarians or Redfriars who had eight houses in Scotland. One of these, at Dunbar, was the site of some small-scale excavations in the 1980s, which revealed that the dovecot that stands at Friarscroft is actually the re-used tower of the friary church. The church building contained the remains of a green and yellow chequered tiled floor which were located on the east side of this structure (Wordsworth 1983). A major hospital also existed at Soutra in the Scottish Borders beside the main southern routeway into Scotland (formerly the Roman road known as Ermine Street). There has been some small-scale excavation at this site, which has concentrated on retrieving as much information as possible about medical practices such as blood-letting and herbal medicines (Moffat 1986) In many parts of Scotland there are place names that contain the element 'Spittal' although this is more likely to indicate lands that were owned by hospitals rather than the location of actual hospital sites.

LEISURE ACTIVITIES

Archaeological excavations have occasionally found evidence of the leisure activities available to the inhabitants of the burghs: a fine example of a bone flute was recovered from an excavation in the Skinnergate in Perth (Cachart in prep). What the feelings of the owner of this musical instrument were when it was ultimately lost or broken cannot be known, but the polish on the object indicates it was well-used.

Other leisure activities were not so peaceful: animals were used to provide entertainment, most of it involving cruelty. There was evidence from PHSE of cock-fighting; the bony spur that occurs naturally on the lower leg of a cock bird was modified by sawing, in a way similar to a nineteenth-century English stuffed prize specimen illustrated by West (1982, 256). A sharp metal claw-like blade would then have been attached to the bony stump, enhancing the bird's capacity to lethally injure its opponent.

Dog-fighting may also have taken place in medieval Scotland: a dog found in a post-medieval cesspit at Mill Street had suffered a suppurating wound to the shoulder blade, which may have been caused by the bite of another dog, perhaps during an organised bout (Smith 1998). A cut bone of brown bear from a medieval context at Castle Park, Dunbar is difficult to explain in any other context than bear-baiting (Smith, 2000, 236). This pastime certainly occurred in England from at least the early sixteenth century (Hazlitt 1905, 36).

THE WAY FORWARD

The archaeology of medieval Scotland has only recently come of age, largely driven by the substantial urban redevelopment boom of the 1970s and 1980s, which allowed the first real opportunity for excavation in the Scottish burghs. The most striking result of urban archaeology in Scotland is the vital evidence that it can provide for everyday life in a medieval burgh, something that cannot be gained when documentary evidence no longer survives. The real challenge for the future is the marrying of the two disciplines of archaeology and history. There is a real and important need for the members of these two professions to work together, particularly as their results will often complement each other.

REFERENCES TO BOOKS AND ARTICLES MENTIONED IN THE TEXT

Bogdan, NQ, Hodgson, GWI, Smith, C, Jones, A, Fraser, M, Heppel, D, Clarke, AS, Jones, AKG, Smart, IHM, Longmore, RB, Cerón-Carrasco, R and McKay, D forthcoming *The Perth High Street Excavation. Fascicule IX. The Environmental Evidence.* Historic Scotland archive report.

Bogdan, NQ and Wordsworth, J 1978 *The Mediaeval Excavations at the High Street, Perth. An Interim Report.* Perth.

Bowler, D and Hall, D 1995 'Kinnoull Street', *in* Bowler, D, Cox, A and Smith, C (eds) 'Four Excavations in Perth, 1979–84', *Proceedings of the Society of Antiquaries of Scotland* [PSAS], 125, 939–49.

*Bowler, D 2004 *Perth. The Archaeology and Development of a Scottish Burgh*. Perth.

Boyd, WE 1986 'Minor Finds of Cereals at Two Medieval Rural Archaeological Sites in North-East Scotland', *Circaea*, 4, (1) 39–42.

Cachart, R in prep. 'Excavations at the Site of the Former Lemon Tree, Skinnergate, Perth'. SUAT archive report.

Cerón-Carrasco, R 1994 'Feathers from Deposit F23 in the Stone-lined Pit (F22)', *in* McCormick, F 'Excavations at Pluscarden Priory, Moray', *PSAS*, 124, 391–432.

Chenery, S, Haggarty, G, Hall, DW, Murray, C and Cameron, A 'A Draft Report on the ICPS Analysis of Scottish Redware Ceramics, 2004–5'. Historic Scotland Archive Report.

Clark, PR and Blanchard, L 1995 'King Edward Street', *in* Bowler, D, Cox, A and Smith, C (eds), 'Four Excavations in Perth, 1979–84', 931–8.

Coleman, RJ 1996 'Burgage Plots of Medieval Perth: the Evidence from Excavations at Canal Street', *PSAS*, 126, 689-732.

Cooper, MR and Johnson, AW (eds) 1984 *Poisonous Plants in Britain and Their Effects on Animals and Man*. Ministry of Agriculture, Fisheries and Food Reference Book 161. London.

Corner, DJ, Scott, AB, Scott WW and Watt DER (eds) 1994 *Scotichronicon by Walter Bower*. Vol. 4. Aberdeen.

Cox, A (ed) 1995 'Backland Activities in Medieval Perth: Excavations at Meal Vennel and Scott Street', *PSAS*, 126, 733–821.

Crone, A forthcoming 'Analysis of the Timber from Perth High Street'. Historic Scotland Archive Report.

Crone, A and Barber, J 1987 'Structural Timber', *in* Holdsworth, P (ed), *Excavations in the Medieval Burgh of Perth, 1979–84*, Edinburgh, 87–8.

Cross, JF and Bruce, MF 1989 'The Skeletal Remains', *in* Stones, JA (ed), *Three Scottish Carmelite Friaries; Excavations in Aberdeen, Linlithgow and Perth, 1980–86*, Edinburgh, 119–41.

Duncan, AAM 1975 *Scotland: The Making of the Kingdom*. Edinburgh.

Evans, D 1987 *Digging up the Coopie. Investigations in the Gallowgate and Lochlands*. Aberdeen.

Ford, B 1987 'The Wooden Objects', *in* Holdsworth, P (ed), *Excavations in the Medieval Burgh of Perth 1979–81*, 141–7.

Fraser, M J 1981 'A Study of the Botanical Material from Three Medieval Scottish Sites'. University of Glasgow: unpublished MSc thesis.

Fraser, MJ and Dickson, JH 1982 'Plant Remains', *in* Murray, JC (ed), *Excavations in the Medieval Burgh of Aberdeen, 1973–81*, Edinburgh, 239–43.

Fraser, M and Smith C forthcoming 'The Botanical Remains', *in* Bogdan, N et al, *The Perth High Street Archaeological Excavation, 1975–77. Fascicule IX. The Environmental Evidence*. Historic Scotland archive report.

Gilbert, JM 1979 *Hunting and Hunting Reserves in Medieval Scotland*. Edinburgh.

Grigson, G 1975 *The Englishman's Flora*. St Albans.

Haldane, ARB 1981 *The Great Fishmonger of the Tay. John Richardson of Perth and Pitfour*. Dundee.

Hamer, D (ed) 1931 *The Works of Sir David Lindsay of the Mount, 1490–1555*, Edinburgh.

Hall, DW 1989 'Perth: the Excavations', *in* Stones, JA (ed), *Three Scottish Carmelite Friaries*, 99–110.

Hall, DW 1995 'Ceramic Building Material', *in* Bowler, D, Cox, A and Smith, C (eds), 'Four excavations in Perth, 1979–84', 968–70.

*Hall, DW 1998 'The Scottish Medieval Pottery Industry: a Pilot Study', *Tayside and Fife Archaeological Journal*, 4, 170–8.

Hall, DW 2005 'What's Cooking? New Carbon Dates from Carbonised Pottery and Structural Timbers from excavations at 75 High Street, Perth', *History Scotland*, 5, 8–9.

Hall, DW forthcoming 'The pottery from the Parliament Site', *in* Moloney, C (ed), *Excavations at the site of the Scottish Parliament, Canongate, Edinburgh*. Historic Scotland Archive Report.

Hannay, RK (ed) 1915 *Rentale Dunkeldense, 1505–1517*. Edinburgh.

Hazlitt WC 1995 *Dictionary of Faiths and Folklore* facsimile of 1905 edition. London.

Hodgson GWI, Smith, C and Jones A forthcoming 'The Mammal Bone', *in* Bogdan, N *et al*, *The Perth High Street Excavation. Fascicule IX*.

Kenward, H and Hall, A 2001 'Plants, Intestinal Parasites and Insects', *in* Cameron, AS and Stones, JA (eds) *Aberdeen. An In-Depth View of the City's Past*, Edinburgh, 280–97.

Lamb, HH 1996 *Climate, History and the Modern World*. London.

Lindsay, WJ 1989 'Linlithgow: the Excavations', *in* Stones, JA, *Three Scottish Carmelite friaries*, 57–93.

Mabey, R 1979 *Plants with a Purpose*. Glasgow.

Milne, R (ed) 1891 *Rental Books of King James VI Hospital*. Perth.

Moffat, B (ed) 1986 *SHARP Practice: Researches into the Medieval Hospital, Soutra*. Edinburgh.

Moffat, B and Penny, M 2001 'Residues from a Ceramic Vessel and Stone Mortar', *in* Cameron, A and Stones, JA (eds), *Aberdeen. An In-Depth View of the City's Past*, 297–9.

Moloney, C (ed) forthcoming *Excavations at the Site of the Scottish Parliament, Canongate, Edinburgh*. Historic Scotland Archive Report

Moloney, C and Coleman R 1997 'The Development of a Medieval Street Frontage: the Evidence From Excavations at 80–86 High Street, Perth', *PSAS*, 127, 707–82.

Murdoch, R and Lewis, J 1999 'Excavations at the St Monans Saltpans, 1990–96', *in* Lewis, J, Martin, C, Martin, P and Murdoch R, *The Salt and Coal Industries at St Monans, Fife, in the 18th and 19th centuries*, Glenrothes, 5–27.

Murray, JC (ed) 1982 *Excavations in the Medieval Burgh of Aberdeen, 1973–81*, Edinburgh.

Muthesius, A 1987 'Silk', *in* Holdsworth, P (ed) *Excavations in the Medieval Burgh of Perth*, 169–71.

Reynolds, PJ 1987 *Ancient Farming*. Aylesbury.

Robinson, D 1987 'Botanical Remains', *in* Holdsworth, P (ed), *Excavations in the Medieval Burgh of Perth 1979-84*, 199–209.

Roberts, J forthcoming 'The Skeletal Remains' *in* Fyles, C, Roberts, J and Hall, D *Watching Brief on Environmental Improvements Around St John's Kirk in Perth*. Perth.

Shaw, J 1994 'Manuring and Fertilising the Lowlands, 1650–1850', *in* Foster, S and Smout, TC, *The History of Soils and Field Systems*, Aberdeen, 111–18.

Smith, C 1995 'The Animal Bone', *in* Hall, DW, 'Archaeological Excavations at St Nicholas Farm, St Andrews, 1986–87', *Tayside and Fife Archaeological Journal*, 1, 48–75.

Smith, C 1998 'Animal Bone from Ladyhill', *in* Hall, DW, MacDonald, ADS, Perry, D R and Terry, J, 'The Archaeology of Elgin; Excavations on Ladyhill and in the High Street, with an Overview of the Archaeology of the Burgh', *PSAS*, 128, 770–74.

*Smith, C 1998 'Dogs, Cats and Horses in the Scottish Medieval Town', *PSAS*, 128, 859–85.

Smith, C 2000 'A Grumphie in the Sty: an Archaeological View of Pigs in Scotland, From their Earliest Domestication to the Agricultural Revolution', *PSAS*, 130, 705–24.

Smith, C 2000 'The Animal Bone', *in* Perry, DR *Castle Park, Dunbar. Two Thousand Years on a Fortified Headland*, Edinburgh, 194–297.

Smith, C forthcoming 'The Animal Bone', *in* Perry, DR and Coleman, R, *Excavations at St John's Square, Perth*. Historic Scotland Archive Report

Smout, TC 1993 'Woodland History before 1850', *in* Smout, TC (ed), *Scotland Since Prehistory. Natural Change and Human Impact*, Aberdeen, 40–49.

Stavert, ML 1993 *The Perth Guildry Book, 1452–1601*. Edinburgh.

*Stones, JA (ed) 1989 *Three Scottish Carmelite Friaries. Excavations at Aberdeen. Linlithgow and Perth, 1980–86*. Edinburgh.

Stuart, M (ed) 1987 *The Encyclopaedia of Herbs and Herbalism*. London.

Thomas, C forthcoming 'The Leather', in *The Perth High Street Excavation*. Historic Scotland Archive Report.

Warden, AJ 1872 *The Burgh Laws of Dundee*. London.

West, B 1982 'Spur Development: Recognizing Caponized Fowl in Archaeological Material', *in* Wilson, B, Grigson, C and Payne, S (eds), *Ageing and Sexing Animal Bones from Archaeological Sites*, Oxford, 255–61.

Whatley, CA 1984 *The Salt Industry and its Trade in Fife and Tayside, c1570–1850*. Dundee.

Wordsworth, J 1983 'Friarscroft and the Trinitarians in Dunbar,' *PSAS* ,113, 478–89.

Wordsworth, J and Clark, PR 1997 'The Excavation at Kirkhill', *in* Rains, MJ *Excavations in St Andrews, 1980–89: a Decade of Archaeology*, Glenrothes, 7–18.

Wyness, F 1966 *City by the Grey North Sea: Aberdeen*. Aberdeen.

Yeoman, PA 1984 'Excavations at Castlehill of Strachan, 1980–81', *PSAS*, 114, 315–64.

FURTHER READING

Items above marked * are recommended for further reading, along with the following:

Cameron, AS and Stones, JA (eds) (2001) *Aberdeen. An In-Depth View of the City's Past*. Edinburgh.

Lynch, M, Spearman, M and Stell, G (eds) 1988 *The Scottish Medieval Town*. Edinburgh.

Perry, D 2005 *Dundee Rediscovered. The Archaeology of Dundee Reconsidered*. Tayside and Fife Archaeological committee monograph 4. Perth.

Rains, MJ and Hall, DW 1997 (eds) *Excavations in St Andrews, 1980–89*. Glenrothes.

Yeoman, P 1995 *Medieval Scotland*. London.

CHAPTER TEN

Rural Society and Economy

Ian Whyte

The study of medieval Scottish society suffers from a severe lack of evidence compared with England. Many of the archives that once existed have been destroyed. Much of what survives relates to the church and is not necessarily representative of what was happening on lay estates (Reynolds 203, 176). Regarding archaeology, there has been relatively little excavation, while the continuation of prehistoric settlement forms such as duns and crannogs into medieval and post-medieval times has complicated interpretations. Excavation has also concentrated on high-status sites; we know little about the settlements of the ordinary population in medieval times (Atkinson *et al* 2000; Whyte 1998). Early historic settlements existed within territorial frameworks whose structures come down to us faintly in documents from the twelfth and thirteenth centuries, and which were important in determining patterns of medieval lordship and landholding. As elsewhere in Britain, territorial organisation involved 'multiple estates' with caputs or central settlements to which rents in produce were brought, and from which authority was exercised over, and justice dispensed to, the inhabitants of dependent settlements (Barrow 1973). Although called by different names in different areas, the essence of the system was similar throughout Scotland. Some of these units in eastern Scotland – called shires, thanages – can be traced back to the seventh century, and may have originated much earlier (Grant 1998).

Place names provide clues to the distribution of different linguistic groups, to settlement hierarchies and sometimes to the evolution of settlement patterns (McNeill and MacQueen 1996; Nicolaisen 1976). Early medieval Scotland comprised a multiplicity of peoples whose political relationships were often warlike, something which tends to emphasise differences between them rather than underlying similarities (Smyth 1984). Picts, Scots, Britons, Angles and Norse had, by the eleventh century, fused into a kingdom – Alba or Scotia – whose leaders had become known as kings of Scots, and the boundary between England and Scotland had been established along the Tweed. Once established, the kingdom of the Scots proved remarkably resilient (Barrell 2000, 10)

POPULATION

Estimates of the population of Scotland at any time between 1100 and 1500 are based largely on guesswork. There are no sources like Domesday Book or the fourteenth-century English lay subsidies to act as a basis for calculations before the hearth tax returns of the late seventeenth century. It is possible, however, to suggest that Scotland may have had around one million inhabitants by the early fourteenth century. Indirect evidence, such as the creation of new settlements and an expansion of the cultivated area, suggests that Scotland shared in the general growth of population in Europe during the twelfth and thirteenth centuries with perhaps a doubling between the eleventh century and the early fourteenth. At their peak, average population densities may have been around 35 people per square mile, a figure that was only slightly greater in the seventeenth and early eighteenth centuries. Medieval Scotland was hardly an empty country then; many rural areas must have been as well populated as they are today and some districts, especially in the north, even more so. To what extent this growth caused pressure on resources is less clear. The evidence for high cultivation levels in areas like the Lammermuirs, and the opening up of royal hunting forests for settlement certainly hints at this (Parry 1975; Gilbert 1979).

There is equally little information on short-term demographic episodes such as mortality crises due to epidemics and famines. We do not know how badly the European-wide famine of 1315–17 affected Scotland, though Scottish raids into England in the 1320s might be seen in this context as an attempt to make up for natural losses by means of plunder. Nor it is clear whether mortality due directly or indirectly to the Wars of Independence checked population growth. Even the scale of mortality due to the Black Death, which reached Scotland in 1349, is unclear. Later chroniclers suggested that a third of the population may have died. A cooler climate and a more dispersed population than England may have reduced mortality but nevertheless the Black Death remains the worst demographic crisis on record, causing a major change in the balance between population and resources. This was reflected in the paucity of subsistence crises during the late fourteenth and fifteenth centuries, in evidence for increases in holding sizes, in falls in rents, in the leasing of demesnes and by indications that the diet of ordinary people included a substantial component of meat and dairy products (Gibson and Smout 1989). After the Black Death there were further outbreaks of plague in 1361–2, 1379–81, 1392, 1401–3, 1430–32, 1439–42, 1455–56, 1468–72, 1475–80 and 1496–1500. The mortality caused by these epidemics must have prevented any significant recovery in population numbers until well after 1500.

SETTLEMENT AND AGRICULTURE

Early charters – our main source of evidence for the medieval Scottish countryside – tell us something about territorial units, but little about the settlements within them. As a result, ideas regarding medieval settlement tend to be based on backward projections from the better-documented sixteenth and seventeenth centuries. Charters and place-name evidence show that even before the medieval rise in population the countryside was far from empty. There is evidence for the growth of existing places, the infilling of the settlement pattern, and the spread of settlement into new areas from the end of the eleventh century. The form of settlement is less clear. Over most of Scotland, as in later times, the pattern is likely to have been a dispersed one of small hamlets and isolated dwellings. It was well adapted to an environment in which extensive areas of well-drained soils, capable of supporting large communities, were restricted, and to an economy oriented towards livestock-rearing. Sometimes the wording of a grant of arable land implies that it had been newly cleared from the waste and is likely to have been associated with the creation of a new settlement. In other instances, references suggest the expansion of arable around an existing settlement. The splitting of townships and their fields to create smaller units can also be identified from as early as written records have survived (Dodgshon 1981, 196).

Charters suggest that there was a greater emphasis on arable farming in the Lothians and the Merse compared with areas further north, although in most areas the improved land would have formed small islands in a sea of waste. In south-east Scotland, when documentation improves in late medieval times, we find nucleated villages similar to those of north east England. Many have regular plans based on parallel rows, sometimes focusing on a central green, similar to examples in the Eden Valley and County Durham (Roberts 1987, 172–77). It seems unlikely that these were created as regular villages with associated field systems during the Anglian occupation of south-east Scotland. It is more likely that they reflect replanning by Anglo-Norman landholders during the twelfth and thirteenth centuries. Elsewhere ferm touns or hamlet clusters appear to have been the usual settlement form. Few medieval peasant houses have been excavated, even fewer securely dated; a terrace of cottages at Springwood Park near Kelso is an exception (Dixon 1998). Sometimes touns were held by single, substantial tenants and sublet; sometimes they were occupied in shared ownership by groups of tenants, a contrast brought out by rentals like one for the Morton estates in 1376 and another for Kelso Abbey c.1300. Where a group of tenants shared a toun, the land could be worked communally and the produce shared or the land could be divided into fractions in terms of the quality as well as the quantity of the land, a system which by the early fifteenth century was known as runrig (Dodgshon 1981, 147).

The farming system involved transhumance with livestock being sent to summer pastures or shieling grounds. In the Southern Uplands, the creation of extensive areas of hunting forest, the spread of commercial sheep farming on monastic estates, and the general expansion of settlement and cultivation seem to have brought the use of shielings to an end in many areas during the twelfth and thirteenth centuries. The widespread survival of farms containing the place name element 'shiel' testifies to the conversion of shielings to permanent settlements (Winchester 2000, 90–93).

Information on agriculture and estate management is sparse, and much of it comes from monastic lands. The quality of monastic estate management before the fourteenth century and its later deficiencies have probably been exaggerated, and it should not be assumed that the monks were necessarily better farmers than their lay contemporaries (Duncan 1975). Open field systems with holdings scattered in fragmented strips can be shown to have existed but details of their organization, such as crop rotations, are few. Wheat was grown in some well-favoured areas but there is no evidence for the cultivation of legumes. Oats and bere (four-row barley) were the principal, and in many areas the only, crops. The great wealth of monastic estates like Kelso and Melrose was not in their arable land but their flocks, possibly up to 12,000 sheep each. Duncan (1975, 431–2) has suggested, however, that even the Cistercians' attitude to estate management was less than optimal with little sign of long-term planning for improvement.

THE LATE MEDIEVAL COUNTRYSIDE

In the Highlands, a perennial problem was the narrowness of the region's resource base in an environment mostly ill-suited to arable farming, although problems due to population growth and pressure on resources become evident only from the sixteenth century. Even in the Lowlands, environmental conditions did not favour cultivation in many areas, with the downturn of climatic conditions from the fourteenth century onwards (Simmons 2001, 70). Nevertheless, from the fifteenth century there are some signs of expansion as population began to build up again. (Dodgshon 1981, 176–7). Much of this was local infilling, as is suggested by place names such as Newton and Muirton. There were also frontiers where larger-scale colonisation was possible. These included royal and baronial hunting preserves that were disafforested. One of the largest of these was Ettrick Forest, which returned to crown hands with the forfeiture of the Douglases in 1455. At this date, it was sparsely settled with forest *stedes* or holdings possessing attached grazing rights. In the late fifteenth century these were converted into large sheep farms, some held directly by the crown, others leased to tenants. At a parish level, some touns grew in size and importance due to the presence of nucleating factors, giving rise to place names containing elements like Milton, Castleton, Kirkton, or Bridgton. Fisher touns – often quite separate from neighbouring agricultural communities – were especially characteristic of the North East from Angus to the Moray Firth.

Field systems also increased in complexity. The distinction between infield and outfield is thought to have evolved only in late medieval times. Initially the difference was a tenurial one (Dodgshon 1981). Infield was the original area of assessed land, laid out in fixed numbers of land units. These units originally denoted fixed amounts of land which might vary from one area to another but which were consistent within individual townships. From the thirteenth century, the assessments of most touns remained fixed. New land taken into cultivation was not absorbed into existing land units but was treated separately so that most touns came to have cores of old assessed land units surrounded by fringes of more recently reclaimed land measured in acres. How did this tenurial distinction produce the differences in farming techniques which led to the creation of infield and outfield? Dodgshon suggests that, by the time the intake of new land was contemplated, the original assessed area would already have been under intensive cultivation, using all the manure produced by the township's livestock during the winter half of the year when the animals were grazed on the stubble and housed. As this manure was already committed to maintaining returns from the existing arable area, any attempt to expand cultivation needed to utilise the otherwise wasted manure produced during the summer when animals were grazed on the common pasture. The solution was to fence the animals on areas of the pasture, allowing them to dung it in preparation for outfield cultivation (Dodgshon 1981, 184–95). The returns from arable farming were modest; although direct data are not available, seventeenth-century evidence suggests that average yields are likely to have been around three or four times the amount of grain sown.

Woodland was a resource that came under increasing pressure during medieval times, although recent research has highlighted the scale of deforestation in later prehistoric times (Tipping 1994). At the start of our period, there is evidence of widespread regeneration, presumably the indirect result of political instability. This provided mature timber to meet the needs of an expanding population in the late twelfth and thirteenth centuries, with the growth of burghs, the construction of castles and the building of churches. Woodland management at this time was directed mainly at the preservation of game for hunting. By the fifteenth century, however, construction timber was in increasingly short supply in the Lowlands, leading to growing imports of timber and attempts by Parliament, from 1424, to protect surviving resources, probably with little effect (Crone and Watson 2003).

THE MEDIEVAL ECONOMY

Despite limited evidence, some broad economic trends can be discerned. A feature of the twelfth and thirteenth centuries was the shift to a money economy and, closely associated, the development of overseas trade and the rise of the burghs. Under David I, around 1136, the first Scottish coinage was minted. During the long reign of William I there was a gradual transition to a money economy, though English coins formed up to 95 per cent of the money circulating in Scotland in the later thirteenth century, emphasising the importance of trade links with England before the Wars of Independence. The development of the burghs as market centres provided a means of turning surplus agricultural produce from demesnes and rents into cash. The role of towns in stimulating arable farming is shown by an assessment of monastic incomes for the Lothians and the Merse in 1293. Religious houses like Newbattle and Holyrood, close to Edinburgh, had larger arable demesnes than abbeys like Melrose, more distant from urban centres (Duncan 1975, 339–42).

How much of this growing wealth filtered down to the peasantry is uncertain. The later fourteenth century, with lower population levels and falling rents, may have been a better time for them than the later thirteenth century, with its evidence of population pressure and declining mean holding size. Nevertheless, the small size of many coin hoards from the later thirteenth century does suggest that money was changing hands among the peasantry as well as higher levels of society.

The growth of the economy was related to the development of trade (particularly wool exports) especially to Flanders but also to France and England. This trade transformed the Scottish rural economy, leading to a concentration on sheep rearing. The wool trade was well established by the thirteenth century, by which time large areas were already given over to sheep pasture. Although of lesser value hides, skins and fish were also significant exports.

War with England began in 1296 and continued until 1323, breaking out again in 1332 and only ending with the Treaty of Berwick in 1357. Damage was severe at times, particularly in southern Scotland, although rural areas were quick to recover from military activity. But, despite the resilience of Scottish society, the economy undoubtedly suffered, not least because contact with England, one of Scotland's main trading partners, was broken. Scottish trading routes across the North Sea were also vulnerable to English attack. Trading contacts with western France, Germany and the Baltic declined while trade with Flanders, especially Bruges, became more significant. Wool exports to the Low Countries continued to be Scotland's most vital overseas link. In European terms, late-medieval Scotland was a major exporter of wool and leather, wool peaking in 1372 when around 9,252 sacks were exported and hides in 1381 with over 72,000 of them exported (Guy 1986).

ANGLO-NORMAN FEUDALISM

The eleventh-century kingdom of the Scots was a mixture of several peoples, languages and cultures to which was added feudalism (Barrell 2000, 10). The development of feudalism was one of the processes, together with territorial consolidation, that in the twelfth and thirteenth centuries changed Scotland from a traditional Celtic society to a kingdom with European status (Barrell 2000, 15).

In Scotland, unlike England, feudalism arrived peacefully, introduced by Anglo-Norman incomers, in a fully-developed form, but spreading gradually and with an uneven geographical impact. Feudalism reached the north-west Highlands belatedly and incompletely. In theory, feudalism contrasted with the tribal kinship-based social structure of Scottish society but in practice many aspects of eleventh-century Scottish society, such as tenure, food renders and military service, were already essentially feudal. David I (1124–1153) established a unified system of feudal lordships and sheriffdoms over much of southern Scotland. His successors, Malcolm IV and William I, extended this into the south-west, west and north of Scotland. Large blocks of royal demesnes were granted to Anglo-Norman immigrants in return for knights' service. Some came from England, others from Normandy, Flanders and Brittany (Barrell 2000, 18).

In the Lothians and the Merse fiefs were generally small: a single village and its territory. In western and south-western Scotland, where royal control was less firm, David I created large lordships; Annandale, some 200,000 acres, was granted to Robert de Brus for the service of ten knights. The new nobles subinfeudated land to their followers. Their settlement is evident today by the earthworks of their motte and bailey castles and by place names incorporating new personal names such as Roberton, Symington (Simon) and Thankerton (Tancard). Under William a new wave of frontier lordships was created in the north-east and even beyond the Great Glen. Stringer's (1985) study of the lordship of Garioch – a 100 square mile block of country between the Celtic earldoms of Buchan and Mar granted by William to his younger brother Earl David of Huntingdon – shows how the strategic and military role went hand-in-hand with economic development.

The social impact of Anglo-Norman feudalism is hard to assess. Cultural differences certainly existed between natives and newcomers. However, the incomers brought only limited numbers of followers rather than a mass of peasant settlers, and there were already marked regional variations in culture (Reynolds 2003, 192). Feudalism had to be integrated with older systems of landholding and social structures (Barrell 2000, 19). Major forfeiture of native lords or widespread displacement of the peasantry was not an option. In the south-west, the occurrence of several Ingliston place names associated with mottes suggests that the incomers were few. Elsewhere, however, their arrival was associated with the foundation of new settlements and the intake of land from the waste. Overall, the economic impact of Anglo-Norman settlement may not have been great and the structure of the lower levels of rural society was probably little affected, though the incomers undoubtedly encouraged the spread of the use of the English language and the retreat of Gaelic. It is unclear to what extent the classic English manorial system was practicable in Scotland where pastoral farming was, overall, much more significant than arable (Barrell 2000, 19). During the twelfth and thirteenth centuries, the organisation of the church was also radically altered. David I rationalised and extended the system of dioceses and, by systematising the provision of endowments for churches and by requiring the payment of teinds (tithes), he created a framework of parishes, many of them using the boundaries of ancient shires and thanages. The network of nearly 1,000 parishes was almost complete by the end of the twelfth century. This involved the extension of a system which already existed in embryo. More innovative was the introduction of continental monastic orders. Although one or two religious houses were founded before his day, David I dramatically increased the pace of new foundations. The Cistercians eventually held a dozen houses in Scotland. Other foundations included houses of nuns and friars, and hospitals. The Cistercians, whose rule forbade them to live off rents, obtained large grants of upland grazings which they converted into extensive sheep farms. By the late thirteenth century, all the main religious orders, apart from the Carthusians, were established in Scotland.

THE NOBILITY OF LATER MEDIEVAL SCOTLAND

From the twelfth century, the independent lordships or earldoms into which Scotland was divided were more closely integrated into the Scottish kingdom. The introduction of feudal tenures allowed the transformation of patterns of landholding, leading to the creation of new secular lordships such as those held by the Bruces and the Stewarts. By late medieval times, these new patterns had reshaped the structure of the Scottish nobility. The nobility of late-medieval Scotland amounted to perhaps 2,000 heads of families, or 10,000 members in all, a little over one per cent of the population, a figure comparable with contemporary France. Within this group there were, at any time, fifty or so magnates who played a significant role in national affairs. Below this were a few hundred substantial landowners. At the lower end they merged into the peasantry, being distinguished by tenure rather than wealth. Unlike England, where the peerage was sharply defined and distinguished from the gentry, a Scottish peerage did not emerge until the mid-fifteenth century. This blurring of distinctions helps to explain why in Scotland a gentry class with a clear sense of identity was so late in developing. Rural society in late-medieval Scotland was more fluid, with greater social mobility, than in many other parts of Europe.

The structure of the higher nobility changed markedly between the mid fourteenth and mid fifteenth centuries. Before the Wars of Independence the nobility was still mainly territorial, with status and power related directly to land. The dozen earldoms were huge, compact blocks of country within which the earls' influence was paramount. The rest of the nobility comprised the barons, who had been granted special jurisdictional powers, and below them the freeholders without special privileges. Within the barons, Grant (1984) distinguishes three groups. First there were those who held great feudal lordships. Some, like Annandale, were as extensive as earldoms. At a lower level were men with groups of baronies. Their importance was greater than the remaining barons who held only one or two baronies each.

Many ancient earldoms and provincial lordships survived until after the Wars of Independence but, by the end of the fourteenth century, this pattern was changing. One important feature was the increasing concentration of earldoms and lordships in fewer hands. By the 1390s, the Stewarts had acquired a dozen of them and the Douglases several more. With the forfeiture of various Stewart nobles by James I and of the Douglases by James II, much of this land came into the hands of the crown during the fifteenth century. By the mid fifteenth century, the nobility was starting to become more distinctly divided between the lords who were parliamentary peers and the lairds, a group which included all other nobles. New earldoms and lordships, instead of having a firm territorial base, were coming to be personal, honorific titles that did not necessarily have close links with specific localities. The earldom of Douglas, created in 1355, was the first of these with territories scattered in nine sheriffdoms. At the same time, many of the old territorial earldoms were disappearing by forfeiture or division among heiresses. As this occurred, the traditional role of the earls in mustering and leading the common army declined. By 1438 only five of the old provincial earldoms survived; the rest had come into the hands of the crown by forfeiture or escheat (the earl dying without heirs).

The great provincial lordships followed a similar pattern. By the mid-fifteenth century many had reverted to the crown, been absorbed by the Douglas earldoms, or been fragmented. It was in this context that the barons who did not hold provincial lordships, but whose lands were nevertheless extensive, assumed greater political importance. The new earls and lords of parliament were drawn mainly from this group. The removal of the Stewart and Douglas earldoms by James I and James II allowed members of this group to rise to the top of the nobility, becoming some of the most important families in Scotland. A distinct Scottish peerage developed in the mid-fifteenth century with the practice of summoning certain lords to attend parliament. These 'lords of parliament' came to form the lower rank of the peerage and were distinguished from the 'small barons' who were summoned as a group.

Grant (1984) has provided interesting insights into the structure of the late-medieval Scottish nobility by calculating the rates of extinction of families and comparing the results for other countries. In England and France the survival rates of noble families were roughly similar. Turnover was rapid. In each 25-year period around a quarter of noble families died out. In Scotland, however, the extinction rate for dukes and earls fell from 27 per cent in the first half of the fourteenth century to between 16 and 17 per cent in the second half of the fifteenth century. The extinction rate for barons and lords of parliament dropped from 24 per cent in 1325–29 to between 5 and 7 per cent for the last three-quarters of the fifteenth century. The aggregate rate of extinction for Scottish noble families fell from 28 per cent in 1325–49 to 10 per cent in 1475–1500, contrasting with England where the rate held steady at around 25 per cent throughout the fifteenth century.

The high levels of extinction of Scottish dukes and earls in the first quarter of the fourteenth century can be attributed to war with England. It is possible that the lack of internal unrest in late medieval Scotland may have aided family survival, but differences in fertility between Scottish and English noble families may also have been important. Marriage with older female heiresses for political and economic advantage was less common in Scotland because such heiresses were fewer. Scottish magnates were more likely than their English counterparts to marry women of childbearing age with a greater probability of producing enough sons to carry on the male line. If the causes of this noble marriage pattern are uncertain, then some of its implications are clear. In England the failure of male lines led to a high turnover of landownership. In Scotland, the estates of the nobility were more stable, and the scope for making large additions to one's territory by marriage more limited. In England, the acquisition of estates by marriage tended to produce a fragmented pattern of land ownership, working against the strong and continued influence of magnate families in particular localities. The prolonged disputes over inheritance that resulted from the marriage patterns of the English nobility – a major cause of local instability – were less of a problem in Scotland. The degree of continuity in the occupation of land in Scotland contributed to stability within rural society. The fertility of the noble families led to a surplus of younger sons who often managed to establish cadet branches.

The creation of cadet branches within territories dominated by existing landed families helps to explain the importance of kinship in late-medieval Scotland. Younger sons of noble families frequently married into the families of local lairds, further cementing kinship links within particular localities. The clearly-defined regional spheres of influence of Scottish magnates, which resulted from the geographical concentration of their estates and the importance of their jurisdictions in baronies and regalities, was powerfully supported by family ties. It is in this context that a switch from a recognition of kinship on a cognatic to an agnatic basis seems to have occurred. Cognatic relationships, acknowledging relationships through the female as well as the male line, produced large, loose kinship groups with weak links.

Agnatic systems, recognising relationships only through the male line and defined by the possession of a common surname, appear to have become typical in Scotland by the end of the fifteenth century, in the Highlands as much as the Lowlands (Dodgshon 1998, 31). Their persistence explains why kinship remained so important in Scottish society.

Agnatic ties were strengthened by geographical proximity. Particular surnames came to be identified with specific localities as, with a lack of heiresses, a family's holdings often remained stable for generations. Another way in which landed families could strengthen their regional influence was through bonds of manrent – written contracts of allegiance and mutual support between two men, usually a lord and a laird. Such bonds extended the influence of magnates and supported lairds in their localities by giving them powerful allies. These bonds did not indicate a new development in terms of loyalty, merely a desire to confirm existing relationships in writing in an increasingly literate age. The relationships involved an extension of the values based on kinship to people who were not related. The possession of clearly-defined regional spheres of influence buttressed by landownership, kinship and ties with non-related families by means of bonds of manrent was one of the most distinctive features of late-medieval Scottish society (Wormald 1985)

RURAL SOCIAL STRUCTURE: THE LOWLANDS

Compared with the wealth of detail for medieval England, the documentation for twelfth- and thirteenth-century Scotland affords only glimpses of the structure of rural society. The terminology for different social strata varied between regions and over time. Rural society in the early fourteenth century seems to have included an upper stratum of free tenants, a substantial class of dependent peasants and an ill-defined group, including smallholders and the totally landless, who may have existed by cultivating lords' demesnes and the holdings of more well-to-do peasants. In central Scotland in the mid-twelfth century we find peasants termed *bondars* paying food rents but only light labour and carriage services. In the early thirteenth century north of the Tay, a class of free tenants is recorded, owing rent in produce to the king's thanes. Below them were unfree tenants or *scolocs*, probably comparable with the earlier bondars further south. Under them were cottagers with small plots of arable and grazing rights but burdened with fairly light labour services. There was no overall contemporary term embracing the mass of the peasantry. *Nativi* or *neyfs*, roughly equivalent to the English villein, was the term most commonly used. The lowest levels of neyfs were known as *fugitivi* in the twelfth century and *servi* (serfs) in the thirteenth. In the twelfth century there may still have been some slaves. The term *neyf* covered a wide social range including relatively wealthy families, but whether *servi* or not they were all considered to be bound to their lord by the places of their birth and the residence of their families. Generalising, the bondars of the twelfth century became the *neyfs* of the early thirteenth century and the husbandman of the late thirteenth, while over the same period the *scolocs* became *fugitivi* then cottars (Duncan 1975).

Even south of the Forth, where arable land was more extensive, labour services were light compared with classic areas of English manorialisation. This reflects the importance of pastoral farming in the Scottish economy and the more restricted extent of demesnes. Demesne cultivation does not seem to have been very important in the early twelfth century, but south of the Forth it increased in the late twelfth and early thirteenth centuries. Given that the quotas of knights' service required from the great feudal lordships were modest compared with England, there may have been less pressure to intensify demesne production for commercial sale. By the end of the thirteenth century, demesne farming on estates like Coldingham Priory and Kelso Abbey was declining, with land being leased to tenants and labour services commuted to money payments (Duncan 1975). Some labour services were nevertheless retained, perhaps as a token of bondage. On the lands of Kelso Abbey in the thirteenth century husbandmen, as well as paying money rents, provided labour at harvest time and did some ploughing and harrowing on the demesne as well as performing carriage services and helping to wash and shear the sheep. Cottagers paid a money rent and harvest labour. Tenants were thirled (required to use) to the estate mill and brewhouse and paid heriot (the best beast, paid on the death of the tenant) and merchet (a payment for permission to give a daughter in marriage). Husbandmen had their holdings intermingled in the common fields of their settlement. Cottars appear to have had separate plots, usually under two acres, often much less. There were also compact holdings, sometimes held free of labour services. The largest of these may have once been ministerial holdings belonging to thanes but the smaller ones were probably recent intakes from the waste. Within peasant society there were marked contrasts in wealth and status, sometimes with a wide gap between husbandmen and cottars, in other cases with more of a range of holding sizes.

LATE MEDIEVAL RURAL SOCIETY

In the late fifteenth century, the volume of evidence on the lower levels of Scottish society begins to increase: the picture that emerges is varied and complex. Most families who farmed the land were tenants, but there was considerable variation in their status. One group – perhaps the majority in many areas – were tenants-at-will, holding from year to year by verbal agreements. In a stronger position legally were tenants with written leases or tacks for a specific number of years or for life. More secure still were rentallers who held a copy of the entry in the proprietor's rental book, so confirming their possession. Rentallers, equivalent in many respects to English copyholders of inheritance, could normally expect to pass on their holdings to their heirs. While population growth was sluggish, it was in a landowner's interest to keep the land occupied in this way. Even where tenants held tacks for only a few years the normal expectation was probably that they would be renewed without difficulty. Even tenants at will had often been established in particular holdings for generations. The customary right of tenants to succeed in this way was known as 'kindness', tenure based on kinship with the previous occupier. Kindly tenants might hold their land as rentallers, leaseholders or at will but their right to succeed, widely recognised by local and royal courts, could be transferred or even bought and sold.

Tenants' holdings varied considerably in size. On estates where detailed records are available – mainly ecclesiastical ones – tenants can be traced moving from one holding to another, leasing extra land and negotiating with neighbours to consolidate land into larger, less fragmented parcels. Below the tenants was a large, poorly-recorded group of cottars and sub-tenants about whom we know little. The picture of rural society is one with elements of both stability and mobility. Rents were paid largely in kind and labour but money nevertheless circulated widely. Tenants could appear as assertive rather than downtrodden, and failure to pay their rents due to adverse circumstances did not automatically lead to summary eviction.

THE EMERGENCE OF THE HIGHLANDS

Highlanders were distinguished by their language, by a more pastoral economy and by the general hardness of their existence. Recent historians have tended to view differences in social structure between the Highlands and the Lowlands as ones of emphasis and chronology rather than of kind. Smout (1972, 39–44) has suggested that Highland society was based on kinship modified by feudalism, Lowland society on feudalism modified by kinship. Barrow (1989) has warned of the danger of drawing too sharp a line between the character of medieval society in the Highlands and Lowlands. The Highlands cannot be neatly isolated as a distinct society (Dodgshon 1998, 32). The balance between Celtic traditions and feudalism varied within the Highlands with a gradient from the more feudalised east and south towards the north and west. Gaelic had been spoken as far south as the Tweed and the Solway in the eleventh century. By the sixteenth century it had retreated from most of the Lowlands. Gaelic may have survived in parts of lowland Aberdeenshire into the sixteenth century and Galloway into the seventeenth but, apart from these isolated pockets, the boundary between Gaelic and English had stabilised along the Highland line by the end of our period (Withers 1984).

If late-medieval Lowland society is thinly documented, the situation for the Highlands is even worse, though rentals from Kintyre in 1505 and Islay in 1506 are useful (Dodgshon 1998, 70–1). This makes it hard to determine just how much Highland society differed from the rest of Scotland. We know that Highland clans were not survivals of primitive Celtic tribalism. They seem to have developed in the fourteenth century when the spread of feudalism into the Highlands was checked by the declining power of the monarchy. Clans arose from a need for local leaders to protect themselves and their followers without the support of central authority. Protection meant, effectively, aggressive expansion that could be legitimised by various means based on feudal authority or kinship.

A clan was, in theory, a patrilineal kindred whose members could trace their descent from a common ancestor. In the west Highlands, clans often traced their ancestry back to Celtic or Norse leaders like Somerled. Where the common ancestor was patently an invention, he was sometimes changed periodically as clans sought more distant and more imposing origins. In the eastern Highlands many clans were feudal in origin, their chiefs descended from Anglo-Norman families established on their lands by feudal charter, who had seen the benefits of augmenting their feudal powers by kinship structures based on local customs.

Clan chiefs had obligations as well as powers: to provide land, protection, welfare and hospitality for their clansmen. Chiefs might give livestock to those whose animals had died, or take elderly people into their own households. Within a clan, there was usually a group of people with close kinship links to the chief: his advisers in peace, his lieutenants in war, a gentry class known as *daoine uaisle* who held land from the chief on a hereditary basis in return for rent and services. Chiefs were supposed to take the advice of the *daoine uaisle*, who might elect a chief from rival candidates or depose an unsuitable one. Most ordinary clansmen were not directly related to their chief, but the idea of such a relationship was a useful fiction that helped clan unity.

Kinship was an important unifying element within clans, but it was not the only one. A sixteenth-century description of clans being united by 'pretense of blude or plaice of thair duelling' neatly expresses the mixture of genuine kinship and geographical propinquity that fostered unity (Dodgshon 1989). Even for later times, relatively little is known about the degree of social differentiation that existed among the levels of clan society below the *daoine uaisle*. The people who leased land from the clan gentry frequently sublet portions in turn to sub-tenants or cottars who, as in the Lowlands, may have formed a substantial proportion of the population.

Work on chiefdom societies in other parts of the world provides a window for understanding Highland clans. Rather than fossilised structures from the Celtic Iron Age, Highland clans were dynamic, capable of evolution and adjustment to external and internal influences. Dodgshon (1989) has emphasised their composite character, showing that they were capable of responding to changing circumstances. When population pressure was low, family groups constantly broke away from the main stems as new settlements were formed. When pressure on resources grew, social structures adjusted by evolving into descent groups linked across several genera-tions, focused around a chief who could organise the tribal economy in a more intensive way. Chiefdoms – and Highland clans – followed a cycle, developing from simple forms into complex structures and then collapsing again. At the start of the cycle, many small chiefdoms competed for status to enhance their power. This was done through feuding and by displays of conspicuous consumption at feasts. Those who succeeded extended their influence by conquest and marrying their sons into surrounding chiefdoms, creating expanding webs of alliances. In time though, such chiefdoms became too large and complex to be sustainable, collapsing into small competing chiefdoms from which the cycle began once more. Before the sixteenth century, the main complex chiefdom in the Highlands was the Lordship of the Isles. Its break-up following forfeiture to the crown in 1493, and its replacement by a number of small clans vying with each other for power in a welter of feuding, followed by the rise of the Campbells, fits the pattern well.

As kinship structures seem to have altered to suit changing circumstances, it cannot be assumed that all clans were organised in the same way. It has been suggested that three types of kinship structure existed. The first, linked with larger clans, involved a single family or chief holding large blocks of land. This was not simply achieved by the chief overriding the rights of his clansmen but by a range of strategies including inheritance, conquest, marriage and grants from the crown. Such territories were often built up rapidly, creating problems of control. This was done by granting portions of the newly-won land to members of the chief's family. The chief's kinship ties gradually spread as new land came within his control. These sub-chiefs would establish their own family groups, working downwards through society, gradually displacing local families which had once held authority.

In the second case, the growth of lesser clans was limited by the availability of land, leading to prestige being attached to feuding and feasting. The spoils of successful feuding provided the means for feasting and the maintenance of fighting men. The status of a chief could be measured by how many days eating and drinking a feast could occupy. Obligations to provide hospitality for a peripatetic chief and his retinue helped to strengthen personal contacts between chiefs and their followers. Feasting and giving prestige gifts helped to cement alliances with neighbouring chiefs. Prospects for territorial expansion by such groups were limited and many were forced to accept the protection and overlordship of larger clans. While large clans tended to diverge as kin groups, much of the growth of smaller clans was achieved by individual families creating their own opportunities through marriage and leases rather than by their chiefs undertaking major expansion of territory. In such situations, women often tended to marry within the clan, men outside it, a system which helped the clan hold on to its existing land and increased its chance of acquiring new areas (Dodgshon 1998, 35).

A third kind of kinship structure was linked to hereditary service. Within many clans were families serving as pipers, bards, doctors, armourers or smiths to their chiefs, receiving land free or at a reduced rent in return for their services (Bannerman 1986). The MacCrimmons, hereditary pipers to the MacLeods, are among the most famous of such families.

Control over land was essential: a clan without land was a broken clan (Dodgshon 1998, 4). Availability of land allowed chiefs to reward kinsmen and supporters. Food rents could be used to cushion a clan against crop failure and famine, emphasising the interdependence of clan and chief. They supported a chief's household, his piper, harpist and other retainers, who gave him status. Food rents maintained a nucleus of fighting men for defending clan territory and pursuing feuds, as well as allowing chiefs to provide feasts and hospitality, which emphasised their generosity. Rents in cattle provided the *tochers* or dowries with which marriage alliances were cemented.

It has been claimed that the spread of Anglo-Norman feudalism into the Highlands undermined the clan system. Feudalism, based on property, has been seen as alien to clanship, based on people. It is unlikely, however, that such considerations bothered Highland chiefs; power was exercised by whatever means were available. The two systems probably reinforced each other more than they clashed. By the end of our period the concept of clan lands as communal property was in decline as the selection of new chiefs from among the most suitable candidates gave way to primogeniture. Feudal lords found the kinship ties of clanship, real or putative, a useful device while clan chiefs strengthened their position by means of feudal grants and powers.

CONCLUSION

Medieval society and economy in Scotland was neither uniform spatially nor unchanging chronologically, though the limitations of the documentary and archaeological evidence severely obscure our perceptions of such variations. On the other hand, many aspects of medieval society continued long after the end of what has been traditionally considered to be the medieval period. Tenant farmers in the seventeenth and even the early eighteenth century were still working their land using farming systems that would have been perfectly recognisable to a medieval peasant. The tacks by which they held their lands still contained feudal obligations such as kain and carriage payments, labour on the mains, attendance at the barony court and thirlage to the estate mill. This underlying continuity was only to be disrupted by the landscape, economic and social revolutions that occurred from the 1760s, with the advent of agricultural improvement.

REFERENCES TO BOOKS AND ARTICLES MENTIONED IN THE TEXT

Items marked * are recommended for further reading.

Atkinson, JA, Banks, I and McGregor, G 2000 (ed) *Townships to Farmsteads: Rural Settlement Studies in Scotland, England and Wales.* Oxford.

Bannerman, J 1986 *The Beatons: a Medical Kindred in the Classical Gaelic Tradition.* Edinburgh.

*Barrell, ADM 2000 *Medieval Scotland.* Cambridge.

*Barrow, GWS 1973 *The Kingdom of the Scots.* London.

Barrow, GWS 1989 'The Lost Gaidhealtachd of Medieval Scotland', *in* Gillies, W (ed), *Gaelic and Scotland*, Edinburgh, 67–88.

Crone, A and Watson, F 2003 'Sufficiency to Scarcity: Medieval Scotland, 500–1600', *in* Smout TC (ed), *People and Woods in Scotland*, Edinburgh, 60–81.

Dixon, P 1998 'A Rural Medieval Settlement in Roxburghshire: Excavations at Springwood Park, Kelso, 1985–6', *Proceedings of the Society of Antiquaries of Scotland (PSAS)*, 128, 671–752.

*Dodgshon, RA 1981 *Land and Society in Early Scotland.* Oxford.

Dodgshon, RA 1989 'Pretense of Blude and Plaice of Thair Dwelling', *in* Houston, RA and Whyte, ID (eds), *Scottish Society 1500–1800*, Cambridge, 169–98.

*Dodgshon, RA 1998 *From Chiefs to Landlords. Social and Economic Change in the Western Highlands, c.1493–1820.* Edinburgh.

*Donnelly, J 2000 'In the Territory of Auchencrow: Long continuity or Late Development in Early Scottish Field Systems'. *PSAS*, 130, 743–72

*Duncan, AA 1975 *Scotland: the Making of the Kingdom*. Edinburgh.

Gilbert, JM 1979 *Hunting and Hunting Reserves in Medieval Scotland*. Edinburgh.

Gibson, A and Smout, TC 1989 'Scottish Food and Scottish history', *in* Houston, RA and Whyte, ID (eds), *Scottish Society, 1500–1800*, 59–81.

*Grant, A 1984 *Independence and Nationhood. Scotland, 1306–1469*. London.

Grant, A 1998 'Thanes and Thanages from the Eleventh to the Fourteenth centuries', *in* Grant, A and Stringer, KA (eds), *Medieval Scotland. Crown, Lordship and Community*, Edinburgh, 39–81.

Guy, I 1986 'The Scottish Export Trade 1460–1599', *in* Smout, TC (ed), *Scotland and Europe, 1200–1850*, Edinburgh, 62–81.

McNeill, PGB and MacQueen, HL 1996 *Atlas of Scottish History to 1707*. Edinburgh.

Nicolaisen, WFH 1976 *Scottish Place Names*. London.

Parry, ML 1975 'Secular Climatic Change and Marginal Agriculture', *Transactions of the Institute of British Geographers*, 64, 1–14.

Reynolds, S 2003 'Fiefs and Vassals in Scotland: a View from Outside', *Scottish Historical Review*, 82, 176–93.

Roberts, BK 1987 *The Making of the English Village*. London.

Simmons, IG 2001 *An Environmental History of Great Britain*. Edinburgh.

Smout, TC 1972 *A History of the Scottish People, 1560–1830*. London.

Smyth, AP 1984 *Warlords and Holy Men. Scotland, AD80–1000*. London.

*Stringer, KJ 1985 *Earl David of Huntingdon, 1152–1219*. Edinburgh.

Tipping, R 1994 'The Form and Fate of Scottish Woodlands', *PSAS*, 124, 1–54.

Whyte, ID 1998 'Pre-Improvement Rural Settlement in Scotland: Progress and Prospects', *Scottish Geographical Magazine*, 114, 76–84.

*Winchester, AJL 2000 *The Harvest of the Hills. Rural Life in Northern England and the Scottish Borders, 1400–1700*. Edinburgh.

Withers, CWJ 1984 *Gaelic in Scotland, 1698–1981. The Geography of a Language*. Edinburgh.

Wormald, J 1985 *Lords and Men in Scotland: Bonds of Manrent, 1442–1603*. Edinburgh.

CHAPTER ELEVEN

Medieval Architecture
Michael Asselmeyer

Scotland enjoys a rich heritage of medieval architecture. The evidence shows that the country in the north-west corner of Europe has been a participant in all periods of European architectural history since Roman times. Amazingly, this relationship has been almost unnoticed by Continental historians. It is typical for the selective view of traditional descriptions that the *Storia dell'architettura medievale* (fourth edition 2002), which intended to provide a holistic picture of the medieval architecture in Western Europe, does not mention a single building on Scottish soil. Stopping geographically at Durham, no notice has been taken, for instance, of its architectural relative, Dunfermline Abbey. Even had Scotland been exclusively at the receiving end of a stylistic genealogy, a complete display of filiations should always include ancestors *and* offspring.

Many Scots have written about the buildings of the middle ages north of the river Tweed since the Society of Antiquaries started unearthing and interpreting the material sources of the past, and especially since the prints of RW Billings drew the appearance of their ruins to wider public attention. We have since been provided with the Inventories of the Royal Commission on the Ancient and Historical Monuments of Scotland, and Richard Fawcett has dedicated his life to an astonishing number of publications on Scottish medieval architecture. The architectural history of medieval Scotland has been recounted chronologically (Cruden 1986), topographically (interwoven in the series *The Buildings of Scotland*), and thematically, by dividing it into building types (Fawcett 1994), raising issues such as form (style) and function (use), structure (technology) and construction (process, finance), and the social and economic contexts. The following chronological discussion tries to respect all of these approaches to some extent, and aims to demonstrate that, throughout the middle ages, Scottish architecture contributed to the diversity of European architecture.

TERMINOLOGY

Medieval architecture in Scotland, as in any other European country, encompasses a period of history and *not* a particular style, although it would be fair to say that most buildings from this period can be attributed as a whole or in parts to either the 'Romanesque' or the 'Gothic'. In order to be able to define the period and thus the range of buildings in question, it is, however, necessary to understand the academic meaning of the term 'middle ages' in this context. This period label makes sense only if seen in connection with the terms 'Antiquity' and 'Renaissance'. It originates in the perception of a rebirth of Antiquity after an intermediate period and consequently results in the chronological sequence Antiquity – Middle Ages – Renaissance. The juxtaposition of 'modern' (starting with the Renaissance) and 'medieval' has always been used to indicate the epochal changes affecting Europe as a whole between the fourteenth and the sixteenth centuries, in particular the events shortly before and after the year 1500. Some of the major changes in connection with innovations, discoveries and the Reformation did not occur throughout Europe simultaneously, which is why in Scotland both medieval history and medieval architecture are traditionally seen as terminating in the sixteenth century, either around 1513 with the death of James IV or around 1560 with the Reformation, almost 150 years later than in Italy. Without mentioning the term 'medieval', even the recently published *Scottish Architecture* sets apart a chapter for the period from 1100 until 1560, with the somewhat un-architectural and misleading title of 'From Christendom to Kingdom' (Glendinning and MacKechnie 2004, 32–63). While considering eleventh-century architecture in Scotland in the same chapter as all previous building including prehistory, the authors point out a striking difference in development compared to its southern neighbours. Unlike the medieval period in England, which followed its ancient history as a Roman province, the Scottish medieval period, at least as far as it is related to the area beyond the Antonine Wall, followed directly after prehistoric times. When does medieval architecture start in Scotland? Does it make sense at all to identify the 'middle ages' and 'medieval architecture'?

The middle ages were characterised in terms of a number of specific elements such as late ancient tradition, the undivided western church, kingship, and feudalism. The architecture of that time reflects these elements. Political history and architectural history are intertwined, but they follow different principles. The terminology to be applied to the architecture of this time should therefore avoid the historical term 'medieval' and, instead, describe and acknowledge stylistic change by using the terms 'Romanesque architecture' and 'Gothic architecture' and their subdivisions and phases on the basis of empirical evidence (Asselmeyer 2002).

The term 'Romanesque architecture' refers to the continuous use of characteristically Roman features in post-Roman times (in Britain after the withdrawal of the Romans earlier in the fifth century) such as semicircular arches, barrel vaults, and other building elements, as well as building types such as the basilica (a nave, often with a flat roof, flanked by one or more pairs of aisles, with or without an apse, mostly on the east end). Typically, a building of this period is architecturally expressed as a composition of geometric forms (cubic, cylindrical etc) with massive, often painted walls and few, narrow or tiny windows. Buildings belonging to this architectural period can very occasionally be found in Scotland from the times of the Celtic or Hiberno-Scottish church onwards, although only archaeological evidence survives for the most ancient settlements, Whithorn and Iona. The term 'Gothic architecture' refers to the distinctively un-Roman (therefore, from an Italian perspective, barbaric or 'Gothic') style between Romanesque and Renaissance architecture, which started in France as early as the first half of the twelfth century and lasted in Scotland until the sixteenth century. Its most characteristic features are the pointed arch, the rib vault, and the buttress. Unlike Romanesque buildings, Gothic buildings tend to emphasise the vertical elements, while their walls almost seem to dematerialise into a perforated network that allows a maximum of light to enter the built space.

THE ROMANESQUE

To base the description of a whole period exclusively on surviving stone structures is risky, since we do not know whether these buildings really represent the mainstream of architecture, or even of ecclesiastical architecture in Scotland. There may have been a multitude of timber buildings, of which virtually nothing is left. In his *Ecclesiastical History of the English People*, the Venerable Bede mentioned a building at Lindisfarne on Holy Island, which was built *'more Scottorum'* (the Scottish way), i.e. in timber. *'Scotti'* in the eighth century means first of all the inhabitants of Ireland. Indeed, Ireland and Scotland were strongly linked even in public perception. Far from being an outpost of Continental culture, from this Hiberno-Scottish world came the missioners who travelled to the heart of mainland Europe, to baptise, to preach, and to educate. That is why there is a *Schottenkloster* (Scottish monastery) in Regensburg (Bavaria) that had filiations all over South Germany.

Two surviving buildings in the Lowlands may indicate that eleventh-century Scotland remained firmly placed not only in the ethnic and religious, but also in the architectural context of Hiberno-Scottish culture. The round towers of Abernethy (Perthshire) (see fig. 1) and Brechin (Angus) display the characteristics of a vast number of round towers that were built in Ireland during the tenth and eleventh centuries. Freestanding, slim stone cylinders, originally with pyramidal roofs and four windows, facing each of the cardinal points of the compass, they have been identified as belfries like their Irish counterparts such as the *cloigtheach* (bell-tower) in Glendalough. Their elevated and narrow entrances indicate that they may occasionally have served as refuges in an emergency (e.g. in 1017 during the Danish sacking of Brechin), since a ladder or other timber structure would be necessary to gain access. Round towers with pyramidal roofs were built about the same time in Germany (St Pantaleon in Cologne or Gernrode in Saxony) and in Norfolk, but on the Continent or in East Anglia they are connected with the church building; the towers at Abernethy and, originally, at Brechin had no link to any other structure. Italian towers such as the campanile of St Apollinare in Classe (Ravenna) and even Islamic minarets have been considered as possible sources of inspiration, but it is unnecessary to go that far. As early as 801, a written source mentions a belfry at York and the specific features of the round towers in Ireland and Scotland certainly point to an indigenous origin (Stalley 2000).

This tradition may have been active even longer on the Orkney Islands, since there is a further round tower on Egilsay, possibly built around the middle of the twelfth century. Although connected to the nave (of St Magnus church) and from this point of view similar to East-Anglian parish churches, the building techniques used for the three components - the tower, the nave with its almost windowless walls and the

Fig. 1 The Round Tower at Abernethy

chancel - seem to resemble the Irish prototypes. The tower shaft tapers like some Irish counterparts and stone has apparently been used universally for walls and roofs.

However, controversy continues regarding the chronology and appropriate classification of the surviving fabric of the round towers in Scotland (Hiberno-Scottish? Pictish? etc.), whether they really pre-date the rectangular church buildings, and whether stylistic parallels to Irish and Anglo-Saxon churches on one and the same building are due to the stylistic diversity of the period (Fernie 1986). Whether the towers of Abernethy and Brechin were built around 1090, not much earlier than the buildings of Anglo-Saxon style, or whether their differences have to be explained with alterations and a difference of age (Cameron 1994), it is worth remembering that 'historical events are nearly always less disciplined than the typologies constructed for them' (Fernie 1986, 405). The ongoing dispute reflects a double dilemma architectural historians and archaeologists have to address when dealing with medieval architecture: firstly the fact that, especially for the earlier middle ages, there are only very few written sources available and secondly that it is difficult to relate the often fragmented and manipulated written information to the surviving fabric of the buildings and the interpretation of sculptural decoration.

Although Scotland north of the Firth of Forth was never part of any of the kingdoms founded by the Angles, Saxons and Jutes, there are a number of buildings in Fife surviving from the end of the Hiberno-Scottish period that have, nevertheless, to be considered in the wider context of Anglo-Saxon architecture. This may be due to direct personal relationships of their patrons, as we will see in the two following cases. When, starting in 1066, the Norman invasion of England swept away the Anglo-Saxon rule, the Saxon princess Margaret sought and found refuge with the Scottish king Malcolm III who married her around 1069. It is not surprising that the building erected near the royal residence at Dunfermline in the late eleventh century reflected Margaret's past in some of its parts. Most of the structure, which was perhaps built but certainly extended by Margaret for the small Benedictine community she founded in 1070, was replaced in the twelfth century by Dunfermline Abbey church (Church III). Yet, archaeological evidence helps us to form a picture of its spatial arrangement. Like other Anglo-Saxon churches, Dunfermline (Church I) was built in a rectilinear form with nave and chancel and later extended eastwards by a third chamber (Church II) that was to become the burial-place for Margaret and Malcolm in 1093 (Fernie 1994).

Another building in Fife marks Scotland's shift from being the northeastern area of a Hiberno-Scottish zone to becoming the northern part of a British architectural context. The similarly small, but exquisite Romanesque church of St Rule beside the ruined Gothic cathedral of St Andrews was probably built by Bishop Robert as a pilgrim church for the relics of the Scottish patron saint, the Apostle Andrew (see fig. 2). It was extended soon after Robert's consecration in 1127, but the new cathedral soon robbed the building of its former importance. St Rule's has an enormous tower of square plan at the west end of a nave, which has lost its chancel and roof, but not the visible traces of the former gable. Although a western addition

Fig. 2 The Church of St Rule at St Andrews

to the tower has also been lost, the surviving central portion of the church is in remarkably good condition and displays, according to common agreement, the finest Romanesque masonry to be found on the British Isles at that time. Similarities to Wharram-le-Street parish church (Yorkshire) are explained by Robert's background as an Augustinian from Nostell Priory in Yorkshire, although the direction of influence is much disputed (Cameron 1994, 372; Fernie 1986, 407). The narrow windows in the nave walls of St Rule's are headed by stone lintels with carved-in arches, a feature that also appears at the tower of Restenneth (Angus). The lower portion of the latter has been dated to the eighth, tenth and eleventh centuries, whereas St Rule's was completed by the death of Margaret's and Malcolm's son, King David I, in 1153. Compared to other churches built around the middle of the twelfth century in Britain, St Rule's stands out because of its unusually slim tower. In size and proportions it rather resembles some of the twelfth century gentile towers in San Gimignano (Tuscany) or Bologna, and, perhaps like the round towers, it may also have served as a landmark to attract the attention of pilgrims at great distance, including those approaching from the sea.

Once the Canmore dynasty (David's I family) as well as Bishop Robert of St Andrews had opened the country to southern architectural fashions, and since Scottish ecclesiastical history under the reign of David I now appeared to be embedded in the European mainstream, architecture in Scotland started to participate actively in the development of every further architectural period. The turn towards the south became most evident when David I commissioned the first building to be attributed to the new style commonly called 'Norman' (Fernie 2000, 208–11), since it is so characteristic of the areas of Norman rule in the twelfth century (i.e. Sicily, Puglia, Normandy, and England). Among the most distinctive features of this style are ornaments such as the chevron (zigzag) and the intersecting arches of interlaced arcading. In 1128, Dunfermline became an abbey and David I apparently benefited from the availability of masons from the cathedral workshop in Durham (Fawcett 1985, 30) when he replaced the small church of his parents in Dunfermline (I and II) with an imposing basilica of one nave and two aisles, which in style, proportion and even dimension was inspired by Durham Cathedral, the prototype of its period in Britain. The massive cylindrical piers at Dunfermline stand comparison with their Durham relatives, with an innovative quality of chevron decoration on some of them.

As a patron of architecture David I bequeathed to Scotland a rich heritage of Romanesque buildings, which all demonstrate the ambition and ability to provide his kingdom with a monastic landscape on a European level – even in architectural terms. There are still significant remains of some of his foundations. The Benedictine abbey at Dunfermline together with the Augustinian abbey at Jedburgh and the Tironensian abbey at Kelso are among the most prominent ones. To these should be added Melrose, an early Cistercian foundation in Scotland, although its plan is only partly known through excavations, and Holyrood Abbey, of the oldest parts of which only the south doorway of the nave has survived in good condition. The existence of many of David's other foundations all over Scotland is known to us

Fig.3 Dalmeny Parish Church

almost exclusively through written sources. The Premonstratensian abbey at Dryburgh was partly a non-royal foundation, but David seems to have been involved.
There are also a number of parish churches which can be safely attributed to the
Norman style. Some of them are so sumptuously decorated with chevrons and
interlaced arcading that it seems Norman fashion was most productive at its
northernmost outpost: the parish churches at Dalmeny (West Lothian) (see fig. 3)
and Leuchars (Fife) are among the most richly decorated, internally as well as
externally. This decoration was not limited to religious buildings, but was also

applied to vernacular architecture, and to domestic structures, including castles. However, in Edinburgh Castle, it is St Margaret's Chapel, built by David I (Fernie 1986, 403) where Norman features such as chevron and scallop capitals survive.

Among the foundations going back to David I's reign, Kelso Abbey is a curious case. Most of its Romanesque structure is irrevocably lost but, thanks to the evidence of a Glaswegian cleric, we know how the abbey church looked before its destruction. The detailed description of Kelso Abbey in a manuscript from 1517 kept in the Vatican Archive informs us that it was built, very unusually, on a double-cross plan. Dimensions and proportions of the abbey church are still evident from the remaining west elevation and the surviving front of the north transept. Although its porch shows the typical features of Norman style such as intersecting arches and, in its pedimented gable above the doorway, even a checked grid similar to some of the wall decoration at the Norman chapterhouse of Bristol Cathedral, the remains of the structure gently indicate a slightly wider background. While the decorative vocabulary is undoubtedly of Norman style, the strong emphasis on the corner, the cylindric turrets, and the projecting porch can also be found occasionally in the 'westwork' of churches in the Rhine valley at that time (Cruden 1986, 45). Cruden is, nevertheless, convinced that Kelso as well as Jedburgh are 'the only two of direct French descent' and concludes: 'It is a tolerable guess that not only did the monks and canons come from France but their architects and master masons came too . . .' (Cruden 1986, 111). The possible successors of the enormously wide arches inside and at the entrance, as a result of which the piers are dramatically reduced either in diameter or in height, are as interesting. It is not the last time that arches whose rise is less than half the span appear in Scotland during the middle ages and even the explicitly un-tectonic positioning of a pilaster above an arch can be found all over Scotland during the late middle ages. The exact opposite of the way in which piers were articulated in Kelso can be found at another of David's grand projects, Jedburgh Abbey, which he founded for Augustinian canons together with Bishop John of Glasgow in 1138. The ground level arcade and triforium are recessed between massive cylindrical piers, creating a giant order through two levels, thus gaining a remarkable height. Romsey in Hampshire, where David's aunt Christina was a nun, has been suggested as either an architectural precedent or successor (Cruden 1986, IX).

We tend to classify and, if possible, to attribute historic buildings to certain periods, although nearly all of them were altered and extended throughout their history. Decay and, even more sadly, demolition can then reduce the remains of a building to something that might seem to belong mostly to an earlier period only because the built evidence of its own middle age has disappeared. St Andrews Cathedral may be added to that group of buildings, since the ruin of its former self tells us more of its earliest Romanesque fabric than of its later history as a Gothic structure. The south transept has decorative intersecting arcading running along the base of the wall and what remains of the fabric is hardly enough to demonstrate that it was part of a Gothic cathedral.

A description of the Romanesque architecture in Scotland in its present boundaries would be incomplete, if it did not take into account the contribution from an
area which, politically, became part of Scotland only when the united kingdom of
Denmark and Norway passed Orkney and Shetland to the Scottish crown (c.1470).
At St Magnus Cathedral in Kirkwall the two lower of three levels expose the original
Romanesque fabric in nave and presbytery and both aisles as well as both transepts
have also kept a continuous band of interlacing arches.

THE GOTHIC

Gothic did not come to Scotland overnight. There was a long period of transition
from the mid-twelfth century when the first elements of the new style appeared in
prominent church architecture, until its establishment throughout the country, on
religious as well as on secular buildings. As in other European countries, these
changes were linked predominantly to the spread of new monastic orders originating
in France, from where they brought their own masons, who then introduced new
techniques and decoration and even a new perception of space to their country of
destination. These orders had been invited by the Scottish kings, who in return
expected their country to benefit from an increase of religious life and culture.
Among these new orders, the Cistercians (originating from Citeaux in Burgundy)
can usually be identified as the earliest transmitters of essential Gothic elements. In
Scotland, their first masterpiece to show the hallmarks of Gothic, including the
pointed arch and a more accentuated verticality of piers and arcades, was Dundrennan Abbey (Galloway). Here, Gothic influence was not of immediate French
provenance, since the Cistercians had already employed the new style at Fountains
Abbey and elsewhere in Yorkshire (Fawcett 1994b).

The first building to introduce the Gothic to Scotland was, however, not a
Cistercian church, but the new cathedral of St Andrews, which was begun in the
early 1160s by Augustinian canons. It is only by looking at its plan and at the
surviving east elevation that one can appreciate the enormous length of the now
entirely ruined cathedral. It certainly reflected the position of the bishop of St
Andrews as primate of Scotland. We can learn more about the structure of St
Andrews Cathedral by looking at its architectural successors, such as the Tironensian abbey of Arbroath whose oldest parts seem to relate closely to St Andrews.
Unfortunately, Arbroath itself is now ruined, and obvious similarities can be
pinpointed only with reference to the east ends of the presbyteries of both buildings.
The largely surviving part of the presbytery at St Andrews, the east elevation of the
cathedral, contains three windows with semicircular arches on the lower level and a
window with a slightly pointed arch and remnants of tracery fillings on the level
above.

Unlike St Andrews, Arbroath has preserved considerable parts of its west
elevation including a blind gallery between both western towers. Rather than being
articulated internally, the external walls of the towers are flush with the external
south, west and north elevations, while the internal corners rest on a pier each.

Fig. 4 Holyrood Abbey

Internally, on ground floor level, therefore, the towers appear as western bays of the aisles and are an integral part of the church interior. Integration is the main theme even of the west elevation, which is in line with the west elevation of both towers, and this underlines the importance of Arbroath Abbey in the evolution of the twin tower façade (MacAleer 1994). Holyrood Abbey, on the eastern outskirts of medieval Edinburgh, is of prime importance for the transitional period in Scotland (see fig. 4). The ruins of the Augustinian abbey church, which became part of Holyrood Palace, show earlier fabric with Norman details as well as early Gothic remains in a nave, the piers of which were described as 'essentially Gothic versions of the Romanesque compound pier' (Hoey 1986, 91).

Transition is, by definition, impure and at times rather inconsistent, but not necessarily loud and often far from unpleasant. Ultimately, one could argue that stylistic purity is just an issue of perception and perception is itself subject to change. Dunstaffnage Chapel (Argyll) is among a considerable number of buildings, which modestly combine Romanesque experience with Gothic experiment. Built probably around 1225 just 150m southwest of Dunstaffnage Castle, the masonry of this small church pays tribute to both styles and still achieves harmony, while brilliantly managing to combine window slots with slightly pointed arches and niches with semicircular mouldings. New motifs such as the pointed arch were filtered and remodelled in a way that makes it difficult to decide whether there is direct or indirect Irish, English or French influence at work. Especially but not only in Argyll, careful combinations of round and pointed and even segmental arches open the most refreshing dialogue. These exhilarating hybrids appear in vernacular as well as in religious architecture, as part of the hall-house within the massive walls of Skipness Castle as well as in the most prominent east elevation of Kilbrannan Chapel. In all these cases, the roughness and defensive strength of rubble contrasts vividly with the fine, sometimes chamfered, and elaborately curved masonry on all window sur-roundings. In Kilbrannan, the theme of pointed arch appears in manifold variations on a rectilinear structure with nave and chancel of great simplicity and homogeneous appearance.

Magnificent cathedrals and abbey churches were built in Scotland during the thirteenth century, when the country shared most characteristic features of the Gothic style with its English neighbour. Glasgow Cathedral (see fig.5), built on the remains of its Romanesque predecessor, best preserves the appearance of a splendid Gothic bishop's church, comparable to the great European cathedrals of its time and the most complete and unified among the Gothic cathedrals in Scotland. Externally, the late loss of two unfinished western towers has given the building a nearly symmetrical appearance. Like many cathedrals in England, its choir and presbytery together almost strike a balance with the nave in length, with a similar number of bays on either side of a massive crossing tower. The rectilinear arrangement of the presbytery rather than a semicircular plan for the ambulatory around the choir like in Germany or France even emphasises this equilibrium. However, the chapterhouse has been positioned in a decisively asymmetric manner in that it is articulated as an independent annex to the structure. Internally, the building reveals its prime function as a shrine for St Kentingern (or Mungo), with a spacious crypt, the piers of which carry a grand rib vault with heavy bosses at their crossing points. The three storeys of the nave elevations with lancet windows in the clerestory owe much to the early forms of Gothic in England, but the samples of tracery in the aisle windows already point to France. There are further indications for the knowledge of building techniques used by French masons as evident in the drawings of vaults in Villard de Honnecourt's sketchbook (Wilson 1998). The even number of bays in plan could well be seen in this context.

The other most important building projects in Scotland during the course of the thirteenth century included the complete reconstruction of the now ruined Elgin Cathedral (Moray) and Dunblane Cathedral (Perthshire), the abbey churches of Sweetheart (Galloway) and Dryburgh (Roxburghshire) and the Valliscaulian priory church of Pluscarden (Moray). However, it should be kept in mind that building went on in many churches, where works had already started during the twelfth century with Romanesque features, and where original plans were abandoned or modified in order to be kept up to date with technological, stylistic and even liturgical developments. Elgin, together with Inchcolm Abbey (Fife), a rebuilding of the Romanesque Augustinian abbey church founded by David I in 1153, and Holyrood Abbey, can be seen as typical for the Gothic in Scotland until the end of the thirteenth century, in that they belonged, stylistically, to the same architectural zone as England. They shared the rather horizontal emphasis of nave elevations in England as compared to France or Germany, and even had an octagonal chapter-house like so many of their English counterparts.

The wide range of secondary literature, based on both groups of primary sources for medieval architecture (i.e. the built fabric along with surviving manuscripts), acknowledges almost unanimously the strong relationship of Gothic architecture in Scotland and in England until the end of the thirteenth century and explains the sudden changes after c. 1300 by the hostilities between the two countries. John Higgitt has even coined the term of a *provincia architettonica* (architectural province), to which both countries belonged from the twelfth until the end of the thirteenth century (Higgitt, 416). In fact, the beginning of the fourteenth century presents a major turning point in the architectural history of Scotland and in many regards the Gothic in the British Isles seems by then to have reached a distance from the previous Romanesque, which makes thirteenth-century Gothic appear classical in its maturity and purity. Structure, form, and function seem to have achieved the momentum of harmony and created the allegedly pure style to which so many of the architects of the Gothic revival in the later eighteenth and nineteenth century referred. But this perception is based on the concept of a tripartite cultural evolution: early (discovery and transition) – high (standardisation and culmination) – late (deformation and decay). The assumption that Gothic architecture, like any other architectural period, experienced these phases appears to be deeply rooted in the minds of architectural historians, and in many ways the architectural record seems to justify this. Of course, there is necessarily a transition from the phenomena we tend to summarise as 'Romanesque' to the phenomena we tend to summarise as

Fig. 5 Glasgow Cathedral

'Gothic' and, of course, there must be then a climax where Gothic appears to be more Gothic, more vertical, more pointed, more un-Romanesque, more un-classical (in Renaissance terms) than ever. Scotland and England are not the only countries where the beginning of the fourteenth century can be seen as a break with the past. The traditional terms 'Early Gothic', 'High Gothic' (in most European countries chiefly during the thirteenth century) and 'Late Gothic' seem to fit national conditions almost universally. But is it necessarily a sign of decline, if the supposed criteria of standard are being abandoned for something else? Is it possible that rather than having reached the point of stagnation, Gothic was only just starting to absorb new architectural influences in a fresh and playful manner?

At first sight, Scottish architecture in the early fourteenth century seems to have entered a long period of crisis. War and internal conflict brought building activity almost to a standstill in many parts of the country, although works were completed at least on the major cathedrals (St Andrews and Glasgow). Many churches and castles in the borderlands are ruins because they were destroyed in this period. In a history of Scottish building activity, the core of the fourteenth century would need to be described, if not as a vacuum between two periods, than at least as a state of deep sleep with regard to ecclesiastical architecture. Occasionally though, there is evidence for new projects and these are among the earliest witnesses of change. However, before the new tendencies in religious building can be discussed, it is important to examine the only type of building activity which tends to flourish in periods of war and unrest, the building of fortifications and castles.

Scotland is rightfully associated with its castles which owe much in stylistic terms to the end of the Gothic and the beginning of the Renaissance. At some stage, it might be interesting to carry investigations further and to ask to what extent the development of castellation in Scotland after 1300 was actually influenced by the knowledge of French and maybe even Syrian crusader castles. Certainly, the reasons for the unfolding of castle architecture in Scotland in the fourteenth and fifteenth centuries can be explained only by major political instability, but it would be incomplete to see the building of castles in Scotland only in connection with centuries of warfare against England. A vast number of Scottish Renaissance castles have been outed as indefensible country-houses with a touch of stronghold (McKean, 2001). There were castles in Scotland even before the Wars of Independence and, in any case, the erection of fortified houses and palaces needs to be seen in the context of the wealth of their owners. The domestic architecture of the secular elites (nobles and monarchs alike) was designed to project images of power, wealth, rank and status as much as it served any practical purpose.

The sheer variety of castle design is evident from the circular plan of Rothesay Castle on the Isle of Bute (late twelfth century) and the triangular plan of Caerlaverock Castle (Dumfriesshire) (see fig.6), although its earliest surviving structure is mainly fifteenth century and only a French poem recorded its shield-like (triangular) plan during the siege by Edward I in 1300. The majority of castles were built on a less regular plan, which was further complicated by continuous expansions and alterations. The impact of pragmatic changes of programme can be

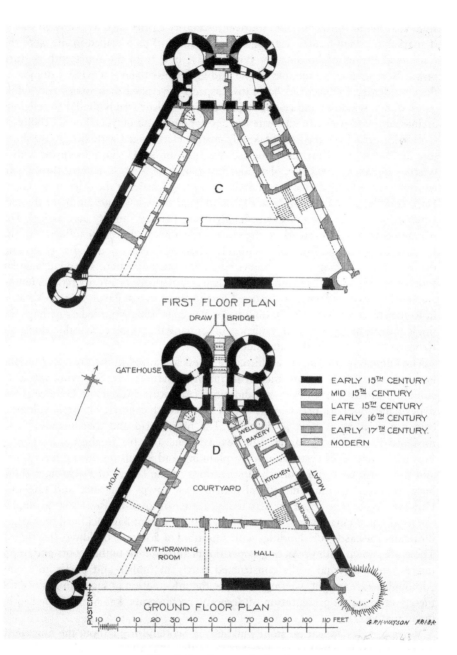

FIRST FLOOR PLAN

DRAW BRIDGE

GATEHOUSE

C

D

WELL
BAKERY

KITCHEN

COURTYARD

MOAT

MOAT

SCULLERY

WITHDRAWING
ROOM

HALL

POSTERN

■ EARLY 15TH CENTURY
▨ MID 15TH CENTURY
▤ LATE 15TH CENTURY
▧ EARLY 16TH CENTURY
▥ EARLY 17TH CENTURY
▦ MODERN

GROUND FLOOR PLAN

10 0 10 20 30 40 50 60 70 80 90 100 110 FEET

G.P.H.WATSON F.R.I.B.A.

Fig. 6 Caerlaverock Castle

studied at major thirteenth- and fourteenth-century castles such as Bothwell Castle (Lanarkshire). Hall-houses (e.g. Dundonald and Rait) on a walled-in site were the traditional means of housing for the nobility, but, from the fourteenth century onwards, it became fashionable for the leading families to erect a massive donjon as their residence. Tactical and decorative aspects developed their own logic, while gates, doors, windows and ceilings still followed stylistic trends similar to religious architecture and perfectly illustrate the development and universal applicability of Gothic features. Even the breathtakingly austere Hermitage Castle (Roxburghshire) (see fig.7) completed for the Douglases by 1400 on an H-shape footprint with a western and an eastern pylon of almost Egyptian dimensions, is entered through an enormous gate headed by a lancet arch. At Stirling Castle, in the oriel of the Great Hall, completed in 1503 by James IV, mullions, transoms, and jambs in the bay window were interwoven in a refreshingly ironic manner - totally un-classical. The triumphal-arch-like Forework to the same castle already shows the influence of the Renaissance. The east front of Linlithgow Palace (1420s, remodelled c. 1500) and the triple fireplace in its Lyon Chalmer hint in the same direction. The quadrangular form of Linlithgow Palace with its four square corner towers directly reflects Italian standards, based on Filarete's treatise: Castello Visconteo at Pavia, Palazzo Venezia in Rome etc. (Campbell 1995). Linlithgow Palace is being regarded as perhaps the finest and one of the last royal residences in Scotland that displayed Gothic alongside Renaissance features in the late middle ages.

The knowledge of secular architecture is less advanced in the area of domestic housing, since there are no medieval timber structures left. Surviving fabric of stone-built town-houses even in Edinburgh (Advocate's Close) or Dundee (Gardynes Land) does not pre-date the end of the fifteenth century, but archaeological evidence gives us at least some clues. The urban grid and dwelling design of medieval Perth is well-known from excavations and fits in the contemporary European context of systematic town-planning and extension during the twelfth and thirteenth centuries from the foundations of the Dukes of Zaehringer (Freiburg, Bern etc) to the symmetrical plan of new towns in France and England. However, ignorance about the actual appearance of town-houses above ground is not total, since a manuscript with a sketch of the Battle of Bannockburn thankfully illustrates the castle surroundings with a number of domestic buildings (see fig. 8). These are shown with projecting upper floors and pitched timber roofs and, most interestingly, external walls constructed partly in timber and partly in stone. Although a rare insight, we ought to take the information at face value, since the merely ornamental presentation of domestic architecture was not intended to be manipulative.

When features appear on stone buildings in Scotland from about the fourteenth century onwards, whether on churches or castles, that allow us to classify them as Gothic, one may notice a slight difference to the previously known form of Gothic, a specific interest in curvilinear articulation. The inspiration for this growing stylistic virtuosity no longer came from other centres in the British Isles, but from the Low Countries, Germany, France, and even Spain and Portugal. The reason for this shift

Fig. 7 Hermitage Castle

of orientation towards Continental architecture may have been partially due to hostility towards the English, but it also reflects the intensifying of trade with the Hanseatic League, especially the rich cities in Flanders and Holland. Gothic in Scotland became more Continental and yet simultaneously more individual.

The beautiful ruin of Melrose Abbey (Roxburghshire) (see fig. 9) shows all the signs of these changes. Rebuilt by Cistercian monks from Rievaulx (Yorkshire) after the destruction of the previous structure in 1385 during the Anglo-Scottish wars, it follows Cistercian rules in plan. The window tracery in the east elevation of the presbytery shows the rather disciplined Perpendicular, overwhelmingly characteristic of the architecture on the English side of the border. But soon after, a slightly different type of Gothic was employed at the south transept window, a curvilinear tracery probably by master-mason John Morow who, according to an inscription still kept in the monastery, convincingly claimed to be from Paris. In the fourteenth century, window tracery clearly departed the common ground with England. France was one place to attract the attention of Scottish masons and master-masons, but the Low Countries soon became another focus of interest. Yet, the avoidance of any Anglicism in favour of decisive Continentalism went hand in hand with conscious references to Scotland's own architectural past. St Machar's Cathedral in Old Aberdeen (see fig. 10) was among the first buildings to pay tribute

Fig, 8 Scottish town houses in Stirling

Fig. 9 Melrose Abbey

Fig. 10 St Machar's Cathedral, Aberdeen

to the stylistic trends in Holland and Flanders, but its cylindrical piers are as much a reference to pre-Gothic church architecture in Scotland itself as to the Low Countries.

This self-interest, as we will see below, seems to have created the most prophetic combination of traditional Scottish castle architecture (rubble, parapet etc) and traditional Scottish church architecture (round piers, lancet windows etc). Round piers on otherwise Gothic structures also appear in the naves of Dunkeld Cathedral

(Perthshire) and Paisley Abbey church (Renfrewshire) (see fig.11). Both buildings even have idiosyncratic nave elevations in common: in the Dunkeld nave (1406–1464), Romanesque tradition (cylindrical piers together with a semicircular triforium) alternates with Gothic tradition (pointed arches in the arcade and in the clerestory) and in Paisley, a triforium composed of segmental arches rests on squat, bundled piers, thus achieving an almost bridge-like appearance. The somewhat encyclopaedic, catalogue-like presentation of variety in horizontal rows of sentences on one and the same elevation strikes the foreign visitor as something rather indigenous, an overture to the proud, totem-like ostentation of heterogenous architectural elements.

Apparently, the widespread use of semicircular arches in fourteenth-century Scottish architecture was not an indicator of a belated stylistic evolution, but an expression of a self-conscious nostalgic movement. Ian Campbell has shown that 'this indigenous Romanesque Revival prepared the ground in many important respects for the Renaissance' (Campbell 1995, 302). Educated Scots were looking back on the 'Golden Age' of national independence during the two centuries of the Canmore dynasty and were engaged in tracing the roots of their nation back to alleged Greek origins. An interest in ancient Greece, Tuscany, and Roman traditions seems to have been premature especially with regards to contemporary England, and served the purpose of national distinction.

This seems to match a rather 'Scottish' preference in the fifteenth century to articulate, to raise, and to sharpen the tower roof of main churches. St Salvator's collegiate church in St Andrews was built with a spire right away, while Aberdeen and Glasgow Cathedrals and even the Romanesque church tower of Restenneth got their spires only then. At the same time, the chapel of King's College, Aberdeen, St Giles, Edinburgh (see fig.12) and St Michael's, Linlithgow were ornamented with a crown steeple, the most exclusive architectural feature to be found in Scotland at the end of the Gothic. Although a crown steeple was erected at Newcastle, the use of this building element in Scotland was certainly meant to be distinctive and we know of plans for its further development at St Mary's, Dundee.

However, it was not exclusively monastic and episcopal architecture or castellated architecture which was the vehicle for new trends, but the growing number of collegiate churches. Their dimensions suited the respectable but not quite royal or episcopal means of private patrons and allowed a hitherto unthinkable number of people to make their mark. The purpose of a collegiate church was chiefly the commemoration of their patrons (Crichton Collegiate Church, Seton Collegiate Church etc), but some projects were so ambitious that they were never finished. The most ambitious among the unfinished is certainly Rosslyn or Roslin Chapel in Lothian, a collegiate church built by Sir William St Clair or Sinclair after 1446, close to his castle on the River Esk. The towers, nave and transepts were never built, but the surviving structure can count as the most lavishly decorated in the country. On a similar plan as the thirteenth century east end of Glasgow Cathedral, the building seems to place itself with confidence in the national tradition, whereas the decorative details seem to confirm the presence of foreign builders. The *horror vacui* seems to match the style of the reign of Isabella I, Queen of Castile and Manuel I of Portugal of the later fifteenth and early sixteenth century and may appear to be untypical for Scottish architecture. But it is typical for the stylistic amalgam in the country given a number of hidden references to both the Late Gothic and the Early Renaissance, from the spiral column to the pseudo-architraves below load-bearing segmental vaults, which separate the bays of the aisles.

We tend to have a static view of historic buildings, although we know that the current state in which buildings are preserved is only a moment in their history. The enthusiasm of nineteenth century restoration all too often led to the desire of 'freeing' a building from the 'ballast' of its intermediate past. Renaissance, mannerist and baroque accretions were all victims of this purist approach to Gothic cathedrals, abbey and parish churches, since they were seen as obtrusive distortions and not as valuable and integral parts in the development of a building. Even medieval fabric has been sacrificed in order to 'build' retrospectively a 'coherent' past. Edinburgh's St Giles' was considerably extended and altered during the middle ages. Built as a parish church for one of the largest burghs in Scotland, it reflected the number of parishioners, their religious fervour, and their civic pride and wealth – on a scale that gave the church a cathedral-like appearance long before it formally reached this status. It is a specific chapter in Scottish architectural history that, in the aftermath of

Fig. 11 St Giles, Edinburgh

the Reformation, large parish churches were subdivided to accommodate simulta-neous services of different congregations under one roof. St Giles', however, seems to have lost more of its historic fabric during more recent restoration: between 1829 and 1833 by William Burn in his pursuit of symmetry; between 1871 and 1884 by William Hoy who removed the dividing internal walls; and between 1909 and 1911, when Sir Robert Lorimer added the chapel for the Knights of the Thistle (Cruden, 186).

The reasons for loss of medieval fabric in Scotland are manifold. Apart from over-restoration during the past two centuries, much damage was been done in the course of English raids. During the Scottish Reformation, especially towards the end of 1559, further demolition was caused by an overzealous mob who turned against the church interior as well as against the built fabric itself. Brechin Cathedral was purged and St Andrews reduced to ruin. The extent of the destruction seems to be due to the removal of lead from the roof, subsequently the decay of the structure and the use of the ruin as a stone quarry.

THE SCOTTISHNESS OF SCOTTISH ARCHITECTURE

We have seen that until around 1100 Scotland and Ireland belonged to one architectural zone and, similarly, that during the twelfth and thirteenth centuries Scotland and England together formed a British architectural zone. Apparently, this geographical change of orientation had nothing to do with the stylistic changes from Romanesque to Gothic. Since the fourteenth century, Gothic in Scotland can be linked to architectural developments in other West European countries, but not anymore to England. From then on, it developed or rather was driven consciously in a different direction. Indications of the adoption of elements distilled from its past have been identified long before the era of the Gothic revival, which gave the country marvellous buildings such as the Scott Monument in Edinburgh. During the fifteenth century, the thirteenth century Glasgow Cathedral had been used as a prototype of national significance to embed a new structure in a manufactured tradition. But would it be justified to speak of 'Scottish Gothic' in the same way in which one uses, for instance, the term 'Italian Renaissance'? The identification of country and style is always in danger of projecting the present onto the past, a method that necessarily leads to distortions. However, there comes a point where it would seem to be over-sensitive to negate the existence of characteristics that help to locate buildings in Scotland rather than anywhere else. There is no reason to object in principle to Cruden's somewhat bold statement regarding 'late medieval ecclesiastical archi-tecture, whether backward or outward-looking to contemporary churches of the Continent' when he concludes that 'it is a totally Scottish architecture . . . it has distinctive characteristics which, taken together, make a national style, however much it might owe to foreign borrowings' (Cruden 1986, 183). One may not follow his judgement that it is of 'inferior' architectural quality and his assumption that the sum of phenomena creates a style could also be questioned. But if we abandon the idea of stylistic purity and artistic leadership as criteria for the existence of a style, we will indeed find the ingredients that justify setting apart the architecture in Scotland. Glendinning and MacKechnie conclude that 'by the time of the Reformation, from 1560, the precocious triumph of the show-castle, in parallel with the retrenchment of orthodox church Gothic, had laid the foundations for a more comprehensive secularization of Scottish architecture. It had also made possible an early and eclectic Scottish embrace of the Renaissance, characterized by a competition between castellar romanticism and pattern-book classicism – a tension that would endure for at least the next century' (Glendinning and MacKennie, 63). There have even been suggestions that it is possible to subsume the Gothic in Scotland and Ireland in the late middle ages as one 'Gaelic Gothic' (Stalley 1986, 108). Whatever the overall framework, one may acknowledge that around 1300 British Gothic split into two branches and that from the fourteenth until the sixteenth centuries there appeared to have been a structurally and aesthetically innovative perpendicular English Gothic, which was consistently avoided by a more conservative curvilinear Scottish Gothic. The stylistically un-dogmatic application of traditional features in the context of the Renaissance then completed a substantially Scottish amalgam, the origin of a national style.

SOURCES

Billings, RW 1845–1852 *The Baronial and Ecclesiastical Antiquities of Scotland.* (4 volumes). Edinburgh.

The Royal Commission on the Ancient Monuments of Scotland, 1956 *An Inventory of the Ancient and Historical Monuments of Roxburghshire.* (2 volumes). Edinburgh.

Theiner, A 1864 *Vetera monumenta Hibernorum et Scotorum historiam illustrantia quae ex Vaticani, Neapolis ac Florentiae tabulariis deprompsit et ordine chronologico disposuit. Ab Honorio PP. III usque ad Paulum PP III. 1216–1547.* Romae.

REFERENCES TO BOOKS AND ARTICLES MENTIONED IN THE TEXT

Items marked * are recommended for further reading.

Asselmeyer, M 2002 'Medieval Architecture by Nicola Coldstream' [Review], *Architectural Research Quarterly*, 6/4, 378–9.

Bonelli, R, Bozzoni, C and Franchetti Pardo, V 2002 *Storia dell'architettura medievale. L'Occidente europeo.* Bari.

*Cameron, N 1994 'St Rule's Church, St Andrews, and Early Stone-Built Churches in Scotland', *Proceedings of the Society of Antiquaries of Scotland*,124, 367–78.

*Campbell, I 1995 'A Romanesque Revival and the Early Renaissance in Scotland', *Journal of the Society of Architectural Historians*, 54, 302–25.

Cruden, S 1986 *Scottish Medieval Churches.* Edinburgh.

Donaldson, G 1985 *Scottish Church History.* Edinburgh.

Fawcett, R 1985 *Scottish Medieval Churches*. Edinburgh.

Fawcett, R 1994a 'Arbroath Abbey', *in* Higgitt, J (ed), *Medieval Art and Architecture in the Diocese of St Andrews*, (British Archaeological Association Conference Transactions XIV, Leeds 1986),61–9.

Fawcett, R 1994b *Scottish Abbeys and Priories*. London.

*Fawcett, R 1994c *Scottish Architecture from the Accession of the Stewarts to the Reformation, 1371–1560*. Edinburgh.

*Fawcett, R 1997 *Scottish Cathedrals*. London.

Fawcett, R 1998 (ed), *Medieval Art and Architecture in the Diocese of Glasgow* (British Archaeological Association Conference Transactions XXIII, Leeds 1997).

*Fernie, E 1986 'Early Church Architecture in Scotland', *Proceedings of the Society of Antiquaries of Scotland*, 116, 393–411.

Fernie, E 1994 'The Romanesque Churches of Dunfermline Abbey', *in* Higgitt, J (ed), *Medieval Art and Architecture in the Diocese of St Andrews*, 25–37.

Fernie, E 2000 *The Architecture of Norman England*. Oxford.

Glendinning, M and MacKechnie, A 2004 *Scottish Architecture*. New York.

Heywood, S 1994 'The Church of St Rule, St Andrews', *in* Higgitt, J (ed), *Medieval Art and Architecture in the Diocese of St Andrews*, 38–46.

*Higgitt, J 1994 (ed), *Medieval Art and Architecture in the Diocese of St Andrews* (British Archaeological Association Conference Transactions XIV, Leeds 1986).

Higgitt, JC, 'Scozia', *in Enciclopedia dell'Arte Medievale*, 10, 413–23.

Hoey, L 1986 'Pier Design in Early Gothic Architecture in Eastern-Central Scotland, c.1170–1250', in Higgitt, J (ed), *Medieval Art and Architecture in the Diocese of St Andrews*, 84–98.

Lynch, M, Spearman, M and Stell, G 1988 (eds), *The Scottish Medieval Town*. Edinburgh.

McAleer, JP 1994 'The West Front of Arbroath Abbey: Its Place in the Evolution of the Twin-Tower-Façade', *in* Higgitt, J (ed), *Medieval Art and Architecture in the Diocese of St Andrews*, 70–83.

McKean, C 2001 *The Scottish Chateau*. Stroud.

McRoberts, D 1962 'Material destruction caused by the Scottish Reformation', *in* McRoberts, D (ed), *Essays on the Scottish Reformation, 1513–1625*, Glasgow, 415–62.

Mentel, R 1998 'The Twelfth Century Predecessors of Glasgow Cathedral and their Relationship with Jedburgh Abbey', *in* Fawcett, R (ed), *Medieval Art and Architecture in the Diocese of Glasgow* (British Archaeological Association Conference Transactions XXIII, Leeds 1997), 42–9.

Rosslyn, H and Maggi A 2002 *Rosslyn: Country of Painter and Poet*. Edinburgh.

Shead, NF 1988 'Glasgow: An Ecclesiastical Burgh', *in* Lynch, M, Spearman, M and Steel G (eds), *The Scottish Medieval Town*, 116–32.

Spearman, M 1988 'The Medieval Townscape of Perth', *in* Lynch, M Spearman, M and Stell, G (eds), *The Scottish Medieval Town*, 42–59.

Stell, G 1988 'Urban Buildings', *in* Lynch, M Spearman, M and Steel G (eds), *The Scottish Medieval Town*, 60–80.

Thurlby, M 1994 'St Andrews Cathedral-Priory and the Beginnings of Gothic Architecture in Northern Britain, *in* Higgitt, J (ed), *Medieval Art and Architecture in the Diocese of St Andrews*, 47–60.

Thurlby, M 1998 'Glasgow Cathedral and the Wooden Barrel Vault in Twelfth- and Thirteenth-Century Architecture in Scotland, *in* Fawcett, R (ed), *Medieval Art and Architecture in the Diocese of Glasgow*, 84–7.

Stalley, R 1986 'Ireland and Scotland in the Later Middle Ages', *in* Higgitt, J (ed), *Medieval Art and Architecture in the Diocese of St Andrews*, 108–17.

Stalley, R 2000 *Irish Round Towers*. Dublin.

Wilson, C 1998 'The Stellar Vaults of Glasgow Cathedral's Inner Crypt and Villard de Honnecourt's Chapter-House Plan: A Conundrum Revisited', *in* Fawcett, R (ed), *Medieval Art and Architecture in the Diocese of Glasgow*, 55–76.

CHAPTER TWELVE

Medieval Literature

Nicola Royan

Medieval Scottish literature is commonly held to begin with *The Bruce*, written by John Barbour and internally dated to 1375. *The Bruce* is certainly the first substantial piece of writing to survive in any form of Scots. Moreover, dealing as it does with such critical events in the formation of Scottish national identity, it seems natural to put it at the head of the Scottish tradition. However, this may not be entirely fair. Firstly, it might suggest that Barbour wrote entirely from inspiration, whereas the sophistication of the references and the literary form indicates that Barbour must have had models for his text and must have been well-read in a variety of literature, including romance, not perhaps entirely to be expected in an arch-deacon. Some of this literature must have originated in Scotland and simply no longer survives. For instance, Barbour invokes a piece believed to date from the beginning of the fourteenth century, preserved in some fifteenth-century chronicles:

> Qwhen Alexander our kynge was dede,
> That Scotlande lede in lauche and le,
> Away was sons of alle and brede,
> Off wyne and wax, of gamyn and gle.
> Our golde was changit in to lede.
> Crist, borne in virgynyte,
> Succoure Scotland, and ramede,
> That is stade in perplexite.

Barbour's lines run:

> Quhen Alexander the king wes deid
> That Scotland haid to steyr and leid,
> The land sex yer and mayr perfay
> Lay desolat eftyr hys day . . . (1: 36–40)

This is only a fragment, however; far more must have been lost.

Barbour would also have been familiar with literature written in English in England; he received safe conducts to travel to England and material circulated quite easily across the border. In comparison to some of the literature being written in the south of England around the same time – Barbour is roughly contemporary with Geoffrey Chaucer – *The Bruce* might seem old-fashioned: its four-stress couplets and formulaic phrases are more reminiscent of earlier English work, as is its emphasis on warfare and chivalry. However, it is in keeping with texts in northern Middle English and there is no doubting its sophistication in structure and argument.

Of course, Barbour would not have been restricted to material written in Scots and English. He would certainly have been able to read and speak Latin and French, with its variety, Anglo-Norman. Latin was the international language of scholarship and religion, and also a language of literature among the Scots into the sixteenth and seventeenth centuries. Anglo-Norman was a courtly and a legal language, and even though the Scots used Latin over Anglo-Norman in their courts, still Barbour may have been familiar with certain texts. There are many romances and other poems written in Anglo-Norman, including one twelfth-century example, *Fergus of Galloway*, that might have been written at the court of William the Lion, or else by someone familiar with it. Most writers of the later Middle Ages would have been polyglot, and would have a European outlook regarding literature.

It is less certain whether Barbour would have been familiar with Gaelic. *The Bruce* makes reference to Gaelic heroes, but whether Barbour knew of those from Gaelic stories or through other material is unclear. Unlike French and Latin, Gaelic was not considered a prestige language by Lowland Scots and a consistent feature of literature in Older Scots is its dismissive attitude to Gaelic culture. For instance, Richard Holland in *The Buke of the Howlat* appears to garble bardic poetry in Gaelic; William Dunbar uses his rival Kennedy's origins in the Gaelic-speaking West as one of the targets of his flyting (a contest between poets in mutual abuse). During the fourteenth and fifteenth centuries, it is also likely that Gaelic-speaking culture looked towards Ireland rather than the rest of mainland Scotland. The political strength of the Lordship of the Isles made this possible, and the mutual comprehensibility of the Gaelic spoken in Ireland and in Scotland supported it. As a result, clear evidence of the influence of Gaelic on Scots literature is slight. The particular time span of this chapter (1375–1513) means that it focuses on literature in Scots with occasional references to texts in Latin; to explore in proper detail Gaelic literature and its relationship with Irish literature would require a separate chapter.

In Scots literature, Barbour's poem is only the beginning. The fifteenth century is a distinguished period in Scottish literature, in range and in quality. *The Bruce* has its counterpart in the *Wallace*; James I and Robert Henryson responded to Chaucer's works in very different ways; Walter Bower extended John Fordun's *Chronica* to produce a huge national chronicle, designed to site the Scots and their history in the world. Scottish writers continued to look outwards: among the translations into Scots is Gilbert Hay's *The Buke of the Law of Armys*, taken from Honoré de Bonet's *L'Abre des Batailles,* itself translated from Ramon Llull's *Libre de Caballeria*. The most famous Scottish Arthurian romances, *Lancelot of the Laik* and *Golagros and Gawain*, also have French sources, but differ significantly from them. Other texts, such as Henryson's *Testament of Cresseid*, clearly looked south and found inspiration in English literature. Scots poets were comfortable with a variety of styles and registers, perhaps most vigorously on display in the work of William Dunbar, whose work encompasses the incredibly ornate 'Haile, sterne superne' and the outrageously obscene *Flyting*. Dunbar was also able to use rhyme and alliteration as structural pinnings in his work; the Scots seemed to maintain an enthusiasm for alliteration later than the English. An almost equal linguistic and poetic range is evident in the work of Dunbar's contemporary, Gavin Douglas. Where Dunbar's speciality was in intense shorter poems, Douglas was expansive and ambitious in his endeavours: his final poem was a translation of the *Aeneid*, complete with prologues to each book and also a translation of a thirteenth book. The *Eneados* stands in the no-man's land between medieval and early modern: Douglas's desire to stretch his language and yet to remain faithful to Virgil's text is humanist, and looks forward to the translations of the sixteenth century; the accompanying glossing prologues and the thirteenth book, to complete Aeneas' story, are typically medieval. Partly for that reason and because it was finished a few weeks before Flodden, the *Eneados* is used to mark the boundary between medieval and early modern Scottish literature. Neither the literary text nor the historical event can be said to mark an absolute gulf between its past and its future, for there are as many continuities as there are differences between the reigns of James IV and James V and between Douglas's *Palice of Honour* and David Lyndsay's *Testament of the Papyngo*. Nevertheless, provided we remember that, this division serves as a useful boundary.

So far, this chapter has emphasised the variety of material surviving and its breadth of influence. Yet, medieval Scottish literature has some recurrent features that form a tradition and suggest an interest in and a view of morality, identity and recreation common across its audiences. Of primary importance to many texts is the nature of virtue and how private morality and public virtue interact. This theme is as significant to comic poems such as *Rauf Coillyear* as it is to *Scotichronicon*, and suggests that it was of primary importance to the audience as well as to the writers. The writers were often clerics: for instance, Barbour, Wyntoun, Bower, Henryson, Dunbar and Douglas were all in orders at various levels. There were also important lay writers, such as James I, Hary and Sir Gilbert Hay, and possibly others, now unknown. But not even the clerical writers were primarily concerned with what we might imagine to be religious virtue, such as piety or even crusading; instead, the concern is for secular virtue, how to behave in society as a layman. (There is very little literature about or clearly for women in Older Scots.) This may have spoken to the interests of the audience. Some poets wrote for the court, such as Barbour, James I, Douglas and Dunbar; of the four, only Dunbar wrote the occasional pieces expected of a regular recipient of royal favour. Others seem to have written for magnates and gentry, such as Richard Holland for the Douglases, Bower for Sir James Stewart of Rosyth, and Hary for Sir William Wallace of Craigie and Sir James Liddale of Halkerston. Bower's composition of a Latin chronicle for Stewart suggests that the common assumption that Latin literacy was primarily limited to churchmen (a view enforced by John Mair's account of noble schooling in Scotland) may not be entirely reliable. Nevertheless, the picture remains one of a reasonably educated, largely lairdly or clerical audience, able to afford the time to read, listen or write and able to gain access to other manuscripts, whether through personal, institutional or employer's patronage. This is the group who expected to participate in public affairs and was concerned with good government. The view of commentators generally was that good government is exercised by good men, and that a degenerate leader will result in a degenerate population, since if he cannot govern himself, he can hardly govern others. For that reason, advising the prince and other rulers to virtue features largely in Scottish literature of this period.

CHRONICLE AND ROMANCE

The *Bruce* has often been regarded as a key witness to the details of Robert I's campaigns and kingship, from Barbour's immediate successors, such as Fordun and Wyntoun, to Geoffrey Barrow's 1965 biography of the king. Barbour himself insists that his tale is 'suthfast' (true), and that this gives it extra value and extra pleasure. Yet he clearly manipulated his portrayal to put Bruce in the best light. For instance, Barbour begins his narrative of Bruce with his betrayal by John Comyn. Leaving aside questions about the exact nature of any pact between Bruce and Comyn, in structural terms, this allows Barbour to ignore Bruce's previously uncertain loyalties and present him as consistently loyal to the Scottish cause. Such spin might be found in any modern biography as well, but Barbour also used tropes from folklore and romance further to glorify his hero. A recurrent example of this is the 'Battle Against Odds', where the hero faces down difficult if not impossible challenges. Bruce faces several of these in Barbour's account, for example, in book 3, lines 93–146, he kills three men who ambush him in a narrow defile, while in 6:453–7:232, Bruce, with the help of his foster-brother, overcomes first five men, then escapes from John of Lorn's party with its tracker dog, and then overcomes another three men, although in the last battle, his foster-brother is killed. It is of course possible that these events took place, in some form or another, but they also have the structure of folktale. Barbour himself seems to suggest this in some of the detail: for instance, he gives two different accounts of Bruce's escape from the tracker dog, one where Bruce and his men wade along a burn in order to force the dog to lose his scent, the other where an archer hangs back in order to kill the dog. The former displays Bruce's wisdom as a leader, the latter the loyalty he inspires in his men, so to elaborate the positive picture of Bruce, it is worth Barbour's while to include them both. Barbour refused to identify one story as more accurate; instead he says:

> Bot quhether this eschaping fell
> As I tauld fyrst or I now tell,
> I wate weill without lesing
> That at the burn eschapyt the king. (7: 75–9)

The truth as fact is that Bruce escaped; but it is clear that this was only part of Barbour's interest. Measured by number of lines, he is obviously keener to demonstrate Bruce's gifts as a leader and to exemplify his character. This is perhaps best regarded as a different kind of truth, which extends Bruce's significance from being a successful warrior in particular circumstances to being a model, exemplifying the benefits of good leadership in such a way as to allow them to be copied by others. It also enables Bruce to stand comparison with legendary romance heroes like Alexander, Charlemagne and Arthur and perhaps also with other mythologised kings, such as Richard Coeur de Lion.

Just like these heroes, in Barbour's poem Bruce is also emblematic of the realm he leads. This is most obvious in Barbour's depiction of Bannockburn. The battle lies at the heart of the poem and is the point on which all other action depends. Barbour maintains Bruce's skills as general, and also foregrounds his personal courage and fighting ability in the despatch of Henry de Bohun. More importantly, though, he gives Bruce speech. In part, this is a traditional pre-battle exhortation, but Barbour makes it earn its place. Firstly, it provides an opportunity for Bruce to be confirmed as leader. Bruce asks his army whether they are prepared to fight, or whether they wish to retreat in the face of a much larger English force. Of course, the Scottish army supports the battle, 'For doute off dede we sall nocht faill/ Na na payn sall refusyt be / Quhill we haiff maid our countré fre' (12:204–6). Their final word, 'fre', connects their position to that core theme of the poem, freedom. Part of the skill of this episode is the manner in which Barbour plays with the concept of freedom, for here Bruce has offered his army a part in their government, a free choice regarding the disposition of their lives. In so doing, Barbour has blurred any distinction between loyalty to Bruce and loyalty to the kingdom. This blurring is taken a stage further when Bruce himself gives reasons for the battle, the second key moment. In this section of the speech, some seventy lines long, the pronouns 'we', 'you' and 'thai' predominate; 'I' is only used three times, where Bruce refers to his own address to the army, and 'me' four times. Bruce constantly identifies his cause with that of his men, his claim to freedom and to the kingship with their claim to freedom, subject to his authority rather than that of the English. This can be seen most clearly in the emotive final reason:

> The thrid is that we for our lyvis
> And for our childer and for our wyvis
> And for our fredome and for our land
> Are strenyeit in bataill for to stand. (12: 245–48)

The desires of the leader are here subjugated to the desires of his followers. After Bannockburn, Bruce's virtues, displayed during his campaigns, and his self-identification with his men combine to make him a good monarch, the guise he takes in the second half of the poem. While Barbour's attention to Bruce as governing king is extraordinary in a romance, it serves to underline the political points that Barbour is making for the benefit of the court of Robert II. Firstly, it provides a platform for advice to princes: to be successful as king, a man should adopt and develop the virtues shown by Robert I. Secondly, in aligning the desires of the king with the desires of his nobles, the poem insists that loyalty to Robert I is the same as loyalty to the Scottish cause, and that the converse is also true. It thus indirectly affirms the right of the Stewart succession and the necessity of loyalty to the king, not a given in the late fourteenth century.

In *The Matter of Scotland* (1993), James Goldstein calls this alignment the 'Brucean ideology' and argues that it is a means of suppressing dissent and rival claims to the throne. Comyn and Balliol in particular are despised in the text: that this has remained the case in some scholarly as well as popular interpretations of the First War of Independence is a tribute to Barbour's skill and success. However, the 'Brucean ideology' did not remain unchallenged in the century following. The chroniclers, Fordun, Wyntoun and Bower, were all familiar with the Bruce back-story as well as Barbour's account, and were impelled by their chronological range to acknowledge the more difficult aspects of Robert I's claim to the throne while praising his heroic achievements. But by including the narrative of Wallace, Bower and Wyntoun were inevitably slightly subversive of Barbour's image of Bruce, since all accounts agree that Wallace's commitment to the Scottish cause was unbroken and that he personally seemed not to benefit from his crusade, contrasting with Robert I's ultimate aim of kingship. Moreover, although his loyalty to the realm and to its nominal king, John Balliol, is stressed, the figure of Wallace does not subscribe to the 'Brucean ideology'. He is not a king, although his loyalty to the realm is equivalent to any king's; he is not particularly deferential or polite to or about his social superiors, including Bruce, and so contrasts with the eventual loyalty of Douglas and Randolph; and he does not, of course, triumph.

While Wallace and Bruce are of key importance to the chroniclers as figureheads for Scottish identity, they are only part of these wider narratives. Although writing in different languages and thus probably for slightly different audiences, both Bower and Wyntoun are concerned to place Scottish history into a world context. These men were roughly contemporary, both Augustinians in Fife, although Bower was abbot of the richer house on Inchcolm, while Wyntoun was prior of a lesser house on Loch Leven. Wyntoun wrote his *Original Chronicle* (so-called because it began with the origins of the world) in Scots, and thus presumably had in mind a local audience rather than an international one. Perhaps because of that, he seems less wedded to a consistently positive view of the line of Scottish kings. For instance, his account of Fimbal, otherwise known as Fenella or Finuele, the assassin of Kenneth III, permits her legitimate motive. According to Wyntoun,

> The Erll of Angus in his dayis
> Conquor callit, the story sayis,
> Had a douchtir Fembal calde,
> The qwhilk had a son yonge and
> baulde.
> At Dunsynnane this Kynede
> The kynge put this man to dede.
> Fra thine his modyr had ay in thoucht
> To get this kynge to dede be broucht.
> (Wyntoun, *Original Chronicle*
> 6. 10. 823–30)

It is not clear from this whether the young man had committed a crime, and so Kenneth is left without a reasonable motive, whereas Fembal's is all too understandable, even if personal. Wyntoun does not particularly approve of her methods – she has to use cunning rather than strength – but he does not condemn her for either for her emotion or for her threat to royal power.

This contrasts strongly with Bower's view, directly inherited from Fordun. In *Scotichronicon*, Finuele is a woman of great cunning and no morals. This is emphasised in the consistently applied epithets: 'versuta' (cunning), 'proditrix' (traitress), 'dolosa' (crafty), even 'maleficta' (witch). She is implicated from the very beginning of the account with illegitimate rebellion; moreover, the text implies that her motive is ill-founded, for 'the king before this had ordered her only son to be put to death at Dunsinane, whether by the severity of the law or because of some crime or any other cause I do not know.' There is no particular emphasis on cause and effect – had the sentence describing the son's death been omitted, the grammatical sense would remain. Rather than focusing on the personal, the presentation here stresses Finuele's dissidence from the greater good of the realm, as represented by the king; the threat that Finuele might have had a case is suppressed.

This narrative is typical of *Scotichronicon* in several ways. Firstly, Bower is regularly misogynist, and his view of allegedly feminine vices, such as cunning and deceit, is always condemnatory. Secondly, he favours strong royal and legitimate government and expects loyalty to the appointed king. This might be attributable to the circumstances of writing, for the *Scotichronicon* was largely composed and revised during the minority of James II. Bower, who had served as a tax collector under James I, was clearly distressed at the factionalism inherent in minority government, and anxious both to educate the boy-king and his nobility on how to govern and how to serve the realm, and to reassert an essential unity of the realm under its rightful king. However, as his depiction of Wallace makes clear, even for Bower, the king had as many responsibilities as rights, and Bruce needed to be reminded of those before he was fit to lead his army to glory.

Hary's *Wallace* borrows from both Barbour and from Bower. The romance structure of the narrative, as well as some key episodes, are borrowed from The *Bruce*. As a result, the contrast between the heroes is forced and writ large, whereas in the chronicles, it was far more muted. Much of the content is derived from *Scotichronicon*, suggesting that Hary was an educated man. This is further supported by the Chaucerian echoes in parts of the poem. This is perhaps most evident at the beginning of Book 6, where Wallace first sees his wife-to-be in a church, reminiscent of Troilus' first sighting of Criseyde. At this point in the poem, Hary also uses rhyme royal, the stanza of *Troilus and Criseyde*, as opposed to the five-stress couplet he uses elsewhere. Such intertextual sophistication enriches Hary's poem, but curiously highlights the inherent brutality of Hary's topic.

While Barbour wrote for a king and his nobles, Hary wrote for two lesser lords who opposed James III's policy of peace towards England. It is not surprising, therefore, that he magnifies the subversive elements of the figure of Wallace. For instance, Hary stresses Wallace's selfless loyalty by having him offered the crown by his men three times. Each time, Wallace refuses, even though on one occasion, his acceptance would precipitate the battle with the English that he had desired for some time. All told, Wallace is the perfect example of unrewarded and unappreciated virtue. Indeed, his devotion to his cause shows up his social superiors, those who claimed authority to guide the realm, such as Bruce and the Comyns. Of course, Bruce comes off the worst for the comparison. Hary turns Barbour's identification of Bruce with the realm on its head by having Bruce declare, in a revelatory moment of guilt when sitting down to eat unwashed in the English camp, that he is accused of eating 'his awn blud' (*Wallace* XI. 536). Here Bruce really does embody the realm, but by consumption rather than by sacrifice. Hary's Wallace is not an untroubled figure, nor indeed one easy to emulate; his virtue is, however, recognisable in his leadership, his own loyalty and in his wit and forward planning, for these are the characteristics of true nobles in both romance and in historiography. The *Wallace* functions successfully because it places itself in a tradition.

DREAM VISION

While the historiographers are concerned to portray virtue in past heroes, The *Kingis Quair* is as much concerned with the future of the narrator as it is with his past. The attribution of this poem to James I is secure enough; the poem seems to have been written towards the end of his captivity in England, around 1424. The attribution rests on a comment in the sole manuscript of the poem, where it says that 'Herefter followis the quair maid be King James of Scotland the first callit the kingis quair and maid quhen his majeste wes in Ingland'; the biographical details seem to tie it even more closely to the young king. The opening of the poem refers to his capture by pirates and his long imprisonment by the English kings, while his future is dependent on the young woman he sees, Jonette, or Joan Beaufort, whose relations supported his release. Famously, C.S. Lewis celebrated the poem as the first about love in marriage (Lewis 1971, 237), but while there is a poignancy in reading the text autobiographically, because of the contrast between the confidence in the future expressed in the poem and James I's eventual fate, to focus on biography is to simplify unhelpfully the complex ideas of the poem.

It is, in part, a dream vision; such texts enabled interior discussions to be played outwith the mind. Whereas Barbour and Hary display character through external action and rarely, if ever, explore their heroes' interiority, James and other writers of dream vision turn the inside out. By recounting a dream, they allegorise internal experience. Here the narrator, in the voice of James, records his encounters with the goddesses Venus, Minerva and Fortune, personifications of Love, Wisdom and Fortune respectively, to explore the best method of dealing with the vagaries of the world. In adopting this genre, James pays homage to Chaucer and John Gower, English poets of the previous generation to whose work he would doubtless have been exposed during his imprisonment. Unusually, though, the Dreamer in The *Kingis Quair* recounts his dream having made sense of its message, instead of describing it in order to make sense of it, which is the usual Chaucerian mode. The influence of English poetry is perhaps evident in the language, which has English features, although that might also reflect James' long captivity in England. Chaucerian evocations are evident throughout, from the choice of stanza (as used in *Troilus and Criseyde*), the captive's sight of his beloved from a window (as in *The Knight's Tale*) and the personification allegory in the goddesses, which Chaucer uses in *The House of Fame*, *The Parliament of Fowls*, and *The Legend of Good Women*. The direct interaction of the dreamer-narrator with his personifications perhaps has more in common with Gower's poem, *Confessio Amantis*, in which Amans, revealed as a figure of Gower himself at the end of the poem, learns from Genius and from Venus the proper way of love.

Love and fortune are the central and intertwined themes of the *Kingis Quair*. The starting point of the poem is the dreamer's reading of Boethius' *Consolation of Philosophy*, in which Boethius, through a dreamed dialogue with Lady Philosophy, comes to terms with his disgrace and imprisonment after a distinguished career. The fundamental assumption of Boethius' text is that Fortune is unreliable, and thus all good fortune should be treated with suspicion since it will come to an end. Such a view of human existence is commonplace in medieval writing, including the romances such as The *Bruce* and The *Wallace*. Its greatest iconographic contribution is Fortune's Wheel, upon which those mortals eager for glory can climb. Once on the wheel, one can either climb to the top, secure only in the knowledge that the only way from there is down, or one can be hurled off into oblivion. From the perspective of one who had power and influence and has lost it, Boethius' text advocates a cultivated indifference; the dreamer in the *Kingis Quair*, whose experience of early imprisonment and then release to potential glory is the opposite of Boethius', disagrees with the earlier text's conclusion and suggests a more active and conscious engagement with Fortune and with life.

From this realisation, that 'In tender youth how sche [Fortune] was first my fo/ And eft my frende', the dreamer recounts his experience. At its heart lies the issue of freedom. The dreamer is physically imprisoned, unfree, and thus unable to make his own decisions or control his own whereabouts. This is focused by the experience of love by the birds around him, who are animal and thus without the divine gift of free will, yet seem better able to act than he does, despite his rationality (183–5). Lamenting this, he begs to be given someone to love, to fulfil his nature, and instantly sees the lady in the garden. This sight makes him a 'free thrall', a man who has chosen his own imprisonment; this is his first act of free will within his physical prison walls. It is interesting to compare this treatment of freedom with Barbour's. Although Barbour is clearly discussing freedom in its political collocations, he uses as one example the thraldom of the marriage debt, a bond taken out willingly but constraining each party to fulfil obligations to the other: Barbour's problem is that men are constrained as much as women, and his point is that English overlordship of the Scots constrained the nobles as much as ordinary life under a lord did lower gentry and peasants. Here the thraldom is all one way, from the man in loyal service to love and to a woman who does not even know that she has been seen. For the dreamer in the *Kingis Quair* and for most medieval dream visions, such service is ennobling, if painful. As Mapstone (1997) points outs, this is a victory of will over wits, but to manage it properly, the Dreamer knows he needs to regain his wits and become educated in self-government.

Learning to love becomes identified with learning to deal with Fortune. Through his dream vision, the Dreamer learns three important lessons. The first is provided by Venus, which is that Love is not enough by itself to overcome his situation, but that it might be part of the solution. Secondly, Minerva insists that he should pursue love, not lust, and 'Be trewe and meke and stedfast in thy thoght' (917). If he does this, then the third lesson will be open to him. This is the means of resisting Fortune:

> Fortune is most and strangest evermore
> Quhare leste foreknawing or intelligence
> Is in the man; and, sone, of wit or lore
> Sen thou art wayke and feble, lo- therefore
> The more thou art in danger and commune
> With hir that clerkis clepen so, "Fortune". (1038–43)

Although expressed negatively, Minerva's 'sentence' suggests that through the development of intelligence, the danger from Fortune can be overcome. Knowing this, and being able to govern himself, enables the Dreamer to accept the risks of Fortune's wheel. This is an optimistic view of the challenge of Fortune, one affirmed by the Dreamer's receipt on waking of a branch of gillyflowers bearing an inscription. The poem offers hope regarding the Dreamer's future, focused on his successful quest for love from the lady. Once that has been achieved, then all else will follow. Such is the optimistic and considered vision of the poem at its end, advocating education and reason as the best way to a successful life of self-governance.

Dream vision is still a reasonably vibrant form at the beginning of the sixteenth century, although its appeal is beginning to fade. Dunbar uses it to diverse ends. In 'As yung Awrora with cristall haile', it becomes a means of satirising a rival for the king's favour, John Damian, as a failed alchemist. The story told here, of Damian falling from the ramparts of Stirling Castle while trying to fly, is a vision and therefore not intended to be taken as true, despite John Leslie's repetition of it in his *History*. But the unchallengeable nature of dream vision makes it a good vehicle for attack. At the other end of the literary spectrum, Dunbar displays his command of aureate language in 'Rycht as the stern of day begouth to schyne' (*The Goldyn Targe*) and 'Quhen Merche wes with variand windis past' (*The Thrissill and the Rose*). Features of aureate or high style include complex grammar, a high proportion of French or Latin derived words and often ornate metrical form. Derek Brewer (1983) compares this style to the contemporary Gothic architecture and notes the care devoted to the form, even when the content seems insubstantial. Some readers find this to be the case with *The Golden Targe*, since neither the dreamer nor his allegorical experience of love are greatly individualised. While the element of love allegory should not be ignored, Denton Fox's suggestion (1959) that the poem may be as much about poetry and its writing offers an additional layer of meaning, where the structure is all.

Such self-consciousness on the part of the writer is a feature of dream vision. Chaucer's narrators all reflect upon their act of recording their visions, as does the dreamer in the *Kingis Quair*. The same is true in *The Palice of Honour*, Gavin Douglas's other work, a poem concerned at one level with the nature of honour and its achievement. Since the Dreamer there finds his protection under the court of Muses, the gaining of honour through writing is paramount in the Dreamer's experience. Like the *Kingis Quair*, *The Palice of Honour* has clear Chaucerian antecedents. Most obviously, perhaps, parallels can be seen with *The House of Fame*, where again the apparently foolish dreamer-narrator finds himself in a desert of inspiration, only partially relieved by what he dreams. *The House of Fame* is unfinished, whereas *The Palice of Honour* ends tidily, if abruptly. Whereas *The House of Fame* seems to question the nature of fame and particularly the nature of authority and truth, even before its lack of conclusion, Douglas's view of honour seems to be much more affirmatory and his view of his poetic career more certain. While the paths of honour may vary – his Dreamer encounters four alternatives, wisdom (Minerva's train) chastity (Diana's train), love (Venus) and finally, poetry (the Muses), nevertheless all meet at the palace and one shared vision of honour.

The Dreamer, a figure of Douglas, has a difficult path, since he hides from Minerva and Diana, and foolishly rejects Venus to her face. His rescue by the Muses occurs in the nick of time; that poetry may be his route to Honour is demonstrated at this early stage by his ability to compose an ode in Venus's praise. This is confirmed later when the Dreamer has the opportunity to look in Venus's mirror towards the end of the poem. Although most people see their beloved in the mirror, the Dreamer sees a procession of historical and literary figures, those who might become subjects of poetry, suggesting that writing might be his true love. Moreover, Venus commissions him to write her book, taken as referring forward to his translation of the *Aeneid*, a poem with which Venus is closely associated. Despite these associations with the personification of love, however, the Dreamer is not primarily moved by the honour of love: the *Aeneid* is far more a political text than it is an amatory one.

Douglas ends his poem with an address to James IV, an acknowledgement of political power over the poetical power of Chaucer and Gower, more common dedicatees. This address has many of the aspects of a modesty topos, for Douglas asserts his humility and his lack of ability, referring to his poem as 'rusty, rural rebaldry' (2150). As Douglas was a scion of one of the most powerful magnatial families, this humility seems out of keeping, notwithstanding a long literary tradition and Douglas's desire for a larger benefice. It serves to flatter, since it juxtaposes James beside the hymn to Honour with which the main poem concludes; but that juxtaposition potentially also serves to warn James about Honour's demands on himself. Ultimately, the Dreamer is unable to look on Honour without fainting, but the image presented in Honour's attendants and his surroundings is kingly, as are three of the members of his court, Kings Kenneth, Gregor and Robert I. James is surely invited to learn about Honour together with the Dreamer, and thus, while The *Kingis Quair* offers a royal model to everyone, *The Palice of Honour*, urges the king to learn from the experience of a noble.

FABLES

Dream vision puts an individual voice and an individual dream at the centre of its narrative. Another form of allegory, beast fable, offers a more general presentation and satire of human foibles and folly. Often in medieval thought humanity is made up of the rational, which is closer to God, and the fleshly, which is closer to animals. Fables point up the qualities that might be ascribed to the animal – lust, greed, sloth, foolishness, even pride – and indicate how they might best be controlled by reason. As texts with clear morals, fables easily escape the condemnation for fiction, lie-telling, that sometimes bothered medieval writers. Barbour and Hary could claim truth for their narratives; the dreamer is the ultimate authority for a dream, so can hardly be accused of lying; but talking animals are clearly fictitious. But as Robert Henryson points out in his Prologue, it is possible to benefit from fiction.

> In lyke maner as throw a bustious eird,
> Swa it be laubourit with grit diligence,
> Springis the flouris and the corne abreird,
> Hailsum and gude to mannis sustenance;
> Sa springis thair ane moral sweit sentence
> Oute of the subtell dyte of poetry
> To gude purpois, quha culd it weill apply. (8–14)

The last line of this stanza is revealing: 'quha culd it weill apply' suggests that some effort is required to extract the corn, and Henryson's *Fables* are not as straightforward as they might initially appear. Henryson plays with narrative convention, offering morals that appear to contradict the fables that go before (as in *The Cock and the Jasp*) or by inserting the narrator into the fable, as he does in *The Preaching of the Swallow* and *The Scheip and the Dog*. Such complexities force the reader to pay attention to the narrative and sometimes to question the moralitas. In Henryson's view, just because fables may be pleasant to read, that does not make them easy.

Henryson's sequence of thirteen fables begin and end with the individual, but most deal with the individual and society. In contrast to the positive approaches taken in the *Kingis Quair* and *The Palice of Honour* towards self-improvement, Henryson's *Fables* become gradually bleaker as the sequence progresses. While in the first five fables, the foolish and the wicked are punished, in the second half, even the innocent are vulnerable to violent death because of the injustice of the world around them. The change is heralded by *The Lion and the Mouse*, the fable that stands in the middle of the sequence. This fable is presented as a dream narrative, where the fable is told by Aesop, the authority for the sequence, directly to the narrator. Aesop does not have much faith in his stories to bring about reformation, but in response to the narrator's demands, he tells a story about rule and kingship, in which the Lion learns the benefit of showing mercy to the small offender, the mice. Attempts have been made to tie this fable to a particular period in James III's reign, since one of the accusations against him was his inequity. However, Lyall (1976) has demonstrated that the advice contained within it is traditional, while the crimes of which James III is accused were also fairly common practice among the Stewart kings. This should not diminish the power of the moral, with its warning to all leaders.

Henryson's political concerns can also be seen in an anonymous text, preserved in John Asloan's manuscript of the early sixteenth century. *The Tales of the Fyve Beasts* inverts the form of the *Moral Fabillis*, for the beasts here tell the stories. One of them, *The Unicorn's Tale*, is concerned with the same theme as *The Lion and the Mouse*, but this time, the victim of unfair punishment takes his revenge. A corrective towards an over-merciful monarch, however, can be found in *The Thrie Preistis of Peblis* and also in John Ireland's treatise, *The Meroure of Wysdome* (book 7, chapter 5). Neither of these texts uses animal fables, but instead their story has a fool as its adviser. A king pardons a man for a murder; the man re-offends and the king has him put to death. The fool's interpretation is that the king is guilty of the second murder, for had he applied the correct punishment initially, then there would not have been a second murder. Remissions for money were common under James III and James IV, during whose rules these texts were written; however, the advice itself is so traditional that it seems risky to posit a direct connection.

Although using different kinds of fables, *The Thrie Preistis of Peblis*, *The Meroure of Wysdome* and Henryson's *Fables* share not only a concern with good government but also the individual soul. *The Meroure* is primarily concerned with the right way to approach God, and only at the end moves towards a focus on the rule of others. *The Thrie Preistis* also ends with a fable of salvation. Henryson's sequence ends with *The Paddock and the Mouse*, interpreted as an allegory of body and soul that which stresses the inevitability of death. All forms of rule are seen to come together as a right relationship between reason and will, and between God and man.

LYRIC

While Henryson seems indifferent to royal approbation, and Douglas requires royal favour only to advance his career, William Dunbar was dependent on James IV and his queen, Margaret Tudor, for his living. While the Treasurer's Accounts do not suggest that Dunbar was ever rewarded directly for his poetry, of all Scottish medieval literature, Dunbar's lyrics are the most obviously those of the court. Some of them often record or respond to events and people encountered within those environs. 'As yung Awrora with cristall haile' is not an isolated example: Dunbar also mocks Sir James Doig, Master of the Queen's Wardrobe, Sir John Sinclair and Walter Kennedy. There are also poems describing tournaments, entrances to burghs and general features of court life, including a preference for Edinburgh over Stirling in 'We that ar heir in hevynnis glorie'. But Dunbar is not only a poet of merriment. Religious lyrics, such as the triumphant 'Done is the batell on the dragon blak' and 'Haile sterne superne' and the penitential, such as 'This waverand warldis wretch-idnes' are an equal part of his repertoire. What is probably his most famous poem, 'I that in heill wes and gladnes', more familiarly known as 'The Lament for the Makars' comes into this category. Only half of this poem is dedicated to com-memorating poets; the rest is concerned with the inevitability of death for all humanity, including the speaker. For scholars, the poem is a treasure trove of names; for Dunbar's original audience, it belonged to a well-known tradition of lamentation.

Dunbar's work offers a huge range of poetry, but there are two recurrent features. Firstly, Dunbar's poetic voice is elusive: indeed, Bawcutt (1992) remarks that 'he speaks with almost too many voices'. Unlike Henryson, whose moral poetry seems to suit the schoolmaster, and Douglas, whose personality is fleshed out through letters, recorded comments and other documents, Dunbar offers no certain voice, and discourages the reader from associating the 'I' of a poem too closely with the writer. Dunbar therefore might serve as a warning against glib interpretations of other poets, for clearly he was not expected to maintain merely one poetic voice, but to change it according to the requirements of the poem.

The second recurrent feature of Dunbar's work is his skilled handling of metre and rhythm. He adopts alliterative metre in one of his most famous poems 'Apon the midsummer evin, mirriest of nichts' (*The Tretis of the Tua Mariit Wemen and the Wedo*), and develops it to suit his own style. 'Hale, sterne superne' is at another extreme: a prayer of praise to the Virgin, this is constructed through highly ornate rhyme, within lines as well as at the ends. Douglas also attempts such virtuosity, but does not do so in short lyrics: Dunbar seems to have been happiest in short stretches and pushes them to the limits. The shortness and the diversity of Dunbar's work makes him quite different from other Scottish poets; it has also probably made his work the best known and the most read of all the early Scottish poets, since even Barbour is primarily read in extracts.

LITERATURE AND HISTORY

From the texts discussed here, it is possible to imagine that nearly all medieval Scottish literature was fixated on political commentary and advice to princes. This is not entirely fair, but it is noticeable that in what survives from the middle ages, material concerned with moral and political virtue is very prominent, perhaps more so than in England. Since the copying of manuscripts is expensive in time and in materials, and since some of these texts are lengthy, the commitment of the readers and scribes to these texts is clear. Moreover, although some texts, such as The *Wallace*, were clearly written in response to particular political circumstances, their appeal stretched far beyond that immediate situation. The relationship between Scotland and England had changed markedly by the end of the sixteenth century, yet there was still an audience for Hary's poem, but by that time for its printed form.

The gap between the date of composition of many pieces and the date of the earliest witness also suggests a lengthy reading and copying history in between. This is equally true of The *Kingis Quair* and *The Palice of Honour*: in both cases, we might assume intermediate copies between the first copy and the first surviving witness. Although we cannot reconstruct the reading culture of fifteenth-century Scotland, we can see patterns of popularity and purpose.

Clearly, these potentially political texts have more obvious connection with the study of the contemporary history than some others, such as *The Freirs of Berwick*, or even *The Testament of Cresseid*. Sometimes they can illuminate specific concerns; Bower's strictures on taxation must reflect the experience both of one taxed as the head of a wealthy house, and also as a tax-collector. More often, however, they reveal long-standing attitudes and concerns, or changes in perspective which are only visible when reading the texts as part of a sequence. Concerns about justice, for instance, haunt many of these pieces: Barbour discusses Bruce's difficulties in the Black Parliament, where he is forced to punish a beloved kinsman in the interests of fairness; it is also a key theme in *Scotichronicon*, and exercises Henryson and the writer of *The Three Priests of Peblis*. At the same time, it is a recurrent theme in the acts of Parliament, where again and again, the king is asked to enact justice fairly. We can no more assume that each writer experienced a breakdown in the legal system than that the members of parliament (many of whom would be acting as justiciars in their own regions) saw catastrophe each time the parliament met.

Rather than read medieval literature purely for illumination of particular events, it is better to see it as an insight into the mindset of an age, a means of identifying difference as well as similarity of experience. We might wonder at Barbour's indignation that Edward I had Christopher Seton hanged (*Bruce* 4. 16–38), but it also provides an insight into the assumptions of chivalry more directly than any treatise. At the same time, we need to be aware of the many things that get in the way of a transparent account or direct reading. Transmission can be problematic. Obviously, many texts have been lost, and some that survive have been damaged beyond comprehension. Less apparent is the interference of a scribe, who miscopied, or who worked from a damaged exemplar, or who misunderstood what was in front of him, and thus introduced variations into the text. The poet himself worked in a frame of literary techniques and traditions, which shape the text produced. All of these affect our reception of any piece of writing, and it is not unreasonable to apply the same cautions to documents as to literature.

Medieval Scottish literature encompasses a range of material, a variety of languages and many genres. It can be highbrow and philosophical, it can be straightforward and educational and it can be scatological and slanderous. Its concerns mirror those of literature everywhere: what is the significance and purpose of writing? How do we express emotion? What makes a good story? What makes a good person? The last seems to have a particularly Scottish spin – namely, what makes a man good at governing other people? This is a recurrent, if not essential thread in Scottish material of the fifteenth and early sixteenth centuries, distinguishing the Scottish tradition from its nearest neighbours. Accounting for this distinction is not easy, for to attribute it to an imagined intimacy and egalitarianism in Scottish society or to a Scottish national character is to champion modern myths. Nevertheless it is a feature, and one that proved pervasive and distinctive in Scottish literature well into the early modern period. Finally, then, like their history, the medieval literature of the Scots is both a part of and yet distinguishable from the wider European and British traditions, and worth attention in its own right.

EDITIONS

Jack, RDS and Rozendaal, PAT 1997 (eds) *The Mercat Anthology of Early Scottish Literature*. Edinburgh.

Duncan, AAM (ed) 1997 John Barbour, *The Bruce*. Edinburgh.

Watt, DER *et al (eds)*, 1987–98 Walter Bower, *Scotichronicon*. Aberdeen.

Parkinson, D (ed) 1992 Gavin Douglas, *The Palice of Honoure*. Kalamazoo. Also available online.

Bawcutt, P (ed) 1998 *The Poems of William Dunbar*. 2 vols. Glasgow.

McKim, A (ed) 2003 Hary, *The Wallace*. Edinburgh.

Fox, D (ed) 1981 *The Poems of Robert Henryson*. Oxford.

REFERENCES TO BOOKS AND ARTICLES MENTIONED IN THE TEXT

Items marked * are recommended for further reading

*Aitken, AJ, McDiarmid, MP and Thomson, DS (eds) 1997 *Bards and Makars: Scottish Language and Literature, Medieval and Renaissance*. Glasgow.

Amsler, M 1982 'The Quest for the Present Tense: The Poet and the Dreamer in Douglas' *The Palice of Honoure*', *Studies in Scottish Literature*, 17, 186–208.

Baird, G 1996 *The Poems of Robert Henryson*. Glasgow.

Bawcutt, P 1970 'Douglas and Chaucer', *Review of English Studies*, 21, 401–21.

*Bawcutt, P 1976 *Gavin Douglas: A Critical Study*. Edinburgh.

Bawcutt, P 1992 *Dunbar the Makar*. Oxford.

Brewer D 1983 *English Gothic Literature*. London.

Fox, D 1959 'Dunbar's *The Golden Targe*', *English Literary History*, 26, 311–334.

Fradenburg, LO 1991 *City, Marriage, Tournament: Arts of Rule in Late Medieval Scotland*. Madison, WI.

*Goldstein, RJ 1993 *The Matter of Scotland: Historical Narrative in Medieval Scotland*. Lincoln NE and London.

*Gray, D 1981 *Robert Henryson*. Leiden.

*Jack, RDS (ed) 1987 *The History of Scottish Literature*. Volume 1. Aberdeen.

Kratzmann, G 1980 *Anglo-Scottish Literary Relations, 1430–1550*. Cambridge and New York.

Lewis, CS 1971 (repr) *The Allegory of Love*.

*Lyall, RJ 1976 'Politics and poetry in Fifteenth and Sixteenth Century Scotland', *Scottish Literary Journal*, 3, 5–29

*Lyall, RJ and Riddy, F (eds) 1981 *Proceedings of the Third International Conference on Scottish Language and Literature (Medieval and Renaissance)*. Stirling/Glasgow.

Mapstone, S 1997 'Kingship and the *Kingis Quair*', *in* Cooper, H and Mapstone, S (eds), *The Long Fifteenth Century: Essays for Douglas Gray*, Oxford, 51-69.

*Mapstone, S 1999 '*Scotichronicon's First Readers*', *in* Crawford, BE (ed), *Church, Chronicle and Learning in Medieval and Early Modern Scotland*, Edinburgh, 31–56.

Mapstone, S (ed) 2001 *Dunbar 'The Nobill Poyet'*. East Linton.

*Patterson, L (ed) 1990 *Literary Practice and Social Change in Britain, 1380–1530*. Berkeley, Los Angeles, London.

Spearing, AC 1986 *Medieval Dream Poetry*. Cambridge.

Spearing AC 1993 *The Medieval Poet as Voyeur: Secrecy, Watching and Listening in Medieval Love-Narratives*. Cambridge.

Spiller, M and McClure, JD (eds) 1989 *Bryght Lanternis: Essays on the Language and Literature of Medieval and Renaissance Scotland*. Aberdeen.

Wallace, D (ed) 1999 *The Cambridge History of Medieval English Literature*. Cambridge.

Index

Note: Page numbers for chapters are indicated by **bold** page numbers and maps and illustrations are in *italics*. Places or people mentioned only once are *generally* omitted.